KNOWING THEIR PLACE?

KNOWING THEIR PLACE?

THE INTELLECTUAL LIFE OF WOMEN IN THE 19TH CENTURY

EDITED BY BRENDAN WALSH

The
History
Press
Ireland

This volume is dedicated to our students
so that they might know …

First published 2014

The History Press Ireland
50 City Quay
Dublin 2
Ireland
www.thehistorypress.ie

British Library Cataloguing in Publication Data.
A catalogue record for this book is available from the British Library.

ISBN 978 1 84588 792 6

Typesetting and origination by The History Press

Contents

Foreword   6
Pam Hirsch

Introduction   8
Brendan Walsh

1.   'Starry Eyed': Women in Science in Nineteenth-Century Ireland   18
    Clara Cullen

2.   'The Fun of Being Intellectual': Helen Waddell (1889–1965) and
    Maude Clarke (1892–1935)   37
    Jennifer FitzGerald

3.   Intellectual Lives and Literary Perspectives: Female Irish Writing at
    Home and Abroad   66
    Kathryn Laing

4.   General Practice? Victorian Irish Women and
    United Kingdom Medicine   85
    Margaret Ó hÓgartaigh

5.   Intellectual Women: Irish Women at Cambridge, 1875–1904   96
    Susan M. Parkes

6.   A Woman's Reply: Women and Divorce Law Reform in
    Victorian Ireland   128
    Diane Urquhart

7.   A Terrible Beauty? Women, Modernity and Irish Nationalism before the
    Easter Rising   148
    Margaret Ward

8.   Knowing Their Place? Girls' Perceptions of School in Nineteenth-
    Century Ireland   170
    Brendan Walsh

Appendix   202
Notes   205
Notes on Contributors   262
Index   265

Foreword

I sat down to write this foreword on International Women's Day, which seemed singularly appropriate. I knew of Maud Gonne – but perhaps rather as the muse of W.B. Yeats than as a woman with her own agency, work and life. Gonne herself spoke of 'an old prophecy which says that Ireland will be saved by the women, and if Irish women will only realise the importance of this work of national education for children, I think this prophecy may come true'. And indeed, the uncovering of previously unsung heroines, the significance of teachers and the pursuit of learning by Irish women, all explored in this book, fills a significant lacuna in historical studies. As I read the book I began to realise that my ignorance was vast and I imagine I am not alone in this.

It turns out that there exists a vast roll call of female Irish intellectuals and, to take just one example, I was reminded of the story of the astrophysicist, Jocelyn Bell Burnell. Burnell discovered the first radar pulsars when she was a graduate supervisor, yet her male thesis supervisor was awarded the Nobel Prize, rather than her. So some of the women in this book have been hidden from history because their worth has been occluded by male rivals, but much more commonly, for many of them, getting the good work done has been more important to them than making a name for themselves.

A letter to *The Irish Times* in 1878 had claimed that:

> Home is the sphere of a woman; modesty is her supreme virtue; softness and sweetness are her true accomplishments; innocence is her best experience; economy is her highest ability; and constancy and self-sacrificing love her only legitimate heroism.

Fortunately, generations of Irish schoolgirls have ignored this. For intellectual girls, prior to the development of higher education for women in Ireland, the Cambridge women's colleges of Girton and Newnham offered opportunities, firstly as students, but sometimes, later, returning as Heads of House. Part of my own failure to realise that a particular woman was Irish is that the story of learned Irish women has – at least in the past – been centrifugal, as Irish women sometimes studied, lived and worked in the United Kingdom and elsewhere in Europe. In that sense they refused to know their place, but followed their ambition wherever it took them.

Dr Pam Hirsch
Newnham College
University of Cambridge, 2014

Introduction

Writing in 1970, Germaine Greer observed:

> It is remarkable how many of today's militant women can remember
> some extraordinary old lady who sought (in vain) to plant the seeds of
> rebellion in their minds. From time to time vivid old women appear
> on TV, or are written up in obituaries in *The Times*, to remind us not
> only of the continuity of the movement but of the tactical address and
> joyful courage of the petticoated, corseted and hatted gentlewomen of
> a lifetime ago.[1]

Perhaps it was not always 'in vain', as Greer suggests, but it is certainly
true that informing much of the modern women's movement are
the actions and words of a small but persistent cohort of women,
particularly in England, in the nineteenth century. This collection of
essays is not intended as a *précis* of that movement, nor is it gender
history; rather it is an attempt to add to the growing body of literature
uncovering and celebrating the achievements of women in the past.
This historical duty should not be taken lightly. Valiulis and O'Dowd
make the point that 'the work of discovery – of digging women out
of obscurity – goes on'.[2] The old adage has it that history is written
by the victors and, in the gender wars of the nineteenth and twentieth
centuries, that history was written by and about men. It was not

until the 1970s that a widespread body of feminist literature began to appear that reflected the varied concerns, but generally unified aims, of the women's liberation movement. It is noteworthy that early titles focused on that sense of coming into the light (or being dug out of the dark), titles such as *Hidden from History* and *Becoming Visible*.[3] These books were concerned with understanding the place of women in history, with *knowing* their place and helping us to know it.

Undoubtedly, women's history is the most significant new field in historical studies in the last four decades. Its appearance and gradual refinement has alerted historians to similar areas of neglect and encouraged them to look to the peripheries, where rich seams of possibility exist in bringing the mute and invisible into the light. This has led to a reimagining of methodologies and, in particular, the use of oral history to capture lived experience and memory. In doing this, women's history has not only invigorated historical studies but added significantly to the way we 'do' history. In Ireland, philosophical debates regarding theory and its impact on method have tended to remain within the academic community and have not permeated mainstream studies, but this is not unusual and, in time, textual analysis, gender theory, poststructuralism and cultural and economic history will possibly impact upon the narrative in more ways than are now evident. For now, Irish historians are busy 'digging' women out from our history, and perhaps when the record is crowded we can begin to allow more theoretical considerations to slightly occlude its vividness. Indeed, the process has already begun. As Valiulis and O'Dowd point out, 'we have now entered a different phase in women's history', evolving from the 'emphasis on great women' to a model where the 'broad historical outlines remain the same except women's participation is noted'.[4] But they correctly note that it is when 'we move beyond that stage that the truly revolutionary potential of women's history is revealed – the potential to challenge what we think is historically important, what we consider the defining moments in history'.[5]

In the nineteenth century, women become involved in great battles. In Ireland, as in England, they campaigned for equal access to education – a liberty that informs all others. They have fought for equality in the workplace, politics, family life, the sporting arena and, perhaps most difficult of all, in the ways in which the notion of 'woman' or 'female' is understood in social, political, moral, public, private and economic settings. The extent to which these battles have been won or lost is not the subject of this book. Without question, those 'petticoated, corseted and hatted gentlewomen' of the nineteenth and early twentieth centuries would look with awe upon the gains made by women in the modern era. How disbelieving my students are when I read for them Mary Hayden's diary entry for 20 March 1880, where she notes that, having spent the day at Trinity College Dublin taking examinations (women were, at this time, allowed sit examinations but not attend lectures or enrol as full-time students), she:

> should like of all things to be a student at Trinity, it would be jolly having rooms to yourself and asking your friends to sprees and playing cricket and football … I'm sure that I wouldn't study much … I should be very wild … I can not [sic] help thinking of it several times a day.[6]

But historical periods must first be measured against their own times and, in order to understand the work of the women considered here, we must take a brief look at the roles allowed and allocated to women in nineteenth-century Ireland – we must look at the 'places' they occupied and those they were banished from. This 'place' was not simply physical but professional and intellectual; private as well as public. Husbands, fathers, politicians and Church leaders knew the 'place' their mothers, wives, sisters or daughters should occupy. The disabilities they suffered are so familiar to us now they have almost lost their ability to shock. But the origins of emancipation are intellectual. The subject reflects on his/her position in relation to 'other' and, realising that their respective 'places' are very different, begins a process of moving from one to the other; slavery to freedom, disenfranchisement to enfranchisement, inequality to equality. The intellectual 'place' occupied by women in the nineteenth-century, before they could access or seize a political or professional 'place' is crucial in understanding the transformation of women's lives in that period. It is all the more pertinent when we consider that, for most of that century, their participation in secondary and university education was deemed unnecessary, if not a threat to the social order.[7] Denied education, women were excluded from those 'places' open to their fathers, brothers and husbands: law, medicine, business, parliament, academia, the church. Their contribution was limited to philanthropic ventures deemed appropriate to middle-class females; their 'place' was restricted in the same way their dress was.[8] Disenfranchised, all women, regardless of class, operated in a 'place' outside the walls of parliament and in struggling to gain access to, and a vote for members of, that institution, they were frequently the terrorised victims of other, darker 'places', such as Holloway Prison where British suffragettes were force-fed both orally and anally.[9] While the first female Member of Parliament was the Irish nationalist Constance Markiewicz (a Sinn Féin candidate who did not take her seat), women were not allowed sit in the House of Lords as life peers until 1958. Markiewicz's identification of the House of Commons as a foreign and politically oppressive 'place' is relevant not only in understanding the legal restrictions imposed on Irish women by Parliament before 1922, but also, as discussed by Mary Ward in this book, in understanding the evolution of nationalism in female circles in Ireland before the Easter Rising of 1916.

Women in the nineteenth and early twentieth centuries knew too well the 'place' allotted to them and recognised those 'places' they wished to inhabit. These were literary, political, intellectual, professional and social. Unquestionably women in Britain were instrumental in winning concessions for women in Ireland but women there were also active and vocal in more recognisably 'feminist' forums such as the Irish Catholic Women's Suffrage Association established in 1915 by Mary Hayden and Mary Louisa Gwynn.

While towards the end of the century cultural and political differences became more manifest, the place occupied by women in Ireland was almost identical to that in Britain and indeed Europe and America. In these arenas, the fundamental differences concerned not gender but class. Joan Burstyn's persuasive study of Victorian education and the ideal of womanhood in England is equally relevant when considering Ireland in the same period. The working class laboured in factories and sweatshops while middle-class women remained at home, consuming the products they generated. Leisured women were 'symbols of the economic success of their male relatives'.[10] With the evolution of the middle class, women were prized as sympathisers and comfort-givers. The man's place was the harsh world of business and trade, the physical world of earning and doing. The woman's place was the home, and in contrast to, but complementing, the male world of 'doing', she came to represent the passive but morally superior listener and advisor. Her place was receptive, inactive, spiritual and dependent. She became the mistress of the home, the Victorian 'angel of the hearth'. She was, in the words of John Burgon, professor of divinity at Oxford, 'the great solace of Man's life, his chiefest [sic] earthly joy', whose 'strength [lay] in her essential weakness'.[11] This 'weakness', understood as moral strength, could only be preserved by remaining removed from the contingencies of the cut-and-thrust of living, and so unworldliness became a prerequisite of moral superiority, almost of a deeper knowledge of the human condition. By remaining uncontaminated by modern living, women could operate in a 'place', a sphere, where they intuited more the profound meanings of existence, and stored them so that their husbands could be rehabilitated and refreshed when worn down by the harshness of the world, and they passed these on to their (female) children in the shape of womanly virtues. It was not just, therefore, that political or economic factors militated against middle-class women engaging more fully in their local or national community; rather, they were enshrined, as if in amber, in a dense casing of theological, social and gender-based *credos* which took absolutely for granted that their role was preordained, defined in relation to men, and that they were in fact superior to men in virtue. This was a silken trap, as it forced early feminists to dispute the place accorded them which society believed was protective, appreciated, fitting, noble, cosseted, financially secure and removed from the brutality of physical work. It is not surprising that working-class women felt little sense of sisterhood, or that early Marxists pointed to class rather than sex as the basis of oppression. Indeed, the case might also be made that the pioneers of education for girls (who rightly won laurels for their efforts) neglected to investigate the social constructs of late nineteenth-century Ireland which allowed the vast cohort of lower middle- and working-class girls to enter shop work, service, factories and so on, with no prospect of securing entry into the select, elite girls' schools.

Newly acquired middle-class status, particularly among urban Catholics in nineteenth-century Ireland, was in most ways identical to that which characterised the same phenomenon in England. The much maligned 'Castle Catholics' and those a few rungs down the social ladder aspired to the financial security offered by the growing wealth of the mercantile class, while also adapting to social developments. For middle-class families, perhaps the most important of these was the development of intermediate education for girls, dealt with in Chapter 8 of this volume. Prior to the evolution of limited employment opportunities for middle-class women in the late nineteenth century, women relied upon fathers, brothers or husbands for financial security. Work indicated modest means and therefore undermined middle-class status, rendering women less attractive to prospective suitors. The frustration of those who saw the possibilities beyond this state of affairs can only be imagined, and historians must hope that diaries and journals lie undiscovered in attics and basements – perhaps those of our 'petticoated, corseted and hatted' ancestors.

For the middle-class girl, no occupation or undertaking must jeopardise her chances of marriage, which meant not only financial security for her but the removal of a burden from her family. Learning and the world of the intellect were deemed to militate against the cultivation of submissiveness and befuddle the much-cherished moral intuition attributed to women, who required training rather than education. They needed to learn to manage the household, and Latin and mathematics were of no use in such a venture. In 1848 *Punch* characterised the 'model daughter' as 'clever and adept in preparing gruel, white-wine whey, tapioca, chicken broth, beef-tea, and the thousand little household delicacies of the sick room ... She knows nothing of ... "Woman's Mission".'[12] In Ireland things were little different. As late as 1878 – the year in which the Intermediate system was established – *The Irish Times* pronounced that 'Home is the sphere of a woman ... and self-sacrificing love her only legitimate heroism.'[13] Restriction characterised all places which women might occupy. Even their garments formed a place of confinement. Tightened waists, heavy fabrics and cumbersome and plentiful underclothing prevented all but the most socially desired feminine movements. Vigorous physical activity was frowned upon. Ladies who took to cycling in Dublin in the 1880s were subjected to verbal abuse. A *risqué* and unladylike activity, it provided women with the opportunity to move about the urban landscape as they pleased and was physically and socially emancipatory. In short, it allowed them expand the 'place' they might occupy.[14]

With the growth of the middle class toward the end of the nineteenth century, understandings of acceptable forms of employment for girls began to change. The social dynamic was altered by, but also reflected in, the inclusion of girls under the terms of the Intermediate Education Act (1878), although, initially, they had been excluded.[15] While schools were eager to grasp the new opportunity, they were also concerned that Intermediate (secondary) education might unsex girls. Their concerns sometimes reveal a hesitancy; on the one hand eager for their girls to succeed yet nervous lest too much education make them unmarriageable, unemployable and unfeminine – a little learning might truly be a dangerous thing! Indeed, the ability of girls to withstand the new examination process ushered in under the Intermediate system was causing concern as late as 1899, when Alice Oldham, honorary secretary of the Central Association of Irish Schoolmistresses, submitted before the Palles Commission that '[i]n the Dublin schools there appears to be an increasing dislike among the most cultured parents to send their girls in for the Intermediate, owing to the high pressure, and to the fear that the girls will injure their health by over-study.'[16] The ambiguity surrounding these issues becomes evident when we consider this submission to the same commission by Margaret Byers, principal of Victoria College, Belfast: 'The examinations have revolutionised girls' education in Ireland. The results fees enable head mistresses to increase the school staff ... accommodation and general efficiency and to offer salaries that secure high-class teachers.' She also reported that 'pupils of Victoria College have been in the foremost ranks at Newnham and Girton, Edinburgh and Glasgow.'[17]

Perhaps the tensions are best captured by the submission of Henrietta White, principal of Alexandra College, Dublin, who, arguing against a separate course of study for boys and girls for the Intermediate examination, urged that:

> girls go in [to the Intermediate examinations], as in the Royal University, on equal terms with the boys ... as there is an increasing idea that girls should be educated to be independent ... and get an education to fit them for the world. In saying this, [she had] not mainly in her mind the professional women, but the mother of sons, for in order to be able to train them properly, a woman's faculties should be developed and cultivated.[18]

The appeal relating to the 'mother of sons' is typical of early feminists, who had to be constantly sensitive to the accusation that freedoms would unshackle women from their 'natural' duties. White, an early and strident advocate of educational opportunities for women and principal of a school that has championed them, clearly understood the risk.

But school was only one 'place', although, undoubtedly, a prerequisite to occupying others. Indeed it was the widening of access that
allowed women such as Maud Clarke and Helen Waddell to develop
their fledgling interest in science; twentieth-century beneficiaries
of those 'petticoated' and 'corseted' forerunners (see chapter 2).
'Place' could be internal, intellectual and private, a space where
women, such as Mary Hayden could contemplate the prohibited
possibilities of a room of one's own at Trinity College. It was a
private topography of imagination and the physical landscape
traversed by women such as those considered by Kathryn Laing in
her essay on female Irish writers. For others it was a combination
of intellectual engagement and alien place as witnessed by those
women who attended Cambridge University in the nineteent
century and discussed by Susan Parkes (chapter 5). Amongst these
were the Irish Dr Sophie Bryant, a key figure in the establishment
of Hughes Hall, Cambridge, and the less well-known Conan sisters
whose high-spirited dislike of 'Cambridge butter' introduced a note
of fun into the busy early days at the first home of Hughes Hall in
Merton Street.[19] For women of this period the 'place' that brought
personal fulfilment, by which they were defined and found the
perfect means of contributing to humanity was deemed, by all
levels of society, to be marriage. Laws emanating from Westminster
meant that, in both Ireland and England, upon marriage, a women
became the property of her husband, a position Mary Wollstonecraft
described as 'legal prostitution'. Upon marriage a woman's property,
including any income she earned, passed into the possession of her
husband. Nineteenth-century marriage stripped a woman of almost
all legal entitlement; custody of children in the case of separation
was customarily decided in favour of the father, while the burden
of proof in divorce cases lay almost entirely upon the female party.
Women such as Caroline Norton in England or Lady Emily Cecil
in Ireland challenged the 'place' accorded them within marriage,
a 'place' that allowed husbands to behave recklessly, immorally and
violently with impunity. In doing so they challenged the sacred
reverence in which the institution of marriage was held and
exposed the hypocrisy and misogyny that informed the contract in
the nineteenth-century. Unravelling aspects of, or reconstructing,
by forcing changes in law, these 'places' meant that women began
to occupy new 'places' – classrooms, hospital wards, observatories,

laboratories, parliament. Later still to occupy the 'flapper' dress, unrestricted and stridently and sympathetically female – as much a statement of intent as the safety-pin of a much later Punk generation. While this volume does not discuss this extraordinary period, the essays of both Jennifer Fitzgerald and Margaret Ó hÓgartaigh's reveal how the achievements of the nineteenth-century provided, at least, a solid foundation for those that followed in the twentieth.

Because we have insisted that the intellectual life of women in nineteenth-century Ireland was complex and potent we wish to conclude by outlining, however briefly, the extent to which intellectual disparity was held to exist between the sexes.[20] This aspect of history is easily overlooked, but the frustrations and achievements of women in this period cannot be understood or appreciated outside this context. The literature pertaining to intellectual inferiority is too vast to consider here, but a few examples may suffice to demonstrate the ingrained nature of 'scientific' thought and social assumption. The artistic, economic and political world had been created by men, not, apparently, because of socio-economic constructs but because men were superior in these areas – men succeeded because they were men, not because they had been afforded limitless opportunities. Shakespeare, Michelangelo, Mozart and Brunel had no female counterparts; hence, men were superior. These assumptions were not limited to the Irish. Writing in the *Christian Observer* in 1865, Oxoniensis [pseud.] suggested that 'the reasoning powers' of men were 'more perfect' than in women. No woman had succeeded in drawing an Othello or Faust because 'it was impossible for her ever completely to know or to realize the tempest of passions which sway' such characters.[21] Again, in *The Lancet* (1868) a contributor notes that 'to apply the same systems of education and training to both sexes alike … would be to act in defiance of natural laws, and to diminish the usefulness and lessen the moral and spiritual influences which women unquestionably exert'.[22] Others argued that if men and women were, in fact, equal, a more even distribution of power would have been found among primitive societies, whereas Victorian anthropologists had not discovered such communities. Craniometry was also employed to scientifically prove the intellectual inferiority of women, leading R.S. Charnock, president of the London Anthropological Society, to declare in 1874 that:

the difference between the sexes as regards the cranial cavity increases
with the development of the race, so that the male European excels
more the female than does the negro the negress; and hence, with the
progress of civilization, the men are in advance of the women, so that
the inequality of the sexes increases with civilization.[23]

Indeed, it was argued that because men had expended so much
energy on developing the modern world and protecting women from
its vagaries, they had inevitably developed a more sophisticated and
responsive intellect. In effect, man had become superior to woman in
order that she might be safe within her subjugation.

These, then, are some of the contexts within which the women
and schoolgirls considered in this volume existed and operated. With
the exception of Maude Clarke and Helen Waddell (see Chapter 2),
the work they undertook and the courses they pursued belong mostly
to the nineteenth century. Without them, we might well have never
had a Clarke and Waddell or, indeed, the 'petticoated, corseted and
hatted gentlewomen of a lifetime ago'.

I wish to convey my deepest thanks to those who have so kindly
contributed to this volume and hope that it might inspire others to
seek out 'hatted gentlewomen', or perhaps to become those of this
generation!

1

'Starry Eyed': Women in Science in Nineteenth-Century Ireland

CLARA CULLEN

Introduction

A recently published book, *How Irish Scientists Changed the World*, covering three centuries, includes essays on just two Irish women: the astronomer Annie S.D. Maunder (1868–1947) and astrophysicist Jocelyn Bell Burnell (1943).[1] This is not unusual. In the 2003 publication *Physicists of Ireland*, covering four centuries, thirty-two men are included but not one woman (although the twentieth-century physicist Kathleen Lonsdale (1903–71) is given a mention in the introduction).[2] A collection about Irish mathematicians from 1560 to 1966 has sixteen essays on various people, none of them women.[3] An earlier compilation on Irish chemists lists sixty-three scientists – all men.[4] Indeed, compilations on Irish scientists in general are sparse in their mention of women who played a part in the development of science or scientific institutions in Ireland. Mollan's recent two-volume work on people with Irish connections born between the early seventeenth century and 1916 who contributed to the development of the chemical and physical sciences contains 118 essays, five of them on Irish women.[5] An earlier compilation of biographies of Irish scientists, *Irish Innovators in Science and Technology*, and its predecessors[6] include eleven women among the 154 'pen-portraits of men and women involved in Irish science and technology'.[7] Amongst them are half a dozen nineteenth-century ladies – entomologist Mary Ball (1812–98) and her sister Anne (1808–72), Mary Parsons, Countess of Rosse, photographer and philanthropist (1813–85), artist and naturalist Mary Ward (1827–69), astronomer Agnes Mary Clerke (1842–1907), lichenologist Matilda Knowles (1864–1933) and Margaret Lindsay Huggins (1848–1915), a pioneering astrophysicist. Susan McKenna-Lawlor, in her 1998 book on female scientists in Ireland, treats the lives and scientific achievements of these same ladies.[8] They also figure in the Women in Technology and Science (WITS) publication, *Stars, Shells and Bluebells*, which records the life and work of sixteen female scientists of the nineteenth and twentieth centuries.[9] A companion WITS publication, *Lab Coats and Lace*,[10] adds to the study of pioneering Irish women who sought to acquire a scientific education and a career in the sciences or technology and includes studies of veterinarian Aileen Cust (1868–1937), Alice Perry (1885–1969) – the first woman to graduate in engineering in Britain or Ireland, the aviator Lilian Bland (1878–1971), the astronomers Annie Maunder (1868–1947) and Alice Everett (1865–1949), the geologist Sydney Mary Thompson (1852–1923), Mary Andrews (1852–1914) and the Boole sisters – the mathematician Alicia Boole Stott (1860–1940) and Lucy Boole (1862–1905), believed to be the first female professor of chemistry in Britain. Four of these women – Agnes Clerke, Margaret Lindsay Huggins, Alice Boole Stott and Annie Maunder – were among the ten women who had achieved a high reputation in different scientific fields and who were shortlisted in a competition in summer 2013 to decide on Ireland's greatest female inventor.[11]

As individuals, most of these nineteenth-century women had to acquire scientific knowledge and expertise without formal training, but all of these women came from aristocratic or professional backgrounds; they were in 'a materially privileged position and had the opportunity to "see" through the activities of their male friends and relatives how professional scientific life was lived'.[12] Their material contributions to science were, for most part, published under pseudonyms,[13] or as illustrators and contributors to the publications of their male friends and colleagues, or in partnership with their husbands. For example, Ellen Hutchins illustrated books and contributed records and specimens to others but did not publish herself, allowing her male

colleagues and fellow collectors to publish her findings instead.[14] These
women's names recur in any study of nineteenth-century science and
one would be forgiven for believing that they were extraordinary in
their interest in scientific subjects.

Historical Context

However, women's interest in science was not a new phenomenon
in nineteenth-century Ireland. Although women had benefited from
the inclusion of girls in the terms of the Intermediate Education
Act in 1878[15] and from 1879 could present themselves for the degree
examinations of the new Royal University of Ireland (RUI), they
were excluded from formal scientific academic education in Ireland
until the 1880s.[16] It was 1883 when the president of Queen's College,
Belfast, J. Leslie Porter, reported that 'the Council of the College, at
the commencement of the Session, resolved to admit women to the
Arts Classes ... This is the first instance in which women have been
admitted as Students to a University College in Ireland; and the result
has been in all respects most satisfactory.'[17] Before that, women with
an interest in scientific subjects attended lectures organised by several
Irish scientific and learned institutions – attendance being available to
those who, or whose families, were members of these societies. From
early in the nineteenth century the Royal Dublin Society (RDS)
had opened its scientific lectures to all and in 1815 William Higgins's
courses of lectures on chemistry were 'so successful that stringent
"ticket only" regulations were enforced for admission to the four
hundred places, some of which were appropriated for ladies only'.[18]
Dublin's Zoological Society from its foundation in 1830 admitted
women as full members, and they, together with the female relatives
of other members, attended the regular scientific papers presented
at the society. When the British Association for the Advancement of
Science (BAAS) met in Dublin in August 1857, 'the total number of
tickets issued to Members and Associates was 2,005, of which fifteen
were new Life Members, 276 Annual members, 900 Associates and 569
Ladies'.[19] Trinity College Dublin admitted the public to some lectures;
by 1868 many of the lectures were open to the public and 'ladies may
attend all of them which are suitable for ladies, but [...] no one can
receive a certificate of instruction unless he be a student in arts of
the college'.[20]

For the less well-connected, local Mechanics' Institutions and scientific societies, established throughout the country from the 1820s, offered the opportunity for self-help and improvement to many ordinary men and women who could afford the institutes' fees. Some of these institutions were unashamedly middle-class in tone but there were many others whose attention was directed at improving the moral and intellectual well-being of the working classes. Dublin Mechanics' Institution, for example, was established in 1824 with the stated aim of promoting the scientific education of artisans. The annual ten-shilling subscription entitled the members to attend lectures on various subjects, including the sciences, and to use and borrow from the institute's library. In 1839 females were admitted and by 1850, the Institution's Reading Room had 'crowded assemblages of readers that frequent it every evening, as well as a large attendance during the day'.[21] The growing popular interest in science was encouraged by regular exhibitions of Irish industry, organised by the RDS from 1834, especially the Great Industrial Exhibition of 1853, organised by the society at its headquarters on Leinster Lawn in Dublin and visited by over a million people.[22] This popular interest was encouraged by Irish scientists such as Robert John Kane, who saw scientific and industrial education as the best way of improving the economy of Ireland and the living standards of its people.

Interest in science was not confined to Dublin. In Belfast, for example, Belfast Academy and Belfast Academical Institution opened their meetings to women, and by 1836 a good many girls attended classes at the Belfast Academy and 'many adults, both ladies and gentlemen, attended the Academy Natural History Society meetings'.[23] In Cork, scientific interest supported the Royal Cork Institution (founded in 1813) and in 1835 Denis Bullen, the professor of chemistry at the institution, could assure a government commission that 'The ladies of Cork have a great taste for scientific reading.'[24]

By the mid-nineteenth century in Ireland, therefore, women were a familiar part of the audience at scientific lectures. For many of these ladies, attendance may have been because of a recognition of 'the importance of maintaining the "benificent activities" of science by their patronage'[25] and they may have been aware of the influence this gave them over their husbands and sons, and the good example that they might set by their interest in science and the support of science. However, for others, their support and attendance was due to personal interest, a desire to learn and, in some cases, the opportunity these lectures offered to improve their employment prospects.

This study will focus not on those women who attended scientific lectures out of social interest, but will instead look at the activities and interests of numbers of other women who pursued scientific knowledge, who were not 'high profile' and whose activities have been barely noted or recognised. It will show that the very active scientific environment in mid-nineteenth-century Ireland was not exclusively male and that although, as in England, a large number of ladies attended lectures and demonstrations on popular science, there were also a significant number who participated in formal courses of lectures on scientific subjects. Their studies were facilitated by two institutions in Dublin: the Museum of Irish Industry and its successor, the Royal College of Science for Ireland (RCScI), which from 1854 until 1926 offered courses of lectures which were equally available to men and women.[26]

The Government School of Science at the Museum of Irish Industry

In the 1850s the management of the provision of scientific education in Ireland changed. The newly established Department of Science and Art (DSA) in London determined that the teaching of science outside the universities should be put on a formal basis. In 1854 a Government School of Science was established at the recently opened Museum of Irish Industry (MII) in St Stephen's Green, with the intention that this new school would confirm that institution's role as a provider of industrial education.[27] The museum building, with exhibitions 'embracing the general range of the industrial arts', contained 'a series of proper museum galleries, a large lecture theatre and laboratories'.[28] When it opened to the public in 1853, the Museum of Irish Industry contained not only galleries holding a wide range of industrial exhibits and a lecture theatre, but offices, a library, the Geological Survey for Ireland and 'a special chemical department, with laboratories, for carrying out such scientific researches as might be required for the public services, and also for giving instruction in practical and analytical chemistry'.[29]

The courses at the School of Science at the MII were intended for a specific constituency, Ireland's 'artisans and the industrial classes',[30] and it was to be 'a centre and a school of Instruction and Research in the

Industrial Arts – a School of Industry for the country'.[31] The director
of the museum and of the new School of Science was Sir Robert John
Kane (1809–90). Kane was a Dubliner, second son of a prosperous
manufacturer, and a Catholic.[32] He was by training and education a
scientist, internationally recognised by contemporaries as one of the
best scientific minds of his day. By the 1840s his interests had moved on
from pure science to its industrial applications and to 'promoting …
industrial knowledge' and scientific education.[33] Robert Kane
believed that the new institution had been 'founded … for the benefit
of the people' and was determined that it would be a place where
'the rivalries of creeds and parties [would] find no admission'.[34]
He carried his commitment to equality of access to scientific
education further when he announced that in 'the formation of the
classes of the present institution they recognised no distinction of
sex'.[35] Kane's commitment was supported by his colleagues, described
in a contemporary newspaper as 'a first-rate staff of professors … Jukes
whose scientific and literary reputation requires no comment … [and]
Professor Sullivan, the talented pupil of Liebig'.[36]

To deliver these commitments, the School of Science offered
courses of popular lectures on scientific subjects during the day, with
corresponding courses delivered in the evening for the benefit of
those whose business prevented them from attending during the day.[37]
These 'popular' lectures were free and were attended by audiences of
hundreds, both men and women. Apart from these popular courses,
the professors and lecturers were responsible for more advanced
courses in botany, chemistry, physics, geology and practical laboratory
work, for which fees were charged. The fee was to encourage serious
students and 'in order to test the reality of the wish to learn on the
part of those attending'.[38] Those who attended these advanced lectures
were expected to have at least an elementary knowledge of the subject,
although W.K. Sullivan on occasion complained about the poor arithmetic of the students in his chemistry classes. From the beginning
the lectures went beyond classroom teaching and the students were
required to apply their acquired knowledge in practical experiments in
the school's laboratories. The courses were detailed and over the years
the core scientific subjects expanded to include other subjects such as
zoology, organic and inorganic chemistry and crystallography. These
systematic courses of scientific lectures might be considered as the first
fully organised arrangement, outside academia, to facilitate the access

of ordinary people to popular scientific education. Examinations were held at the close of each session. The majority of the students who presented themselves for the museum's examinations were those for whom a certificate of proficiency in one of the industrial sciences might assist their future career, and successful students had the opportunity to recoup their fees by winning one of the monetary prizes awarded to the most successful students.

Very few records of the School of Science at the MII and its students have survived and the original student registers no longer exist. The printed annual reports of the MII to its paymaster in London, the Department of Science and Art (DSA), give only the numbers of students attending the various courses and the names of those who excelled in the examinations. These lists of prize winners, together with the reports of the annual presentation of prizes published in Irish newspapers from 1855 to 1867, remain the only constant, albeit incomplete, source of information regarding those students whose attendance at the museum's educational courses was more than passing or casual.[39] It is from these reports that we know of the numbers and some of the names of the women who attended the courses of lectures in the School of Science. Out of the 330 students who were successful in the examinations at the Museum of Irish Industry and for whom there are records, at least forty female students are listed as having been awarded prizes or certificates. We have no idea what percentage of the student body were women – but, given the proportion of women among the prize winners, we can assume they attended in significant numbers.

At the school's first prize giving, on 28 May 1856, Kane congratulated these women students as follows:

[h]itherto it had been the practice not to include the female portion of the community in their educational arrangements, and, generally speaking, the whole scheme of education had been to supply scientific education to gentlemen only; but in the formation of the classes of the present institution they recognised no distinction of sex. Consequently, several ladies had been students, and in the competition for prizes distinguished themselves in a high degree … The commencement that had been made that session in developing female talent in the pursuits of industry could not but be productive of the most beneficial results.[40]

Fifteen students registered for the first course in natural history; in examination in May 1856 there were four women among the ten successful students and of these 'Miss Halgena Hare's answering was remarkable for its excellence, general correctness, and number of answers'.[41] Her sister, Miss T.S.A. Hare, was awarded a certificate in the same examination and both women gave their address as 76 St Stephen's Green, where Mathias Hare, LLD was the proprietor of Dublin High School.[42] Halgena continued her scientific studies, being awarded prizes in geology, chemistry and physical science in 1857 and 1858 as well as first place in the overall 'general' examination in 1858.[43] She was described by Robert Kane at the 1858 prize giving as 'the most distinguished student of the present session', and the Lord Lieutenant, when presenting Halgena with her prizes, expressed his 'gratification at being enabled to confer the most distinguished honour on a lady, and his admiration of the gallantry of the gentlemen students in permitting themselves to be beaten by the ladies'.[44] Frances Annie Hare joined her sisters as a student at the School of Science in 1857, winning prizes in zoology and botany, whilst also being awarded prizes at the RDS School of Design. The educational efforts and scholastic attainments of the three Hare ladies may have been intended to contribute to the family enterprise, the Dublin High School, but by 1862 the school had been closed.

Amongst the other ladies who had been successful students in 1856 were Frances Elizabeth Armstrong and Katherine H. Egan, both of whom were awarded prizes or certificates in various subjects. Frances Elizabeth Armstrong was almost certainly the daughter of Francis Thomas Armstrong, builder, and both lived at the same address at 55 Baggot Street, Dublin.[45] She was awarded prizes and certificates in geology and physical science in 1856 and 1857 and may have been pursuing her studies for her own interests or in preparation for an educational career. She was probably one of the 'young ladies' described by Robert Kane in 1859 who 'are themselves more or less connected with education, and will go forth to diffuse through society, by the most powerful and favourable influence, sound scientific truth'.[46] These first prize winners are typical of the women who followed them as students at the Government School of Science at the MII. The majority were Irish and middle-class and, although the institution's records do not include the religious affiliation of the individual students (as it was open to all regardless of creed), the surviving records indicate a range of religious backgrounds – Catholic, Quaker, Methodist, Presbyterian and Church of Ireland.

From 1854 to 1867, every year, without exception, saw the names of female students appearing in the lists of prize winners, and almost every year they also figured in the lists of students awarded medals by the Department of Science and Art. Three Harman sisters, Hester, Harriet and Henrietta, were notable among the prize winners at the School of Science and at the RDS School of Design at the end of the decade. Between 1858 and 1860, Harriet was awarded prizes in zoology, practical zoology and botany and a certificate in geology, and Hester was a prize winner in zoology, practical zoology and botany. During these years they also participated in classes at the School of Design at the RDS, along with Henrietta, who was appointed as a pupil teacher at the RDS in 1858, causing the Lord Lieutenant to comment that he was glad to observe that in this, as 'in the twin institution in Stephen's Green, the young ladies have at least borne their part in obtaining the honours'.[47] All of the Harman sisters made good use of their qualifications and knowledge, and were employed as required at the Museum of Irish Industry, drawing diagrams to illustrate lectures during 1858 and 1859 and possibly later, and making quite a good living.[48] They may also have been teachers, although this is impossible to confirm. In 1901 'Harriette' and 'Esther' Harman were living in London, aged 65 and 73 respectively, and maintaining themselves by 'drawing and archaeological work', working from home.[49]

Other students' addresses were registered to solicitors, to private schools, to widows, to merchants, farmers and bank managers. Many of them were teachers, either in the model and national schools or in private 'seminaries'. Robert Kane and his colleagues continually emphasised the educational role of many of the female students, and the majority of those who attended courses at the MII were intent on a career in the field of education. In 1862, for example, Kane told the Treasury Inquiry that 'Practically all the ladies who attend the day systematic courses are either governesses or persons preparing to be governesses. They receive here an instruction which they would get nowhere else, and similar to that which is given in the Ladies' College [Queen's College, London, founded in 1848] in London.'[50] Miss Adelina Rorke, who took first prize in botany in 1865, was one of those who derived her income from education. *Thom's Directory* for 1864 noted John Rorke, 'teacher of English and Science', and Miss Rorke's 'ladies academy', both at 4 Pembroke

Place in 1864 and at 7 Pembroke Road in 1866, where the academy was still situated in 1872.[51] Certainly some the women were of the group described by Anne O'Connor as 'young women of the middle classes, living in reduced circumstances', who were forced to earn their living.[52]

Although many of the students were in, or intending to join, the teaching profession, there were others who probably attended courses at the School of Science from personal interest – students like Miss Eleanor Cope, 'periodical dealer' of 34 Castle Street, who was awarded certificates in zoology and geology in 1860 and 1861 respectively. There were some families who may have attended the courses at the MII in order to expand their scientific knowledge, like John F. Murray, Mrs J.F. Murray and Hannah Murray, who between 1859 and 1860 were awarded certificates in physical science, botany and geology.

Apart from the Hares, the Harmans and the Coneys, there were other family groups (probably sisters) registered as students at the museum. There were Clara A. and Gretta D. Stritch, both of whom were awarded prizes in botany and medals at the museum examinations between 1865 and 1867, and Mary L. and Gertrude Hayes, prize winners in botany in 1867. Others are typified by Jane Anne [Jeannie] Leeper, the daughter of the secretary of the Church Education Society and sister of Alexander Leeper, the first warden of Trinity College, University of Melbourne, who won prizes in botany (1863) and geology (1864).[53] Jeannie Leeper, who, like her mother before her, greatly resented that, as a woman, she was barred from higher education, attended these courses as her only option in furthering her education. By 1876 Jeannie had taken over as housekeeper for her family in Dublin and had become involved in the movement for women's rights. She maintained her interest in science and education, heard Huxley's address to the British Association for the Advancement of Science when it met in Dublin in 1878 and, with her sisters, attended the 'strange sight of nine ladies in caps and gowns receiving degrees',[54] although she believed that Trinity College Dublin should have taken the lead in admitting women to higher education in Ireland. Jane Anne Leeper typified the corpus of female students who a few years later benefited from the establishment of Alexandra College and similar educational institutions. In 1921 her family described her as the 'only member of the family here who had any brains; it was a pity she lived in the wrong generation'; they believed her to be 'extraordinarily clever and if only she had been born in this generation, would have been really happy working for exams and honours'.[55]

Robert Kane was very proud of the achievements of these women. He took every opportunity of referring to them and to their achievements in official reports, in evidence given to various government committees, and at the annual distribution of prizes. In 1868, for example, in his evidence to the Commission on the Department of Science and Art in Ireland, he described the audience at the science lectures as:

> attended by large numbers of girls and ladies of the middle class, and thus they supplemented in a most valuable manner the ordinary elements of female education. I think that the system of public instruction of an elementary and popular character in Dublin has exercised, for the last couple of generations, a most valuable influence upon the training of female society in the middle classes.[56]

The Earl of Carlisle, who as Lord Lieutenant attended several of the distributions of prizes at the School of Science and who was a supporter of Kane's ideas regarding technical education, also frequently referred to the successes of the female students. In 1859, he described the school as:

> the serene temple of knowledge ... the rivalries of creed and parties can find no admission here ... no distinction of class, or creed, or opinion, can find admission, so likewise there is no monopoly of sex. The laurels that are to be gathered here are twined around fair as well as around manly brows.[57]

Two years later, in 1861, he remarked that 'in every other quarter where we hear of classes and competitive examinations, the actors in these operations are exclusively of the sterner sex, while here, without any departure from the rigid rule of impartiality, the lists are entered and the palm, as we have seen, frequently carried off by the gentler aspirants'.[58]

Carlisle and Robert Kane were justified in emphasising the examination successes of the female students. These women did not confine their studies to the 'softer' sciences and were very successful in the more technical subjects. Robert Kane seemed to have been particularly proud of this. He told the Treasury Inquiry in 1862 that the ladies:

> [c]ompete with the best of the male pupils and carry off a great number of the prizes ... their greater sensitivity and power of appreciating differences secure to them a proficiency in Zoology and Botany; but their success is not confined to those sciences. In Natural Philosophy, Chemistry and Geology, some of the highest prizes have been taken by ladies.[59]

One of the most determined of the women who studied at the Museum of Irish Industry, Matilda Coneys, was also a teacher, and in at least one of the years she was a student, her address was that of Miss Rorke's academy, presumably because she was teaching there. Matilda and her sister, Zoe Leigh Coneys, regularly appeared in the prize winners' lists, both at the School of Science and later at the Royal College of Science for Ireland (RCScI). Matilda was awarded first prize in practical chemistry in 1862, in chemistry in 1863 and was a medal winner in both years. Zoe Leigh Coneys was awarded prizes and certificates in botany and chemistry between 1858 and 1862 and, like Matilda, was awarded a medal in 1862.[60] It was probably Matilda Coneys, writing as 'M.C.', who published a description of her experience as a student at the School of Science at the MII:

> We are so proud of it because it is, I believe, the only one in the kingdom where, as our much esteemed Dean Sir Robert Kane said to me ... 'woman is in her proper intellectual position, on a perfect equality with man' ... The most perfect harmony, courtesy and good feeling has always existed there. We sit on the same benches in the lecture theatre and read in the same library [as the men] ... I was the first lady who worked in the laboratory, and I found my fellow students as ready to tender me any little civility I needed, as if I were in a drawing room.[61]

It was Matilda Coneys who was instrumental in ensuring that when the new College of Science was established in 1867, women should be admitted to the courses at the RCScI 'as heretofore to the Classes of the Irish Industrial Museum'.[62] There is a letter from 'Miss M. Coneys', dated 27 November 1867, in the council minutes

of the college, 'requesting to know whether Pure Mathematics forms
a distinct Course from Applied Mathematics, and whether she would
be permitted to join it'. On 'a motion from the Chair' (the new dean,
Robert Kane), the council agreed that:

> Female students be admitted to all courses of lectures to be delivered
> in the Lecture Theatre, but not to those in the classroom without
> special permission of the Council. Resolved also, in reference to
> the application of Miss M. Coneys, that considering the circum-
> stances of her case the Council approve of her attending Professor
> Ball's Courses.[63]

Tracing the story of the women who attended the courses at the
Museum of Irish Industry is frustrating and most of these women
have vanished from the printed record. The Hare sisters, for example,
had returned from the United States with their father in the late
1850s and, following the closure of Mathias Hare's school in 1862,
probably left Ireland. Frances married and later studied at the Female
Medical College, London.[64] Many others, like Matilda Coneys,
married, and for the most part they have vanished from the record.
What is certain is that these students at the Government School of
Science were strong-minded, intelligent and well-educated women.
The success they achieved is even more remarkable in the context
of the standards and quality of education for girls of the time when,
apart from private tuition, there were few opportunities of education
beyond the elementary level. Before the establishment of the Queen's
Institute in 1861 and Alexandra College five years later, education for
women was rarely seen as a gateway to employment but rather as the
opportunity to acquire useful accomplishments and as a preparation
for marriage. Subjects such as Latin, mathematics and science did
not figure in the curricula of these educational establishments for
girls. Anne Jellicoe, in her submission to the Commission of Inquiry
into Primary Education in Ireland in 1869, described the level of
education she encountered amongst the students when Alexandra
College was founded in 1866:

> in the constant recurrence to the underlying foundations of knowledge
> needed in a thoroughly sound educational process, the experience
> of a few weeks only was required to bring to light, the inaccurate,

vague, and fragmentary nature of the education generally given to girls, the neglect of the rules of spelling, of the principles of grammar, the downright ignorance of arithmetic, the absence of any training of the mind, the meagreness of the so-called accomplishments on which so much time and energy had been wasted.[65]

Female students (such as the Hare sisters and Jane Leeper) would have had access through their families to scientific knowledge and expertise, but all of them were excluded from formal academic courses in mathematics and science.

The Royal College of Science for Ireland

In 1867 the Government School of Science at the Museum of Irish Industry ceased to exist and was replaced by a new and more formal institution, the Royal College of Science for Ireland (RCScI).[66] The RCScI had its origins in the recommendations the Select Committee of Scientific Institutions of 1864, which had recommended that a new college of science should be established in Dublin that would be an independent institution 'of great utility' to Ireland.[67] The 'first comprehensive attempt made in the United Kingdom by the British Government to give State-aided higher scientific and technical education',[68] this new college predated the Royal College of Science in London by twenty years. A more formal institution than its predecessor, it offered courses in scientific education at a number of levels. The full-time course was a three-year one and successful students were awarded the diploma of Associateship of the Royal College of Science for Ireland (ARCScI). Interested students could also register as Occasional students for single subjects in the RCScI's academic or laboratory courses and this was an option taken up by significant numbers of Irish students. Four faculties – mining, engineering, manufactures and agriculture – were established and by the end of the century practical courses in many subjects, including zoology, physics, spectography, engineering and electro-technology, had been added to the original curriculum.[69] In all of these subjects the principles of scientific education established in the Government School of Science continued – practical instruction in the college's laboratories supplemented classroom lectures. Robert Kane was the first dean and new professors of mining, applied mathematics, applied chemistry,

agriculture, botany and zoology joined the staff of the RCScI.[70]
Despite the new title, expanded choices of subject and a number of
new professors, until 1911 the new college continued in the converted
Georgian building in St Stephen's Green that had been home to the
Government School of Science at the Museum of Irish Industry.
Described in 1868 as 'an institution which ... is more complete as a
pure school of science than anything of the kind existing in Scotland
or England',[71] the RCScI had other claims to farsightedness and innovation, as from 1867 it provided access to science education for all,
without any discrimination of religion or gender.

Robert Kane, in his first annual report as the dean of the new
college to the Department of Science and Art, wrote:

> The question of the admission of female students to the College having
> been considered it was decided by the Council that such students
> should be admissible to all courses of instruction given in the lecture
> theatre, but not to those given in the classrooms, unless by special
> authorization of the Council.[72]

As discussed above, this decision had been taken following the request
of one of the star pupils at the old Government School of Science,
Matilda Coneys, who applied to attend a course in pure mathematics
in this new college. On the recommendation of Robert Kane, her
application was accepted, thus ensuring that 'female students should
be admitted to enter for the separate courses of the Professors as
heretofore to the Classes of the Irish Industrial Museum'.[73] Given this
opportunity, that year Matilda and three other women, her sister Zoe
L. Coneys (Botany), Emily McGusty (Theoretical Chemistry) and
Henrietta Pepper (Theoretical Chemistry), were among the thirty-six
students who attended the new College of Science.[74]

Matilda Coneys did not disappoint the RCScI's faith in her and in
1868 Robert Kane reported:

> My Lords are aware, by previous report, that the Council had arranged
> for the admission, under certain regulations, of female students to attend
> the lectures of the professors. The utility of this concession in favour of
> higher female education is satisfactorily shown by the high position
> taken in the examinations by a young lady who obtained the 1st prize in
> the class of pure mathematics.[75]

In 1874 all remaining restrictions on female students were lifted when Alice Stopford (later the nationalist historian Alice Stopford Green), Louisa Digges La Touche (later Lady Principal of Alexandra College) and Camilla L'Estrange, the approval of the council having been obtained, 'were admitted to the Physics course, and took a high place in the Sessional examinations'.[76] Women were excluded from competing for scholarships until the end of the century and none of the women registered for the full Associateship course until October 1901, when Anne Frances Farrell and Aileen Frazer were entered in the RCScI books.[77] However, the Coneys and their fellow students in these early years of the RCScI were trailblazers for numbers of other women who subsequently attended courses there. From the opening of the college in 1867 a significant number of women attended the courses offered on a wide range of scientific subjects and competed equally (and successfully) with men in the examinations. By the 1880s, after the RUI was established and opened its examinations to both men and women candidates, up to one sixth of the students on some courses at the RCScI were women.

Like their predecessors at the old School of Science, the majority of the female students were middle-class, the daughters of solicitors, naval officers, bankers, Presbyterian and Methodist ministers, librarians, academics and government officials.[78] Many of them were students at Alexandra College (founded in 1866) or at the other second-level women's colleges, such as the Dominican College of St Mary's (founded 1882), Loreto College (founded 1893) in Dublin, Victoria College Belfast (founded 1859) and St Angela's College in Cork (founded 1887), and a number were teachers in these or in other schools. Others, like Alice Stopford and Camilla L'Estrange and her sister Jane, entered the courses at the RCScI out of personal interest and a desire to learn. Many took up careers in teaching, like Mary Scarlett, Margaret Johnston and Mary Robertson, who later taught in Alexandra College.[79]

Others had academic ambitions. The first female graduates of the RUI in 1884 (the 'Nine Graces') included four women who had taken practical physics courses at the Royal College of Science for Ireland: Isabella Mulvany, Alice Oldham, Mary Sand and Eliza Wilkins.[80] Some female students continued in the sciences, like the chemists Mary Robertson and Genevieve Morrow. By the end of the century some were making a career in the sciences, like botanist Matilda Knowles who, with her sisters, studied at the college between 1895 and 1896.

From the 1880s, when the barriers to the admittance of women to
the medical professions were lifted, there were a number of women
who attended courses in the RCScI as part of their medical studies,
many of them students at the Catholic University School of Medicine
and the Royal College of Surgeons (RCSI), which admitted female
students from the 1880s.[81] The female medical students at the RCScI
included the first woman to register at the RCSI, Agnes Shannon
(one of three sisters to attend the RCScI), and Emily Winifred
Dickson, the first woman to be elected a fellow of the RCSI in 1893
and who later became assistant master of the Coombe Hospital. Eva
Josephine Jellett, the daughter of a provost of Trinity College Dublin,
one of the first women admitted to courses at the Catholic University
Medical School and later a medical missionary in India, studied at the
RCScI. Like a later medical student, Lily Baker, Eva Jellett transferred
to Trinity when it admitted women in 1904. Kathleen Lynn (1899),
Katherine Maguire (1904), Isabella Ovenden (1904) and Ada English
(1904) were amongst others who studied at the college whilst students
at the Catholic University Medical School.

Amongst those whose later careers did not follow a scientific,
teaching or medical path were two sisters who attended the science
courses at the RCScI – Camilla Alicia Vincentia and Jane Sophia
Frances L'Estrange – the daughters of Sir George Burdett L'Estrange
of Moystown, County Offaly. Camilla never married and, apart from
an unsuccessful attempt to become a Lady Supervisor at Alexandra
College, spent the rest of her life writing letters and visiting relations.
Jane founded the Dublin Workingman's Club, as she wanted to do
something useful with her life. Through her work there she met and
married the archaeologist George Coffey, and their home at Harcourt
Terrace was a meeting place for many of the Irish nationalists in the
period before 1916.

The twentieth century brought changes to the RCScI. In 1900
the responsibility for the college was transferred from London to a
new Irish department, the Department of Agriculture and Technical
Instruction (DATI). The curriculum was revised and new courses
introduced. Fellowships and scholarships, open to both men and
women, were established and for the first time women entered into
the full Associateship programme at the college.

In the first decade of the twentieth century the profile of women
at the RCScI changed. The opening of the universities to women

students meant that the number of women attending the college dropped. Those who attended the courses were more focussed on the sciences and a possible career in these areas. From 1901 women were eligible for scholarships and for the first time they entered into the full Associateship programme. A new building was approved and in 1911 the RCScI moved into new and very palatial premises in Merrion Street (now Government Buildings).[82] Among those present at the official opening were several women, now teaching as well as studying at the RCScI, including Belinda Dawson, Anne Hemphill, Louise Bermingham and Genevieve Violet Morrow.

Conclusion

The period in which the first generation of women studied at the Government School of Science at the MII (1854–67) was a time of educational change and new opportunities for women. All of these opportunities for higher education or a career in anything apart from teaching came too late for the female students of the Museum of Irish Industry. Their younger sisters attended Alexandra College and it was the next generation of female students at the school's successor, the RCScI, who were among the first graduates of the RUI. When Jane Leeper and her sisters watched nine ladies in caps and gowns receiving degrees in 1884 she may not have been aware that among them were some of the women who had succeeded her as students at the college at 51 St Stephen's Green. The female students of the RCScI benefited from the successful campaign for higher education for women which culminated in 1880 with the opening of degrees at the RUI to women. However, none of the existing universities in Ireland allowed women to register as students until 1883. It was 1904 before Trinity College Dublin admitted women and the passing of the 1908 Universities Act which finally completed the struggle for equal access of women to higher education. Before then women had to organise their own university classes.

It was the Government School of Science at the Museum of Irish Industry and its successor, the Royal College of Science for Ireland, that provided access to scientific education where otherwise for many there was none, from 1854 until 1926. This was particularly important for the 50 per cent of the population who were female and who, until the twentieth century, had little access otherwise to advanced courses in scientific subjects. Until 1911 these courses were provided in the most challenging of circumstances – poor facilities, an unsuitable building and, in the early days, a very ambivalent attitude on the part of its managers in London.

We may not know the identity of many of the first women who studied at the School of Science or the RCScI or what direction their subsequent lives took. What is certain is that they were representative of a significant number of women, mostly unknown, who had acquired sufficient scientific knowledge and skills to participate in courses of lectures in advanced scientific topics, had enough self-confidence to compete on an equal footing with men in examinations and frequently to take the top prizes in the two institutions that provided access to all in scientific education.

2

'The Fun of Being Intellectual': Helen Waddell (1889–1965) and Maude Clarke (1892–1935)

JENNIFER FITZGERALD

Joys of the Intellect

Maude Clarke shared 'the fun of being intellectual' with her best friend Helen Waddell.[1] Their parallel journeys began at Queen's University Belfast, where Helen attained a first class honours BA in English literature and language in 1911, followed by an MA by thesis in 1912. Maude graduated with first class honours in modern history in 1913, proceeding to Oxford in January 1914 to a second history degree, again with first class honours.

Maude's academic career began almost at once; from 1916 to 1919 she substituted at Queen's for Professor F.M. Powicke who had moved to London for war work. In 1919 she returned to Oxford as a history tutor at Somerville College, was appointed Oxford University lecturer in 1930, vice-principal of Somerville in 1933 and was in line to become the next principal. By the mid-1920s her publications began flowing, giving promise that she would become one of the leading medievalists of her generation.[2] But breast cancer, diagnosed in 1933, killed off that promise in November 1935.

Helen's career began in stasis. After her brilliant degrees, the Queen's Professor of English, Gregory Smith, recommended strongly that she move to Oxford or to the British Museum in London to edit a text from manuscript sources, the route *par excellence* to university employment in literature. As the only child left at home, Helen felt she could not 'vex' her widowed stepmother 'and leave her alone', so in 1912 she assumed the role of Mrs Waddell's permanent companion-housekeeper, undertaking research based on books in the Queen's library.[3] Helen was 31 when, on her stepmother's death, she moved to Oxford and later to Paris and London to continue the work which eventually became her literary history, *The Wandering Scholars* (1927). Its unexpected success and the offer of part-time publishing work, combined with her failure to obtain a university post, led her to opt for a career as an independent scholar. Her translations, *Mediaeval Latin Lyrics* and *Peter Abelard: A Novel* cemented her reputation. She was conferred with honorary DLitts from the universities of Durham, St Andrews, Queen's and Columbia, received the A.C. Benson medal from the Royal Society of Literature, was made an Associate of the Irish Academy of Letters and a Corresponding Fellow of the Medieval Academy of America. In her time 'she was the best-known medieval scholar in the English-speaking world'.[4]

The fun that Maude and Helen derived from their studies goes hand-in-hand with serious commitment. Belonging to the second generation of women to attend university, they relished the opportunities it offered. A fellow undergraduate described Maude as 'first and unforgettably a scholar', for whom the search for knowledge was 'the vital interest of each day, the central reason for waking and for staying awake, the promise of a complete reward for wakefulness'.[5] For Helen, too, the attractions of scholarship were strong: she was at home in 'the familiar oak-scented darkness' of the Queen's library, 'the long quiet empty spaces, and the dim shelves row on row down the passages where only the likes of *me* are allowed to go'.[6]

In 1915 Helen and Maude co-authored *Discipline*, a marriage-problem novel whose Oxford-educated heroine, Elizabeth St John, rebels against her husband, participating in suffragette window-smashing and spending a night in custody. She publishes a scholarly work which contradicts her academic husband's well-known views on the Bacon–Shakespeare authorship controversy. Like Jane Austen's Elizabeth Bennet, she is deeply discomfited when the repercussions of her actions confront her with her own pride and prejudice. The novel in the end 'disciplines' the heroine while drawing attention to sexual politics. Elizabeth's methods and even her grievances may be misguided, but she expresses the frustration of many university-educated women faced with the restrictions of traditional patriarchal marriage.

The obscure references interspersed on almost every page of *Discipline* reveal the novel's origins in the authors' learning. The characters are scholars at heart, so steeped in the intimate details of their material that the boundaries between work and pleasure dissolve. The collaborators tried hard to get their novel published but by 1918 they had second thoughts: it now seemed 'so terribly undergraduate in its cleverness'.[7] If the novel shows off the authors' erudition, it also reveals their delight in its acquisition. Other women, newly enfranchised in the republic of learning, put it on display in their writing. Dorothy Sayers's detective fiction bristles with classical, Biblical and literary allusions.[8] The novels of O. Douglas (the pseudonym of John Buchan's sister) are equally intertextual, including a reference to Helen's own *Wandering Scholars*.[9] George Birmingham, aka the Belfast-born clergyman, James Hannay, features Helen's *Mediaeval Latin Lyrics* in his novel, *The Hymn Tune Mystery* (1930), one of whose characters is hard at work trying to improve on her translations.[10]

Maude's research also had literary repercussions. Her essay, 'The Deposition of Richard II', overturning the accepted narrative of Richard II's renunciation of the throne, appeared in January 1930. Gillian Olivier's novel, *The Broomscod Collar*, also published in 1930, follows this interpretation.[11] Olivier no doubt heard Maude's revolutionary reading from the horse's mouth; Maude taught her in 1926/27, and we know she discussed her research with her students.[12] In 1931 she told another student about her discovery of the first recorded mention of what we now call a handkerchief.[13] This appears in *The Broomscod Collar*, although the publication in which Maude identifies it postdates the novel.[14] In February 1933, Gordon Daviot's play, *Richard of Bordeaux*, opened at the New Theatre, London, making its leading actor, John Gielgud, a star.[15] The tremendous success of the play focused attention on its historical sources; Olivier sued Daviot, the pseudonym of Scottish writer Elizabeth Mackintosh (who wrote detective stories under the name of Josephine Tey), for plagiarism. The case was settled when the arbitrator, Charles Oman, Oxford's Chichele Professor of Modern History, decided that both authors had researched the subject independently, although the historical community continued to believe that the play utilised Maude's work.[16] She herself played a role as the model of the Irish don, Patricia O'Neill, in *The Dark Tide*, a novel by her student Vera Brittain.[17]

Experiencing, as did so many women of their generation, the joys of the intellect, for Helen, as for Maude, scholarship 'was not work; it was *fun*, it was *life*, it was the happy hunter's day'.[18]

Helen Waddell

But studying also involved engaging with distasteful material. In Belfast, Helen embarked on *Woman in the Drama before Shakespeare* – or, as she told her sister, 'the evaluation of US' – a book which she expected would be 'an abiding joy'.[19] Gregory Smith felt that her feminist views eminently fit her to the subject.[20] Almost immediately, however, she was forced to confront the notorious misogyny of Jean de Meun's thirteenth-century French *Roman de la Rose*, representative of an important strand of medieval literature. Smith accepted 'cynical fun at the expense of women' as routine; other scholars dismissed it as little more than the 'host of somewhat inane jests against one's mother-in-law' which 'time-honored custom has sanctioned in our own day'.[21] It was the rare female researcher who subjected misogyny to scholarly analysis, disentangling personal from cultural attitudes.[22] Helen knew that she should view Jean's brutality in the *Roman de la Rose* from this perspective, but she could not help her revulsion:

> I do not know what to say of him save this – I do not like him. It may be unjust, but in spite of all his philosophy the taste left by his precious *Roman* [*de la Rose*] is not savoury. I had rather read the English Drama from start to finish than go through him again![23]

Such unpleasant reading made her yearn for distraction, so she took one of her father's books off the shelf. This was a volume of the *Chinese Classics, The She King, or Book of Odes*, translated by James Legge; she found herself adapting his ponderous translations into compressed lyric form.[24] Gregory Smith approved and helped her find a publisher.

Helen's *Lyrics from the Chinese*, published in December 1913, was reviewed by the English poet Walter de la Mare and the Irish Æ. Incited by misogyny, it is not surprising that many of the poems focus on women's exclusion and emotions. Æ recognised the subversion lurking beneath the lyricism: 'Who after this book can say that the feminist movement is new or that it is a temporary phase? Had we not better give the vote and settle a grievance that now appears is considerably older than two thousand years old?'[26] Helen compresses, conflates and improvises on Legge's literal translations, drawing the attention of those at the forefront of the Imagist movement who identified her as a kindred spirit.[27]

In 1914 Helen received financial support from Revd George Pritchard Taylor, a Presbyterian missionary in India who had met her while on furlough in Belfast. Aware that she was sacrificing her talents to her stepmother's care, he subsidised her studies; in return, she wrote to him weekly, detailing the progress of her research. At the same time she met George Saintsbury, Britain's most famous man of letters, who had acted as the Queen's external examiner for her BA and MA. They conducted an academic-cum-flirtatious correspondence until his death in 1933. His support would be significant in launching her scholarly career. With the encouragement of her brother Sam, the playwright Rutherford Mayne, member of the Ulster Literary Theatre, she also began to write creatively, eventually publishing in prestigious journals.[28] The decision was practical – 'my paymasters are likely to be publishers and not universities, and I don't like to shut any door. Even if the hole in it is a hole for the kitten, and not for the cat'[29] – but it was also a choice. As Helen's whole writing career would prove, she was never willing to keep the scholarly and the literary on opposite sides of an unbreachable divide. From undergraduate days onwards, and against the norms the academy imposed more and more strictly, Helen would write 'with the mind of a scholar and the graceful pen of a wit'.[30]

Woman in the Drama before Shakespeare proceeded slowly, interrupted by the sudden deaths of the two brothers closest in age to Helen. In November 1914 Billy was lost overboard from the ship on which he acted as medical officer; George, just ordained as a Presbyterian minister, suffered a sudden heart attack in June 1915 on a visit to his fiancée in Cork. Her stepmother would not hire a housekeeper so Helen's 'own work had to begin when what other women would count a good day's work was done'.[31] Mrs Waddell had never liked Helen to go out; in 1916 she was declared an invalid and Helen became captive to her whims and needs, a situation that became hellish when Mrs Waddell, prescribed whiskey for medicinal reasons, succumbed to alcoholism. Battles over the bottle could go on all night; physically and emotionally exhausted, Helen believed that she would never escape. Her academic career faded into a mirage: although Maude was back teaching at Queen's, Helen was not. Gregory Smith was 'dead against the appointment of women' to university posts, so that even the position of assistant lecturer in English literature, to which promising new graduates were usually appointed, was given to a younger and less qualified man.[32]

When her stepmother died in June 1920, on Maude's advice, Helen moved to Oxford to finish her book, whose subject had shifted. The surviving chapters of *Woman in the Drama before Shakespeare* reveal what was lost in this change; Helen's subtle close literary readings suggest that she would have made a sophisticated feminist literary critic, prompting favourable comparison with female Shakespeareans in later years.[33]

She was now committed to investigating the non-liturgical sources of English drama, surviving from the close of the Roman theatres to the medieval mime, a term covering both actor and play. In 1921 she delivered a series of eight lectures, 'The Mime in the Middle Ages', sponsored by the Cassell Trust at St Hilda's College and organised by Oxford's Board of Advanced Studies.[34] Taking up a temporary lectureship in the English Department of Bedford College, University of London for the academic year 1922/23, she changed focus once more. Among the inheritors of the mime whom she had studied were the *scholares vagantes*, clerical students educated in the classics whose songs of inebriate conviviality, joy in nature, sexual pleasure and romantic love were sung in Latin. She had encountered references to the *Carmina Burana* and other collections early in her research but it was only when she recognised the marriage of sacred and profane in their songs that she became 'irretrievably' a student of medieval Latin poetry.[35] Awarded the Susette Taylor Travelling Fellowship by Lady Margaret Hall, Oxford, Helen studied at the Bibliothèque Nationale in Paris from October 1923 to December 1924, reading for herself, 'with a mind emptied, what the ordinary medieval student would have read, to find the kind of furniture his imagination lived among'.[36]

Oxford stipulated two more years' residence for a DPhil dissertation with an altered subject; Helen demurred, believing that a substantial research book in press would help her find an academic post.[37] She delivered another set of Oxford lectures, 'The Wandering Scholars: Ninth to Thirteenth Century', in the 1926 Trinity term. But she was competing with the post-war influx of former servicemen at a time when men were explicitly preferred and women's colleges were beginning to hire men.[38] A female academic's best chance was a residential post, combining supervision (administrative, pastoral and disciplinary) of the female students with teaching and research – although precious little energy, not to say time, would be left over for the latter. Helen resolutely refused to apply for such posts.[39] In May 1926 she set her hopes on the position of head of English at Westfield College, University of London, but her lack of teaching experience (attributable to Gregory Smith) cost her the job. She was 37 when, on the publication of *The Wandering Scholars*, Constable's director, Otto Kyllmann, offered her a part-time position with a salary close to that of a university lecturer. No longer knocking on closed doors, she became, like some other university-trained women in the first half of the twentieth century, an independent scholar.[40]

The Wandering Scholars, published in April 1927, traces the humanist heritage, 'that divine doctrine of reconciliation between body and soul', explicitly contradicted by the teleological ideology of the Middle Ages, which yet peeks out from behind the severest denial.[41] The Church continued to teach the classics and exposed new generations to the enticement of human – as distinct from theological – values. The book traces subterranean manifestations of humanism from the fourth century to its explicit flowering in the twelfth, not only in the revival of classical learning but in the rediscovery of the goodness of the earth, sensitivity to beauty and to human love. Helen weaves her literary history from a dense web of quotations and paraphrases gleaned from this reading, specificities which bring the remotest figures to life through cameo biographies, domestic details and heartfelt comments. She makes even the most austere and esoteric aspects of the Middle Ages accessible to her readers. With her selective focus on the human and the humane, 'she goes deep into the regions of the medieval Latinists', said *The Times*, 'but, unlike certain sapless professorial commentaries, her discoveries are both exciting and charming'.[42] Reviews were ecstatic, appreciating 'that kindling enthusiasm that can make the dead live again'.[43] Within three days of publication, *The Wandering Scholars* was a best seller; by the end of 1927 it was rated one of the year's six best literary books.[44]

However, its stylistic exuberance appeared incongruous to the academy: scholarship was meant to be objective and detached, clearly distinguished from literary subjectivity. It is only with postmodernism's epistemological paradigm shift that critics are beginning to address what Helen Waddell's idiosyncratic methodology actually achieves. The failure of *The Wandering Scholars* to adhere to scholastic protocols such as structure of argument and clarity of focus, even to deliver what its title indicated – the goliards only appear in the last chapter – perplexed its academic audience. Its undoubted learning is not marshalled to convince; the book's thesis is not spelt out but rather implied by means of narrative. Even more disconcerting are the constant allusions scattered throughout the text. Professors complained: 'Scraps of Chinese poetry, stray allusions to Rabelais and Peacock, and out-of-the-way Elizabethan learning, incessant quotations from the poetry of all times and peoples are brought to bear upon these medieval figures and we are supposed to know at once what every distinct reference means.'[45] These literary and cultural references facilitate the reader unfamiliar with medieval thinking by providing more contemporary analogies but they require a different reading strategy than that demanded by academic argument.[46]

Helen's translations, *Mediaeval Latin Lyrics*, published in 1929, were almost universally praised: readers understood that her fidelity was to the spirit of the originals.[47] She is attentive to the music of her verse, replicating Latin rhythms as closely as possible and attempting to keep her English as concise as is the Latin. Scholars recognised the linguistic, historical and cultural learning which went into comparing different Latin texts, but she took liberties in translation, condensing, omitting from, even adding to, the originals, transposing stanzas from one manuscript version to another. It was inevitable that academic critics, committed to the integrity of source texts, would challenge such freedoms.[48] Many objected to the anthology as unrepresentative since it omitted medieval Latin hymns. Helen's own defence, 'I tried to translate them, and could not', did not convince those who held a brief for gravity and piety.[49]

John Scattergood offers a re-evaluation of the strengths and weaknesses of these translations, noting that for Helen the overall meaning took priority over local accuracy.[50] New attitudes see translation as a matter of 'freeing the linguistic sign into circulation', or, as Susan Bassnett puts it, releasing the energy of the source text as it blossoms again.[51] This is precisely what Helen Waddell attempts: 'to give, not a reproduction, but an English echo of the music and feeling of the original'.[52] The unanimous verdict of reviewers was that these were poems in their own right. Helen indeed claimed the creative prerogative: 'A man cannot say "I will translate," any more than he can say "I will compose poetry." In this minor art also, the wind blows where it lists.' Even when she recognised a mistranslation, she couldn't correct it, 'because the mould of the verse had set and I was too obstinate to break it'.[53]

She had planned to write a book on the humanist philosopher, theologian and lover, Peter Abelard, since undergraduate days.[54] The Belfast years of frustration, when her family expected her to repress her academic ambitions in the interest of filial duty, helped her identify with Abelard's struggle as an intellectual upstart, whose works were condemned as heresy by those who did not understand them. Having fallen in love with Constable's director, Otto Kyllmann, whose two failed marriages constituted for her an unbreachable obstacle to sexual union, she also understood Abelard's personal dilemma.[55] An extraordinary night in a Paris hospital in 1924 cemented her identification with Abelard's lover, when, as she wrote:

> I passed, fully awake and not I think delirious, into some strange state of being. For suddenly I was Heloise, not as I had ever imagined her, but an old woman, abbess of the Paraclete, with Abelard twenty years dead: and I was sitting in a great hall lecturing to my nuns on his *Introductio ad Theologiam*. It was near the end of the lecture, and I pronounced the benediction, and sat watching them go out, two by two. And one of them, the youngest and prettiest of my nuns for whom I felt some indulgence, glanced at me sideways as she went out, and I heard her whisper to the older sister beside her, 'Elle parle toujours Abelard'.[56]

The academy was not bound to apply scholarly criteria to a novel. Nevertheless, T.B. Rudmose-Brown, the Professor of Romance Languages at Trinity College Dublin, gave *Peter Abelard* the academic third-degree, ascertaining 'the meticulous accuracy of [Helen's] facts and dates' only to take exception to some of them.[57] She defended herself vigorously, reserving 'the fundamental right of the novelist to invent' – not 'in contradiction to actual fact' but drawing on probabilities thrown up by exhaustive research 'plausible enough for a novel, though not for a monograph'.[58] The interwar years saw a flowering of historical fiction; this had long been the purview of female writers, but their newly acquired education prompted much more extensive research, resulting in exceptional historical novels.[59] Helen's thorough immersion in the twelfth century means that *Peter Abelard* exceeds even this high standard. Her sources include not only the events recounted in the letters of the historical Heloise and Abelard, often in their own words, but she integrates into the dialogue and action the humanist philosophy, canonical gossip, theological debate and troubadour lyric she had absorbed in her reading. These provide the meat of the action, rendering the extreme emotions of the famous lovers – Abelard's arrogance and competitiveness, Heloise's resolution to live as Abelard's whore rather than to jeopardise his career by public marriage – theologically as well as emotionally plausible.[60] Helen does not contextualise the action with period description; instead, snatches of liturgy and fragments of prayers echo as a matter of course through the minds of Abelard the cleric and Heloise, niece of a canon of Notre Dame, occasionally surfacing to provoke a spiritual crisis.

Peter Abelard is rightly valued as historical fiction but it can also be read as a challenge to history, or at least to the positivist historiography championed by the academy. As Stephen Kelly argues, stories and myth keep the dead living alongside their communities; historiography removes them into a secondary discourse of historical contextualisation, 'displac[ing] myth and the cultural work that myth undertook, of gathering to itself the variety and intensity of human experience. As a "practice of meaning", historiography thus leads to existential disorientation: the destruction of experience.' He suggests that it was precisely because Helen realised that the sort of historical analysis demanded by the academy 'would create a breach or rupture between her desire to experience the past and the past's irredeemable distance' that she chose instead to performatively re-experience the lives of Abelard and Heloise in fiction.[61]

Helen's intense identification with both Abelard and Heloise allows her to penetrate not only the lovers' personal dilemma but its spiritual significance for the historical Abelard. *Peter Abelard* weaves the tragedy of Heloise and Abelard's love affair around the themes of suffering and redemption pioneered in Abelard's atonement theology, particularly in his commentary on the Epistle to the Romans.[62] Her novel dramatises the struggle which leads to his theological epiphany, the conversion which replaces his passion for Heloise with an overwhelming devotion to God. The result for Heloise, however, is devastating. True to his new love, he rejects her completely, while she never wavers from her total commitment to him. She may appear devout but that is mere façade: she took the veil not for God's sake but for Abelard's. Here, too, Helen's own experience of emotional imbalance – the depth of her love for 'O.K.' was not equally reciprocated – helped her to identify with Heloise's agony. 'Think for a moment what it would be like if you weren't sure you were loved,' she wrote to a friend. 'That is the real torture. And that is what happens to Heloise at the last.'[63] Not quite the last: Helen invents a scene in which Heloise's grief distresses their mutual friend Gilles de Vannes. Seeing his hurt, she assures him that her agony is momentary, words meant merely to placate but which once uttered become true. As each suffers vicariously for the other, they achieve some relief of pain – maybe even the redemption promised by Abelard's atonement theology.[64]

Peter Abelard was a great success; Helen was in demand as a lecturer and reviewer, fêted and celebrated, invited to meet the great and the good – breakfasting with the former prime minister. Such socialising, combined with her paid work, interfered with her writing. She never completed her monograph on the English humanist John of Salisbury nor the two sequels she planned to *Peter Abelard*. In 1934 she published *Beasts and Saints*, a volume of translations of 'the mutual charities between saints and beasts, from the end of the fourth to the end of the twelfth century'.[65] This was followed in 1936 by *The Desert Fathers*, from Herbert Roseweyde's *Vitae Patrum*, a Latin translation of accounts of the hermit monks of the early Church, much originally written in Greek. *The Wandering Scholars* and *Mediaeval Latin Lyrics* had, of course, focused on the secular joys so abjured by the Church, so that the decision to translate anecdotes of third-century hermit monks famous for extreme asceticism appears rather incongruous. But she chooses to highlight not the desert fathers' solitude or fanaticism but their 'humility, their gentleness, their heart-breaking courtesy', recognising that 'inhumanity to oneself had often its counterpart in an almost divine humanity towards one's neighbour'.[66]

The political climate of the 1930s disturbed Helen profoundly. Events across the globe – the Japanese invasion of Manchuria, the Italian occupation of Ethiopia, the Spanish Civil War and 'the final surrender to the Fascist powers at Munich' – alarmed her; even worse was the failure of the rest of Europe actively to champion the oppressed.[67] The outbreak of war, and especially the fall of France, struck a very deep blow, sending her to translate Latin lyrics 'of the graver sort'.

But wartime strains prevented her squeezing 'the last ounce of courage that will get them into a book'.[68] The death in combat of two of her nephews was an overwhelming grief, prompting her to translate Milton's 'Epithaphium Damonis'.[69] Soon another insidious enemy encroached: intermittent loss of memory. She discovered these poems anew, having forgotten that she had translated them; they were published posthumously in *More Latin Lyrics: From Virgil to Milton*.[70] It took an enormous effort for her to prepare and present 'Poetry in the Dark Ages', a public lecture in October 1947, whose account of the sack of Troy, Rome laid waste by barbarians and Britain invaded by Danes, interspersed with some of those verse translations, paralleled the horrors of the war just ended.[71] Helen's progressive dementia was heartbreaking, for herself and for her family and friends; by the late 1950s she no longer recognised them. Her death on 5 March 1965 was a blessed release.

Maude Clarke

Maude Clarke's early career stands in conspicuous contrast to the bitter years of Helen's Belfast captivity.[72] When Maude was offered the history tutorship at Somerville College, Oxford, Helen felt that she was 'face to face with a phantom self that might have been' herself. 'I didn't know,' she wrote, 'when I refused Oxford ages ago that it was going to hurt like this.'[73] But Maude's job, a college rather than university appointment, was extremely onerous. She gave tutorials eighteen hours a week but also supervised thirty-two other students, helping them select the classes in other colleges that would best fit their studies; these appointments could be scheduled as late as 10 p.m.[74] When, seven years after Maude's appointment, there was talk of a similar tutorship for Helen, Helen was appalled: 'even Maude', she wrote, 'who was broken into it young, has got almost more than she can bear'. Maude herself tried to escape in 1926 by applying for the chair of modern history at Bedford College, a women's college affiliated to the University of London, but a male candidate was preferred.[75]

Eventually, however, Maude's research got underway, while teaching allowed her to communicate her intellectual passions. She began training a whole generation of female academics: May McKisack, professor of history at Westfield College, University of London; Mary Macaulay (Lady Ogilvie), principal of St Anne's College, Oxford;

Agnes Headlam-Morley, the first woman to be elected to a full profes-
sorship at Oxford.[76] Dominica Legge, professor of Anglo-Norman at
the University of Edinburgh, was not formally Maude's student, but
Maude planned a joint research project with her. It was Dominica's
grandfather, James Legge, whose translations of *Chinese Classics* Helen
had adapted with such success in *Lyrics from the Chinese*.[77] In 1927,
Maude's student, Lucy Stuart Sutherland, became a tutor in economic
history and politics at Somerville and Maude's closest friend after
Helen. Her career as an eminent eighteenth-century historian culminated in the principalship of Lady Margaret Hall.[78] Naomi Hurnard,
history tutor at Lady Margaret Hall, Margaret Griffith, the Deputy
Keeper of the Public Records in Ireland, and Betty Murray, principal
of Bishop Otter Teaching Training College in Chichester, were also
Maude's pupils.[79]

Maude urged her students to think for themselves rather than to
base all their arguments on their reading, preferring 'the open mind'
to the relentless defence of a hypothesis.[80] Betty Murray reported
Maude's view of history 'as a reconstruction of particular facts
as seen by a particular mind – your own – and the only essential
thing is to be true to that mind and not to distort things for the
sake of show or be misled by memories of what others have said'.[81]
She constantly tried to bolster her students' confidence, the lack
of which she felt was 'a feminine vice'. She pointed them beyond
the curriculum, advising them to visit medieval buildings around
Oxford so that they could engage with the material context of their
studies.[82] She fostered her students' research abilities; Betty grumbled
that 'apparantly [sic] … one ought to spend every minute till ones
[sic] dying day in PURE RESEARCH'. She brought promising
undergraduates to meetings of the Medieval Group, an informal
gathering of tutors and graduate students to read papers and discuss
historical problems organised by F.M. Powicke, Regius Professor of
Modern History.[83] Powicke referred to her 'almost passionate reserve
which she treasured like a private possession'; this was mitigated by
her charm and wit, but students could feel, as Vera Brittain and Betty
Murray did, that she was only interested in her students' intellectual struggles, not their personal problems.[84] Betty found Maude's
male colleague, Vivian Galbraith, the only academic 'who takes any
trouble to really know one & doesn't just stick at the product of ones
[sic] mind'. Yet Betty suspected that Galbraith, paid three guineas a

term to supervise her BLitt thesis, never read it while 'Miss Clarke really does all my supervising and for nothing.'[85] Graduates who left Oxford disillusioned with the quality of the teaching remembered Maude as an extraordinary exception.[86]

Maude also travelled: in 1919 she accompanied her brother Brice to the Pyrenees to recover from wartime gassing; she went to Italy in the summer of 1920 with her youngest brother, Stewart, known as Chang. She visited him in Greece in 1924, as he was undertaking archaeological exploration; on a visit to Delphi she was thrown from her mule and broke her leg. Chang accompanied her on the journey back to Athens, organising her homeward travel. She had just arrived in Oxford when she heard that he had drowned while sailing with other researchers to the island of Salamis.[87] The shock was terrible: Chang, who shared her academic commitment, was the brother closest to her heart. She escorted her father on a visit to Palestine in September 1925 and in December 1930 to visit her brother Harry, who was an army chaplain in Jamaica.

As a postgraduate Maude had chosen ecclesiastical history as her research field, planning a BLitt thesis on the Irish Franciscans, but scarcity of material forced a change of focus. While teaching at Queen's she began investigating the Anglo-Norman settlement in Ireland; the Chartulary of Tristernagh Priory, Westmeath, an unpublished manuscript she had discovered in the public library in Armagh, would form a central case-study.[88] Her new area was constitutional history, considered the most rigorous and significant of historical fields, dominated by William Stubbs, founder of the Oxford School of Modern History. Over time, however, Stubbs's central thesis, that 'the great characteristic of the English constitutional system is the continuous development of representative institutions', was challenged by a new approach examining the actual day-to-day business of government and the civil servants who carried it out.[89] Incorporating the perspectives of F.W. Maitland and T.F. Tout, this new approach investigated legal and administrative processes to find out what parliament actually did.

Maude belongs to this group of medieval constitutional historians, including her teacher, F.M. Powicke, her colleagues, J.G. Edwards and J.E.A. Joliffe, her student, May McKisack, her contemporaries, Helen Cam, H.G. Richardson and G.O. Sayles and her successors, B. Wilkinson and S.B. Chrimes. Maude's work stands out, however, for an equally relevant input of political theory. Her *Medieval City State*, for example, examines democracy in practice in late-medieval Italy, Germany, the Netherlands and Switzerland, discovering that local populations which controlled their own government often produced tyrants, as the majority chose to trust a strong leader rather than to leave themselves exposed to invasion.[90]

This first book was based on secondary sources; the ten essays she published between 1926 and 1934 offer instead close studies of primary texts which meticulously establish the facts of a certain event. Her expertise in tackling manuscripts and her knowledge of diplomatic (the critical examination of the protocols and formulae of historical documents, especially important in establishing the relationship between actual historical facts and what the documents claim to report) are remarkable, but even more impressive is the lucid narrative she builds out of data so scrupulously established, allowing her to tease out far-reaching implications. According to Helen Cam, these papers contribute to Maude's reinterpretation of English political and constitutional development in the fourteenth century, which in time she would have integrated into 'a full synthesis'.[91]

Some of Maude's papers changed the historical landscape. In 'The Deposition of Richard II', she collaborated with Vivian Galbraith to edit a chronicle by a monk of Dieulacres Abbey near Chester. Offering independent corroboration of a suspect account of Richard II's abdication, this document proved that the version recorded in the Parliamentary Roll 'must be false, deliberately concocted to gloss over the capture and coercion of the reigning king'.[92] Turning the accepted narrative of Richard II's deposition on its head, this essay provoked an editorial in *The Times* and affected all further scholarship.[93] Maude applied iconography to another 'text', the Wilton Diptych, a painting of Richard II kneeling in front of the Virgin, newly acquired by the National Gallery. Since 'Richard's subjects could read a coat more easily than they could read a letter', she argues that the painting's heraldry provided valid interpretative evidence. By means of what a commentator calls 'ingenious detective work', she deduces that the diptych's symbolism translates into recruiting propaganda for a new crusading order.[94] Although this remains Maude's only iconographical work, its findings, supplemented by John Harvey's in the 1960s, have remained fundamental to all subsequent scholarship on the subject.[95]

Maude intended to write a monograph on Richard II, but she had also launched herself into research on Edward II and Edward III. It was fitting, then, that in 1931 she should be asked to write the fourteenth-century volume for the *Oxford History of England* series, the only woman and the only Irish person to be commissioned. She also worked on Irish history: one of her papers investigated the turbulent administration of William of Windsor in Ireland. Under pressure to fund Edward III's French wars, William attempted to collect revenue not by levying taxes locally but through parliament. This was normal practice in England but not in Ireland, leading the colonists to accuse him of illegally coercing their consent.[96] In another paper, Maude examines the introduction during the reign of Edward III of several statutes to limit the jurisdiction of the Crown and of parliament by invoking subjects' rights to 'the due process of law'. This common-law privilege, however, involved archaic, clumsy court procedures; remedies were therefore developed outside common law to punish the king's servants for abuse of power. She analyses in detail each step of this process, impelled in contradictory directions and perhaps influenced by the model of the Anglo-Irish Parliament's indictments of William of Windsor. The result was a totally new procedure, in which the speaker, in the name of the commons as a body, formally prosecuted members of the king's council. The essay pinpoints the moment when parliament makes the transition 'from procedure by petition, with all its implications of grace and favour, to procedure by indictment, which is an assertion of right'.[97] Yet another paper investigates the deposition of Edward II, responsibility for which was shared by the three estates – clergy, nobility and common people – acting together in committee. This was the climax of a long process of change from hierarchical control by the aristocracy to co-operative action, neatly exploiting the rights of the commons by extending not so much power as accountability.[98]

Maude's insight into the constitutional repercussions of specific episodes and processes such as these would be particularly beneficial in a large-scale enterprise such as *The Fourteenth Century*. But first she had to finish a book she had begun in 1930. This was a study of the *Modus Tenendi Parliamentum*, written in Latin and surviving in both an English and an Irish version. Autumn 1932 was indeed the high point of Maude's research career: one book half-completed, another influential tome commissioned and, as Betty Murray commented, 'umpteen other articles on hand. How she ever does it all I fail to understand'.[99] But there was a sudden interruption: in the spring of 1933 Maude was diagnosed with breast cancer. Treatment and illness took their toll; despite her determination to finish the *Modus* book at all costs in the summer of 1934, it was only submitted to the publisher in July 1935, four months before her death.[100]

Medieval Representation and Consent: A Study of the Early Parliaments in England and Ireland, with special reference to the Modus Tenendi Parliamentum challenges the established view that the *Modus* was an idealised account of how a parliament should be conducted; Maude argues instead that it reflected actual practice. Carefully adducing multiple layers of evidence, she posits that it was composed in 1322–23, just after the statute of York had asserted the role of the commons in parliament. She suggests that the *Modus* was the working model for Edward II's deposition in 1327, the abstract notions of harmony and equity it presents translated, in practice, into the rougher justice of dominance and subordination. By 1337 the elimination of the clerical proctors produced a parliament that deviated from that of the *Modus* but the Irish parliament retained the older form, emphasising the principle of consent especially in areas such as taxation. In 1419 the colonists forced the Deputy Lord Lieutenant to certify the *Modus* under the Great Seal of Ireland, an action which made concrete 'the general principle that even the representative of the king himself was below Parliament'.[101]

Maude roots her political theory in the actions of flesh-and-blood functionaries and the mechanics of institutional processes on specific occasions. But its central thesis, that the *Modus*, which grounded the authority of parliament in its application of the principles of representation and consent, was the working basis for constitutional practice, brought her analysis very close to Stubbs'. Recognising the controversial, if not heretical, nature of her argument, she supports her hypothesis of an unusually early date for the emergence of democratic principles by examining the evolution of notions of representation and consent from classical times. But she also provides exciting, convincing evidence that the principle relating taxation to representation and consent has ecclesiastical origins, in a doctrine laid down in the Lateran Council of 1215.[102]

It is not surprising that *Medieval Representation and Consent* was reviewed as risky, provocative and idealistic.[103] Writing under different circumstances, Maude might well have dug deeper into the evidence or modified her conclusions. Although her Whiggish interpretation was out of kilter with the prevailing consensus, she nevertheless contributed substantially to later research. Her thorough, detailed investigation into the English and Irish versions of the *Modus* (texts published in an appendix) applied to significant incidents in medieval history carry historical weight. Her account of the symbolic role played by the *Modus* in 1419 in the resistance of the Anglo-Irish colonists to the administration of the executive became part of the Irish historical consensus.[104] *Medieval Representation and Consent* is referenced by scholarship on the *Modus Tenendi Parliamentum* throughout the twentieth century and into the twenty-first.[105]

Illness and the drive to complete *Medieval Representation and Content* precluded progress on *The Fourteenth Century* but Maude mapped out ideas in a notebook, identifying the century's 'energy and complexity, the restlessness of greed, the cunning, the individualist resistance to the common good – all fighting against a general will to order and a general conviction that the world is God's world and ought to be a better place'. Her theme would be the 'blind purpose', the dynamo powering institutions, 'vastly more significant' than the immediate intention of individual participants. She would face compositional challenges, including 'the danger of treating the great institutions in detachment instead of merging them into the personal conflict, showing them both of it and above it'.[106] Over the Easter vacation of 1935 she 'read nothing but Chaucer', hoping that literature's historical parallels would flesh out fourteenth-century social history. 'For the psychological side,' she resolved, 'every detail of biography that can be scraped together must be pressed to service.'[107] But she could make little headway with the volume as a whole; the commission would pass to her former student, May McKisack, who completed it in 1959, prefaced with an acknowledgement to Maude 'whose book this should have been'.[108]

Maude's premature death came as 'a blow to Somerville, to Oxford and to the cause of historical studies' in England and, as we shall see, in Ireland.[109] *The Times* called her 'our finest scholar on the constitutional and Parliamentary history of England in the fourteenth century and its parallel development in Ireland', comparing her, as did others, with Mary Bateson, whose brilliant research career was also brutally cut short thirty years before.[110] Powicke felt 'privileged to number [her] among the first and most brilliant of [his] pupils'.[111] Helen described Maude's mind as 'extraordinary ... I think she forgets nothing, and yet she reads enormously: but it's not chaos. It's just as though the creative intelligence brooded over the mass.' Her reading was wide-ranging, thorough and up-to-date; according to her friends, 'on her table lay poems and plays so recent that the wonder was that they had in fact been published'.[112] Onboard ship in 1930 she read eight books in eight days, including war memoirs, political biography, popular philosophy, newly published historical monographs and older texts. This 'insatiable zest in wide reading' might be eclectic but it was always purposeful: she copied extracts into a notebook, using them as catalysts for her own reflections.[113]

While Maude was teaching at Queen's, Helen reported that 'someone told her she should have gone into Science, instead of History: she has the same "humility before the fact" that is rare in historians'.[114] But she was also a philosophical historian.[115] Some of her surviving papers recall the writings of Benedetto Croce and R.G. Collingwood. For Maude, successful history 'implies a projection of personality into the past so complete that the events actually repeat themselves and become an experience of the mind. Facts must not only be known but experienced or else they are not alive. This is an individual process. Only a great artist can do it for another.'[116] This echoes her Oxford colleague R.G. Collingwood's famous lectures on 'History as Re-enactment of Past Experience'. These were delivered after Maude's death but she may well have attended the 1928 lecture when he first proposed the concept;[117] she may also have been exposed to his ideas through personal contact.[118]

She was equally up-to-date in her literary reading. She applies Virginia Woolf's intimations of the subconscious to reflections on historical data, first quoting the thoughts of the character Cam in To the Lighthouse: 'here one could let whatever one thought expand like a leaf in water; and if it did well here … then it was right'.[119]

To expand like a leaf in water. Something like this happens to facts in one's head when they have been soaked for a time by a subconscious process in the imagination. Only they are long dead leaves and they grow and come green again in the water, so the miracle is greater than Cam's because what one thinks has always life and the facts are really dead until they are soaked again. But two disasters seem inevitable. When the leaves are picked up and shaken they gradually dry and shrink up again; though one cannot forget that one saw the miracle, it becomes only a memory. Worse than that, everyone must soak his [sic] own: the memory of life coming back never seems strong enough to convince another. If one wrote with the leaves in water it would only be a slop, because soaking is one thing and thinking another.[120]

For Collingwood too, in an essay Maude read, historical thought is 'living thought, a thought that goes on within one's own mind, not a dead thought that can be treated as a finished product, cut adrift from its roots in the mind that thinks it, and played with like a pebble'.[121] Echoing Croce, she insists that 'Dead History is no History'.[122] She relates Woolf's stream-of-consciousness to her own historiographical purposes, reminding herself to 'draw on [her own] subliminal activities' and to recognise the value of 'marginal or fringe thoughts'.[123]

The titles of some of Maude's surviving notes indicate her focused reflection on historiography: 'Methods of Thinking about Historical Problems'; 'Stages of Mental Development Necessary for Historical Study (or better) The Equipment of a Historian'.[124] She articulates the necessity of imagination in historical enquiry, which must be 'sensitive as well as strong. Responsive to every subtle suggestion & half-shade.' She also recognises 'what emotion working on knowledge and controlled by art can do for historical writing', applying it as a historiographic principle: 'To write well, at least to write history well, some emotion must be allowed to work on the heart.' The scientific historian then intervenes: 'Is this too much or too dangerous?'[125]

Given Helen's own exuberant style, it is not surprising that she should find Maude's prose austere, but others did not agree, drawing attention to her 'flashes of brilliance'.[126] Maude's arguments are conspicuously multi-layered, so she puts a premium on meticulous logic and clarity of exposition. She has a gift for disentangling from befuddling technicalities, such as variants in manuscript sources, a clear account which compels the reader's attention. The result is a narrative style which, 'working from the known to the unknown', resembles the detective story, a characteristic which Maude herself recognised. In the full flow of composing *Medieval Representation and Consent* she played with the genre under the title *The Mystery of the Modus*, fantasising chapters such as 'The Scene of the Crime', 'A Clerical Suspect', 'Murder by Committee'.[127] Indeed, Galbraith assessed Maude's achievement using the same term that was applied to Helen's: 'great learning lightly borne'.[128]

In June 1935, Maude left Oxford, telling no one at Somerville that it was for the last time. It was left to Helen to tell Maude's father that there was no hope.[129]

Irish Intellectuals

Helen and Maude pursued careers in England but identified strongly as Irish. Helen followed in her father's Home Rule footsteps, even if it put her at odds with her extended family.[130] The 1916 Rising caused her great pain; she understood (without endorsing) those who believed their goal could not be obtained by constitutional means and pointed to Unionist complicity: 'I believe with all my heart that Ulster is not guiltless of the blood of the rebellion ... How in decency were they to allow the Ulster Covenanters to drill and parade for two years, and then pounce on Sinn Fein [*sic*] volunteers for doing exactly the same thing?'[131] Her 'Irish and republican sentiments' made her ambivalent about meeting the dowager Queen Mary, although she 'loathe[d] the IRA and all its works'.[132] Palpable injustice meted out to Irish rebels moved her to public comment: 'there's something about one's own country that takes the guts out of you'.[133] Maude's family was Unionist: during the Ulster crisis, her father served as one of several clergymen vice-presidents of the East Antrim Constitutional (Unionist) Association and signed the Ulster Covenant.[134] Yet the Clarkes were distinctly liberal, to the point that her brother Brice's friend, E.R. Dodds, remembered them as 'Protestant Home Rulers'. According to Helen, Brice, who signed the Covenant as a teenager, returned from the First World War on the verge of socialism.[135]

Helen straightforwardly accepted her Plantation origins, deeming however that '300 years of Irish climate and Irish land has so profoundly modified [the Waddells] that we are no longer Scottish'.[136] Home was her sister Meg's farm, Kilmacrew House near Banbridge in County Down. This was, of course, the property of Meg's husband, but the Revd J.D. Martin was also Meg's and Helen's mother's first cousin. Kilmacrew had belonged to their great-uncle; their mother grew up on a farm five miles away and their great-grandparents lived in Ballela, just three miles from Kilmacrew.[137] The Waddells had settled in the late seventeenth century in the townlands of Ouley and Courley near Newry; Helen inherited a share of the Ouley farm in 1917.[138] Her father's cousins lived in Ballygowan House outside Banbridge; when Helen was 3 years old, one of these, Martha, became her stepmother. In her writings Helen would treat Ballygowan as her ancestral home: 'what is bred in the bone comes out in the prose,' she commented in 1934, 'and mine was bred in an old house in Down'.[139]

But being Irish did not preclude identification with English culture, its literature and history, all the stronger when Irish and English dovetailed. Jonathan Swift had ridden along the 'Broad Road' in Banbridge from Kilroot to Dublin. Helen would be buried, along with her mother and great-grandmother, next to 'the ruins of the old church where Patrick Brontë's father came galloping to marry the girl on his pillion before her relations overtook him: the girl who was to be grandmother to Charlotte and Emily and Anne'.[140] A closer Brontë connection came through the Waddells, whose old house in Ouley was only a few miles from Patrick's birthplace; whom, indeed, her ancestors might have known personally.[141] Helen compared her perspective on England – which, she said, 'I love passionately because I so often see it from outside' – with the 'double life', 'the sense of being "in" and yet not "of"' she imagined was experienced by English Jews.[142] Welcoming Irish literature's desire 'once again to drink the nature of the soil', she felt they were mistaken 'in the assertion that the Irish spirit could only fully express itself in *Irish*. For one cannot turn back the sun dial ten degrees.' Her own language, and that of the Irish Literary Revival, 'is English with the Irish idiom'.[143]

Helen became friends, first through her brother Sam and later through her publisher Constable's, with several major figures of the Irish Literary Renaissance: Æ, Yeats, Shaw, James Stephens, Stephen Gwynn, Patrick Kavanagh. She was an associate member of Yeats's Irish Academy of Letters and for a time vice-president of the Irish Literary Society of London.[144] But Helen's purview was not only national, even when that nation encompassed Britain as well as Ireland: her upbringing had given her a transnational outlook, not only from her childhood in Japan but through the crosscultural confidence she inherited from her missionary father and the comparative-literary perspective of her education.[145] Her research into English literature sent her backwards in time to its European origins and to the latter's *lingua franca*, Latin. While Irish was one of the languages in which she had 'no skill' and of whose literature she had 'no right to speak', her work is always alert to the Irish presence.[146] In *The Wandering Scholars* she creates a cameo of Irish monks working in the scriptorium from Old Irish glosses written in the margins of a ninth-century manuscript of Priscian's *Institutiones Grammaticae*.[147] In *Peter Abelard* the hero applies to his own dilemma of conscience an Irish prayer she found in Douglas Hyde's *Abhráin Diadha Chúige Connacht: The Religious Songs of Connacht*, published in 1906.[148] The final words of the novel come from another prayer, reportedly by St Columban, this time in Latin. The lines are taken from the Bobbio missal, published in 1924.[149]

The Irish Golden Age heralds in the wandering of scholars, the centripetal influx of students from the sixth to the eighth centuries from across Europe, 'driven like thistledown before the barbarian blast' to monastic centres such as Bangor and Clonmacnoise, complemented by the centrifugal emigration of the Irish who chose the 'white martyrdom' – *peregrinatio pro amore Dei* – to found monasteries across Europe, 'some of them the greatest strongholds of learning in the Middle Ages'.[150] If the Irish were the true *Vagantes*, Charles Lock shows that their symbolic role is even more extensive: never part of the Roman Empire and therefore never exposed to its culture, they encountered the classics through the teachings of the Church. Unlike the rest of Europe, they did not feel the need to demonstrate fidelity to Christianity by abjuring the pagan legacy. Thus for Helen, Ireland represents the dual heritage, religious and literary, which flowers in the education and poetry of the *scholares vagantes*.[151] Helen's medievalism was seen as a special compliment to Ireland, so much so that *The Irish Times* reviewed *The Wandering Scholars* twice in six weeks, presumably due to its escalating reputation.[152]

If Maude had pursued her original topic of the Irish Franciscans, she would have confronted the split in the order at the end of the thirteenth century when the indigenous Irish who had joined various religious orders were accused of holding secret meetings with their chiefs, instigating rebellion against the colonial English. The hostility between 'English' and native Irish Franciscans triggered the complaint to Pope John XII: 'Not only the laity and seculars among [the English], but even some of the religious, heretically maintain that it is no more a sin to kill an Irishman than a dog', an accusation which Maude quotes.[153]

Although Gaelic Ireland was not the area of Helen and Maude's expertise, it lay at the forefront of their consciousnesses as medievalists. While finishing her research for *The Wandering Scholars* at the British Museum in 1925, Helen got to know Robin Flower, assistant in the museum's Department of Manuscripts, who was completing its catalogue of Irish manuscripts. Brought up in England but of an Anglo-Irish family, he had learnt Irish as an adult, living for periods on the Blasket Islands off Kerry to attain fluency. His emphatic and dismissive manner was off-putting, and Helen herself was 'always scared of him, because he knows such a terrible lot, and is very truculent', but he seemed to like her.[154] He read *The Wandering Scholars'* Irish chapter in proof; he gave her his translation of the ninth-century Gaelic poem 'Pangur Bán', found in the margins of the St Gall Priscian manuscript. This now-famous version first made its public appearance in *The Wandering Scholars*.[155] He also no doubt provided her with the epigraph which appeared in the first edition of *The Wandering Scholars*, a quotation in Middle Irish from the *Vision of Mac Con Glinne*, with English translation.[156] But it was the popularity of Helen's work which made Mac Con Glinne recognisable as 'an example of the type of truant scholar, the *scholaris vagans* of European literature, the happy-go-lucky vagabond who goes singing and swaggering through the Middle Ages' when Flower lectured on him in 1938.[157]

Maude's predecessor and successor as history tutor at Somerville were also from Northern Ireland: Florence McLoughlin had been in class with Helen at Victoria College, Belfast; May McKisack was born in Belfast but brought to be educated in England by her widowed mother.[158] But neither made Ireland a focus of study. As a constitutional historian, for Maude, Gaelic Ireland was inevitably a side issue: it was Goddard Orpen's *Ireland under the Normans* on which her Irish research initially relied, not Edmund Curtis's *A History of Medieval Ireland*, which 'devoted more attention to the native side'.[159] She may well have known Curtis personally, since he was a close friend of her brother's friend, E.R. Dodds.[160] But she cited the sparse evidence of Anglo-Norman constitutional arrangements that emerged from native sources.[161] She drew attention to newly published documents which showed how, 'partly by infection and partly in self-defence, the Anglo-Normans came to assimilate much of the culture and methods of a vigorous Celtic society at an earlier stage of development'. She highlighted the significance of details such as whether, as the open field system developed on the Anglo-Irish manor, the soil was tilled by colonists, Hibernici, or together.[162] She refuted Orpen's 'eulogy of the *Pax Normanica*', which suggested that the Norman conquest of Ireland conferred the benefit of civilisation on an essentially anarchic population, pointing to evidence of complaints against the Normans for 'oppressing peaceful persons ... protecting and abetting felons ... constantly waging war with each other'.[163] Echoes of his cultural bias, however, can be occasionally discerned: 'The influences of English models or of English ideas ... once admitted, seemed to fossilise into stone, to lose all meaning and to stand as in a magic circle, held fast by the Celtic genius for restless movement in the same place.'[164]

Maude was often asked to review Irish history for English periodicals.[165] In her own work, she got as many Irish medieval sources into print as she could.[166] Her profile appears to fit the academic genealogy linking Edmund Curtis, Jocelyn Otway-Ruthven and James Lydon, whose Stubbsian training was similar to hers, dubbed 'The Lecky Professors' from their tenure of that chair of history at Trinity College Dublin.[167] The Oxford-educated Curtis taught Otway-Ruthven at Trinity, and Otway-Ruthven proceeded to Cambridge to research under Helen Cam, a sincere admirer of both Stubbs and Maude.[168] James Lydon, described as embodying the 'unique blend of the best of Curtis and Otway-Ruthven', worked at the Institute of Historical Research in London. There he became the protégé of Maude's colleague, J.G. Edwards, and was also mentored by F.M. Powicke, who had of course taught Maude at Queen's.[169] All three drew on her work.[170] In 1939 H.G. Richardson drew the attention of Irish historians to the fact that the bombing of the Four Courts in 1922 had not destroyed all medieval sources: a good deal of material had been previously copied or preserved in England.[171] Maude had made the same point in 1933, indicating that the assiduous researcher could retrieve Irish material from English archives.[172] If she had lived it might have been Maude, rather than Richardson, whose recognition of these surviving resources is acknowledged as 'present[ing] Irish medievalists with a research agenda' lasting decades.[173]

While Maude's historiography did not include Curtis's native side, her attempt to establish ancestral links between the County Cavan Clarkes and the Ó Cleirighs, hereditary bards and historians of the O'Donnell clan of Donegal, suggests a certain identification with it. Her biographer claims that the Clarkes' name was originally O'Clery and connects them directly with the contributors to the *Annals of the Four Masters*, the seventeenth-century compilation of the historical record of Gaelic Ireland from ecclesiastical and secular sources.[174] Tadgh Ó Cleirigh, known by his name in religion, Friar Micheál, left Ireland sometime after the Flight of the Earls, becoming a lay Franciscan brother in the Irish College of St Anthony in Louvain, in today's Belgium. There he committed himself to collecting records of his native history, returning to a Franciscan house in Donegal whence he travelled widely, transcribing manuscripts. The *Annala Rioghachta*

Éireann, compiled by Ó Cleirigh and his collaborators between 1632 and 1636, was edited by John O'Donovan and published in 1851, when he was Professor of Celtic Languages at Queen's College, Belfast.[175] But for her early death, Maude might have accessed the influence of the Gaelic Middle Ages through her just-begun study of Irish high crosses and figure sculpture, which prompted visits to Monasterboice in County Louth and elsewhere.[176]

Like Helen, Maude felt equally at home with English or Irish material. Her work paralleling corresponding developments and divergences in England and Ireland shows affinity with the all–Britain historiography of Rees Davies which encourages 'breaking down barriers between the histories of England, Ireland, Scotland and Wales and ... seizing the opportunity to enrich our historical understanding between them'.[177] Robin Frame also suggests that 'a view that takes in the British Isles as a whole may highlight themes and relations that otherwise are only dimly visible'.[178] Interestingly, the Welsh Davies was taught by Maude's student May McKisack while the Irish Frame studied with Otway-Ruthven as an undergraduate; his DPhil supervisor was James Lydon.[179]

Bluestockings Have Fun

As learning and femininity were deemed categorically incompatible, the caricatured bluestocking was earnest, humourless, unattractive and badly dressed.[180] Helen Waddell was spared this stereotype, but perhaps not entirely to her benefit. When the Irish press dubbed her 'Ulster's darling', it was not to pay considered homage to her intellectual achievement; she was more easily identified with the sensitive poet than with the exceptional scholar. Her personality – spirited, compassionate, striving to please – contributed to this image. Her relations with older men of letters such as Saintsbury were filial or flirtatious; they were more likely to treat her as a clever protégée, not a serious rival. Maude could more easily be typecast as the female don prevailing in popular literature until the 1950s.[181] Her students referred to her 'aloofness'; her reserve and dignity could be alarming.[182] Helen commented that Maude was 'like an acid when she isn't satisfied'.[183] Her intolerance of self-pity could translate as lack of sympathy (although Helen once called her 'the most exquisitely sympathetic person I know').[184] There was, however, another side, 'the caressing Maude that you so seldom see'.[185] Betty Murray described her as burning with quiet enthusiasm, 'more like religious fervor than anything else', when she talked about her favourite subject of parliament. Nevertheless, she did not live in an ivory tower, taking 'a rich and catholic delight in the whole business of living'.[186] The young Maude could be 'freakish'; her Oxford colleagues talked of her 'kindly malice' and her 'dancing humour'.[187] Unlike the blue-stocking, she was stylish, or at least 'the best dressed of the dons ... in a very exquisite black dress', reported Betty (although she herself 'wouldn't be seen dead' in any of Maude's hats).[188] She did conform to the sexless stereotype: Helen believed that 'physical passion was left out in her'.[189] But Maude's sensitivity to the feelings of others could be acute. As she returned to Carnmoney to die, her Somerville friends, incapable of accepting what was about to happen, fell prey to misunderstandings and mutual irritation. The letters Maude wrote in her last few months reveal her deep affection and the tact with which she handled their raw emotions and hurt feelings. She was also open about herself: 'I think most about my family and friends and how they love me. This is the big thing in my life.'[190]

Helen died thirty years later, the last twenty spent in an intensifying fog of dementia. She knew what was happening; her cross was heavy to bear.[191] What lives on are the intellectual achievements of these best friends. Helen's celebrity status faded but her books continue to be read, although not necessarily as part of the academic curriculum. Thomas Pynchon, reading *The Wandering Scholars* in college in the 1950s, found a parallel between the goliards and 'alternative lowlife data filtering insidiously through the ivy'.[192] In Columbia University in the 1970s, 'Helen Waddell was a name murmured passionately by future medievalists outside the classroom but was usually absent from their professors' reading lists.'[193] However, she also attracted the praise of scholars of the calibre of Etienne Gilson and E.R. Curtius.[194] Despite conflicting responses – 'effusive loyalty along with dismissive criticism' – her influence has proved widespread and enduring.[195] Contemporary scholarship no longer judges the imaginative intensity of her engagement with the medieval world as unprofessional. In an unfinished essay on translation she quoted Edward FitzGerald's maxim, 'at all costs a Thing must Live', as her own; her practice, which involved taking considerable liberties, is vindicated by current attitudes to translation. Selections from *Lyrics from the Chinese* and *Mediaeval Latin Lyrics* continue to be anthologised and used for scholarly purposes;[196] above all, over fifty composers have set them to music. These include Herbert Howells's version of her translation from Prudentius, 'Take him, earth, for cherishing', commissioned for John F. Kennedy's memorial service in Washington DC. The significance of Helen Waddell's work to literature and to scholarship is not in question.

Maude's legacy is equally permanent. Her impact on those who knew her – and on those who didn't – was great, influencing the work of her immediate successors and resonating throughout twentieth-century scholarship.[197] A list of citations would be one measure of her achievement but an inadequate one, since her research has become 'part of the mainstream in the understanding of the fourteenth century', even when it is not separately cited.[198] But, as a historian who had never known her noted, Maude was 'a scholar whose influence went very much further than her published work'.[199] Her influence as a teacher, although no longer identifiable, lives on through the genera-tions of scholars trained by her own academically eminent students, May McKisack, Lucy Sutherland, Dominica Legge and others. In 1960 an American academic surveying the history of late medieval England from 1939 was reminded by Helen Cam to include Clarke's work, even though Maude died in 1935.[200]

Given the impact of Helen and Maude's achievements, it comes as a shock to realise that their publishing careers were so brief. Maude's publications span ten years; her 1937 *Fourteenth Century Studies* reprints earlier material. Helen's most memorable works cover 1927–36; *Poetry in the Dark Ages*, a lecture, was delivered in 1947. The poems she translated during the Second World War were published post-humously. But their final tragedies – and the shadow of the joyless bluestocking – should not eclipse the fun Helen and Maude had as scholars. Helen's 'piggy' refusal to review a book came from a dread of its dullness: 'I do like a sense of humour and of humanity in handling medieval stuff.'[201] The historical mysteries Maude unravels from the mind-numbing technicalities of diplomacy are kissing cousins to the detective story. The learned repartee of *Discipline*'s characters reflects how thoroughly its authors had absorbed the content of the books that were their passion. The 21-year-old Maude described herself to Helen in a second-hand bookshop, with 'a minute and a half to catch an imperative train', looking for:

books of the genuine kinds – chronicles, law books, first editions. In a flash I was in the midst of wonders. A Renascence Plutarch in nine volumes: glorious Greek type; Black's Tasso in two white velume [*sic*] volumes; 'The Clergyman's Lawbook'; Newcastle's letter. I made a hasty selection. The book man made a rough calculation. I hurled the money – also counted roughly – at him and fled incontinently for the station. Now hear the sum of my treasure. Algernon Sidney's 'Discourse of Government' – a first edition. Sir Philip Sidney's 'Arcadia' – slightly imperfect, but at least a 16th century copy. This is for you if you are very good. 'Ecclesiastical Documents', Camden Society. 'The Pylgrymage of Sir Richard Guylforde to the Holy Land, A. D. 1506', also Camden Society. Now tell me quickly that I have the book lover's flair.[302]

Helen, making the case to borrow 'an exceedingly valuable edition' of the sixteenth-century dramatist Robert Greene from the Queen's library, describes a 'final scene'

in which [assistant librarian] Mr Salmon was called in to protest that Greene would lose his back – his valuable quarto back – if he were read at all. And I told them they were behaving like custodians, instead of librarians, and [librarian professor] Gregory [Smith] turned upon Mr Salmon. 'Behold, she rails upon us like a fish-wife.' I'm afraid we all three shouted at that point. And I knew Greene was mine.[306]

Helen Waddell and Maude Clarke could attest to the fun of the intellect.

Intellectual Lives and Literary Perspectives: Female Irish Writing at Home and Abroad

KATHRYN LAING

One of the ways in which to examine the intellectual lives of female Irish writers of the Victorian period is to consider them within broader European contexts. The aim of this essay is to map out how some of these writing lives were enhanced and shaped through travel and often residence in Europe, and how experiences of cultural exchange through observation of other societies were reflected in their writing about gender and national identity formation.[1] The reasons for travel across this turbulent and politically uncertain period for Ireland varied, from economic necessity for many, to the practices of the more privileged who sometimes sent their daughters abroad for education, or made the equivalent of the 'grand tour' themselves.[2] Reflections on these diverse experiences of being abroad took the form of a range of publications including fiction, travel writing and journalism.

Hannah Lynch's *fin-de-siècle* and New Woman novel, *Jinny Blake: A Tale* (1897), provides a useful point of departure. In conversation with her friend about culture and customs regarding women in Spain, the eponymous heroine, the impetuous 'wild Irish girl' declares:

Races as well as classes and sexes have their own tram-lines, of which they have the air of bolting for accident and disaster. Boys are simply asked not to be cowards, and women are simply recommended to be chaste. Yet the pure woman may be the meanest and biggest liar unthrashed, she may have a taste for brandy, and knock all the other commandments into smithereens. And your man of courage may be a bestial ruffian and drive a dozen women to the grave. It isn't only the Spaniards who are topsy-turvey. I'm afraid, Nannie, we're all wrong and so besotted with our different conventionalities that there is no getting hold of a clean and reasonable aspect of virtue that will do for all weathers, all nations, all sexes, and equally for public and private use.[3]

Following a thwarted romance and a shock discovery (the nature of prostitution), Jinny has been persuaded by her father to travel instead of entering a convent as she has threatened to do. Despite 'breaking her heart over the sorrows and degradation of her sex',[4] she agrees to embark on a journey that takes her through France and Spain to Genoa and Constantinople, Greece and back to London. Connecting race, class and gender in her exasperated outburst about topsy-turvey convention, Jinny's observations on the limiting ways in which men and women's lives are constructed are central to much *fin-de-siècle* women's writing. Her bitter commentary is also a continuation of concerns voiced by female writers earlier in the nineteenth century. This example of transcultural exchange and the transnational European contexts in which Jinny's revolt against social conventions takes place, especially in relation to expectations about the lives of women, is central to my overall argument.

The essay will be limited to a detailed discussion of various works by Hannah Lynch and the mid-nineteenth-century writer Julia Kavanagh, with brief reference to other authors such as Kavanagh's contemporary, Kathleen O' Meara (pen name Grace Ramsay), and later writers including M.E. Francis, Emily Lawless and Somerville and Ross. The intellectual lives, and specifically female and sometimes feminist literary perspectives, of all of these writers were shaped and even enabled by experiences of life abroad, but many others could be included. For there were numerous female Irish writers publishing during the Victorian period, some of whom in recent years have begun to receive a great deal of critical attention following decades of neglect.[5]

Many of these writers with transnational experiences were avid readers and indebted, often consciously acknowledging their debt, to two key 'literary foremothers' in Ireland. The fiction and non-fiction of Maria Edgeworth and Sydney Owenson (Lady Morgan) offered a legacy of cosmopolitan insights gleaned from travel as well as reading. They also initiated a distinctive form of Irish writing and the origins of an Irish female literary tradition. This legacy, which will be briefly traced in the work of selected authors in the final section of the essay, marks a starting point for further study.[6]

Models and Frameworks

Joe Cleary has argued for alternative readings of the shaping of the nineteenth-century Irish novel including a transnational dimension: 'nineteenth-century Irish culture must be seen not just in terms of diachronic development, but also in terms of a complex series of intellectual negotiations conducted between several shifting cultural centres: England, continental Europe, the wider world of the British Empire, the American diaspora'.[7] Recent studies that pay attention to the transnational and notions of cultural transfer both within the broader contexts of European women writers and more specific Irish contexts provide useful models to draw on. For example, in her intro-duction to a selection of essays that 'examine transnational questions in women readers, and in women writers (by definition readers themselves) seeking to explore the influence of writers from abroad', Gillian Dow notes the increasing importance across the humanities of '[t]ransnational approaches to the long eighteenth and nineteenth centuries' in the past three decades.[8] This attention to transnational contexts has shifted to later in the nineteenth century and is an area of newly emerging scholarship in Irish contexts, evident in the title of a recent conference panel on 'The Cultural Mobility of the Irish in Europe in the Long Nineteenth Century'.[9] The newly published *Reading the Irish Woman: Studies in Cultural Encounter and Exchange, 1714–1960* offers another important model that intersects with and builds on studies of 'cultural encounter and transfer'.[10] Focusing on particular 'points of cultural encounter' using three case studies (the enlightenment, emigration and modernism), there is an exami-nation of, amongst other things, reading practices and the possibility of assessing the impact of educational developments on 'the public image and construction of the Irish Woman' during the eighteenth century.[11] Considering the reading practices and education of Irish women and women writers during the Victorian period is material for a much larger project. Instead, the models offered by scholars working in these fields provide a framework for a narrower focus on cultural exchange or transfer through an analysis of selected Irish women authors whose European travel and/or residence shaped and informed their writing, as well as a limited consideration of 'cultural encounters through reading'.[12]

Nineteenth-Century Irish Literature – Critical Contexts

Following on from the ground-breaking publication of volumes 4 and 5 of *The Field Day Anthology* offering key insights into the range of material produced by women writers in the nineteenth century, a range of publications have appeared: books, chapters and articles about the long nineteenth century and more on specifically Irish women writers who were published in Dublin and London during the period.[13] That London offered more opportunities for publishing and making a living, especially for Irish female writers, is one of the many reasons cited for emigration during the nineteenth century in studies such as Loeber and Stouthamer-Loeber's 'Literary Absentees'.[14] Attention to the broader and more contentiously labelled period – 'Victorian Ireland' – has also inspired focused attention to some earlier female writers, such as Eileen Fauset's more recent *The Politics of Writing: Julia Kavanagh 1824–77* (Manchester University Press, 2009).[15]

Renewed interest in Irish *fin-de-siècle* culture beyond or outside the Literary Revival, and the New Woman project, has generated broader as well as single-author studies on both more canonical and less well-known writers. For example, Emily Lawless has become the focus of several New Woman studies and is the subject of a detailed examination in Heidi Hansson's *Emily Lawless 1845–1913: Writing the Interspace* (Cork: Cork University Press, 2007). Somerville and Ross, the subject of study in Irish Big House, Anglo-Irish and New Woman contexts, have also been the focus of a fuller study by Julie Anne Stevens, *The Irish Scene in Somerville & Ross* (Dublin: Irish Academic Press, 2007). The recovery of May Laffan's neglected fiction, published towards the end of the nineteenth century, has begun. Jill Brady Hampton has drawn attention to its often satirical focus on 'social issues resulting from Ireland's sectarian bitterness' and on the 'contradictions and complexities facing writers in this volatile period',[16] and her life and work is the subject of Helena Kelleher Kahn's monograph, *Late Nineteenth-Century Ireland's Political and Religious Controversies in the Fiction of May Laffan Hartley* (Greensboro: University of North Carolina Greensboro ELT Press, 2005).

Laffan's contemporary, Hannah Lynch (1859–1904), who shared her Dublin origin and hybrid identity (Catholic and Protestant parents), and who was also educated abroad, features in several recent general surveys of the period and in more focused studies.[17] Daughter and then stepdaughter of Irish Catholic fathers with strong nationalist connections, her experience as an active participant in the Ladies' Land League as secretary to the London branch and the hostile reactions to this nascent feminist movement also served to shape her observations about women, nation and identity.[18] Like many of her female contemporaries whose middle-class family suffered economic difficulties, Lynch took on governess work in Ireland and Europe before making travel writing and fiction her sole and often precarious source of income. The hybrid, feminist and transnational contexts of Lynch's writing are shared with other writers too, from Lady Morgan to George Egerton, also restless travellers and commentators on the international and national scene. Egerton's narratives 'move between a variety of cultural and social settings, establishing transcultural connections between Irish and European literary practice, and thus address a wider European audience at the end of the nineteenth century'.[19] Transcultural connections, but also displacement and expression of rebellion, the assertion of an Irish and feminist identity as well as a 'Europeanized field of view' enabled and provoked by European travel, and the motif of wandering, are all features of Lynch's writing.[20]

Hannah Lynch and Julia Kavanagh: Two Case Studies

Jinny Blake: A Tale, published at the very end of the nineteenth century, is an evocative work to begin a consideration of aspects of the intellectual lives and literary perspectives of some of the numerous female Irish writers of the Victorian period. Firstly, this novel embodies the 'spirit of the age' through its conflicted and contradictory heroine who exhibits all the characteristics of the contemporary New Woman figure, and whose sense of fracture and instability of identity – 'We are all, you as well as I and others, made up of a heap of inconsistencies' – gesture towards a latent modernist sense of self.[21] The instability of identity is not only personal but political, not simply a gender issue in this and other novels by Lynch but an issue of nation too.[22] Such concerns featured in the fiction of many other female Irish writers published at the *fin-de-siècle* and earlier, and preoccupied many of the writers themselves. This fluidity of identity impacted on notions of what constituted authentic Irish writing. As Heidi Hansson has noted, the 'unstable political identity of many nineteenth-century writers such as Lady Morgan, Emily Lawless or Rosa Mulholland' is one of the several obstacles 'to forging a women's tradition in Irish litera-ture'.[23] Alternative ways of approaching the writing of this period are offered by Margaret Kelleher, who has highlighted how '[t]he years 1830–1890 … mark a period in which differentiations of "English" and "Irish" writing, whether in prose or drama, are not easily made', but that rather than this being a negative feature of the period, 'cultural hybridity is instead where much of the richness of nineteenth-century Irish literature in English lies'.[24] The notion of cultural hybridity can be extended beyond the English/Irish nexus to a Europeanised or more specifically French/Irish identity. For example, Kathleen O'Meara, born in Tipperary (1839) but living most of her life in Paris (died 1888), is described as a 'gifted Irishwoman' who was, in many respects, 'more French than Irish' in the obituary published in the *Irish Monthly*.[25] O'Meara's near-contemporary Julia Kavanagh, also born in Tipperary but living and travelling abroad most of her life and also the subject of an *Irish Monthly* obituary, might have been described likewise. While Kavanagh was keen to assert her Irish identity, she also described the rewards of living in exile and establishing a European hybrid identity:

> If all the O'Donnells had stayed at home, would one have married a member of the Royal Family? – would the other hold the destinies of Ireland in his hand? The fate of those who preferred home to the splendid chances of exile gives the answer to this question. The senior representative of the O'Donnells, the Reverend Constantine O'Donnell, now holds a living in Yorkshire; in the junior branches we find a Henry O'Donnell, who married a cousin of the Empress Maria Theresa – and another who, under the name of Duke of Tetuan, now wields the destinies of Spain.[26]

A fictionalised version of this history of Irish exile resulting in European hybridity makes a brief and comic appearance in Lynch's *Jinny Blake*, where Jinny describes her various encounters in Spain, including 'a descendant of the Irish Princes, Don Fernan O'Neill. But he is quite a Spaniard, and speaks only broken English, while the remote Irish strain asserts itself in a hospitality and extravagance so lavish the he is never out of debt, and the family silver rarely out of the keeping of the family jeweller.'[27] A comic glimpse into cultural transfer is given in the portrait of the little Duke of San Carlos who, because of his Irish nurse, speaks broken English with an Irish accent. Lynch, who grew up in Ireland but was schooled abroad and ended up living in Paris, epitomised this Europeanised hybrid identity, associating herself particularly with the 'Parisianised foreigners' she discusses in one of her numerous cultural commentaries on France: 'But the passion, the earnestness, of all these Parisianised foreigners in the adoption of the several prejudices and aspirations of Paris prove the truth of my assertion, that Paris absorbs us in her furnace of ardent sentiments and theories as no other place does.'[28]

Lynch's most striking portrait of hybridity and also of revolt is in fact that of a little girl in her best-known work, *Autobiography of a Child*. This child, 'the Dublin Angela' and 'the English Angela' whose rebel identity is shaped both by her experiences of oppression and restriction at home in Ireland as a girl, and in an English convent as an Irish girl, is the younger version of the many rebel women of Lynch's other fiction.[29] If Angela is a fictional version of Hannah Lynch, the double identity of Irish/English is further multiplied by Lynch's own travels and by her eventual settling in Paris. In novels such as *Rosni Harvey* and *Jinny Blake*, Lynch deploys conventions of travel writing as well as of the adventure and romance novel, melding these sub-genres into works that can be described as anti-marriage and anti-colonial. The popularity of travel writing during the late nineteenth century, and the proliferation of travel writing especially by women, have been well documented. Blending the genres of travel and adventure was particularly attractive for female writers engaged in forging new roles and new possibilities for their female characters. The evocation of 'distant and exotic locations', characteristic of numerous New Women fictions, allowed writers to explore taboo topics without connecting them directly with 'home'.[30]

Lynch's landscapes of France, Spain and Greece might not be as exotic and distant as Egerton's Nordic settings, or another Irish contemporary Beatrice Grimshaw's South Seas, nor are these landscapes deployed to displace and distance taboo topics. They are, however, geographies of potential liberation, both in terms of gender and national identity. The nature of travel itself, of being in transit, enables the heroines to reinvent themselves and allows Lynch, a writer described by one of her reviewers as '*déracinée*', to take a mobile, shifting position on a number of subjects.[31] Lynch employs the figure of the vagabond consistently in her journalism, noting, for example, in a travel piece on the Canary Isles, how she knows 'nothing more cheering to the vagabond than this readiness of friendship among common people … They seem to delight in outlandish acquaintance and if you happen to be a woman, you instantly appeal to their better selves.'[32]

As the significant body of scholarship dedicated to women and public spaces (that is, mainly urban spaces) in the late nineteenth century has revealed, the *flâneuse* is a complex and contradictory figure. But Lynch's version of the *flâneuse*, the Irish female vagabond, is not only urban. She tramps through forests and up mountains, travels by ship and train, often unaccompanied, and, as a solitary figure exploring on foot remote Spanish and French rural villages, is at times tantamount to a spectacle.[33] Lynch's vagabond heroines in her fiction create similar sensations, setting off abroad and flouting expectations of their sex. Rosni Harvey, after the death of her parents and only sibling, has ambitions beyond that of marriage: 'Instead of marriage, she wanted a private purse to carry out vast plans for the improvement of the race.'[34] Her desire to study medicine sets her travelling. She was going to 'an alien land, in pursuit – not, O ye gods! of a husband, but, sad to tell, of a diploma'.[35] Travel, in this novel, becomes as an alternative to marriage and sets Rosni on a course far from Ireland, although she returns there in the end and marries the Greek Ulysses, met on her travels. In a similar way, Jinny Blake has ambitions for social reform rather than marriage: 'Women were to be rescued by other women, the poor and trodden [*sic*] by the wealthy and honoured.'[36] Ultimately, for Jinny, and perhaps for Lynch herself, '[e]scape had become almost a permanent instinct in her life' – escape from the condition of femaleness itself. In Lynch's oeuvre, escape is realised through travel and residence in foreign countries.[37]

Jinny Blake is staged across a range of European countries, revealing and examining a cosmopolitan Irishness through which Lynch voices her double criticism of the fact that 'the Saxons [are] still ruling over in Erin' and that women can only move 'from vexed liberty to servitude'.[38] Schooled at a French convent along with a Spanish princess and the English 'Miss Brown' who she meets again in Spain, Jinny's education epitomises the experience of transnational contact

and cultural transfer. She recalls teaching her foreign friends about
Ireland as they celebrated a St Patrick's Feast: 'We all wore shamrocks …
and we sang a rebel song, just as heartily as if we were all conspiring
against England.'[39] Jinny describes herself as 'your wild Irish girl' who
comes from 'a perverse and rebel race'.[40] Through her story, Lynch
deliberately deploys these stereotypes of Irishness as she holds up for
examination the notion of national identity against a variety of other
national types – life for Spanish women, for example, is described as
'Dress, love; love, Dress' and 'British erectness and stiffness' is mocked
as Jinny travels through Spain.[41]

In several of her travel pieces on Spain, Lynch also attacks the
position of women there, one of her most trenchant critiques of the
gender inequalities of the nineteenth century being voiced through
her impressions of life for Spanish women in 'The Senora of Today':

> within what mean and intolerable limits of action, thought and
> education she is confined by tradition … She is furthest from being
> happy from any woman I know of, and I have listened to her confi-
> dences, married and maiden … All over Spain the life of the street and
> that of the house is fashioned exclusively for the convenience of men.[42]

Asserting an intimacy with the lives of Spanish women, 'I have listened
to their confidences', an intimacy enabled through her understanding
of the language, she writes with the authority of an insider and the
international perspective of an outsider.

Lynch's insider/outsider perspectives on women's lives in Ireland
and Europe were informed by education, travel and, of course, reading
(she reviewed and commented on a range of writers – French, English
and Irish – for publications in all three countries). Although there is no
evidence of her being a reader of mid-century writers Julia Kavanagh
and Kathleen O'Meara, all three writers shared the experience of
growing up or being educated and living in France as well as travelling
across Europe. All three remained single women who depended on their
writing for a living. While Kavanagh's work was mainly published in
London, she was also popular with American readers.[43] O'Meara and
Lynch also contributed to Irish periodicals, including the influential
Irish Monthly edited by Father Russell, although the travel pieces Lynch
published there seem to have met with less approval than those by her
predecessors and other contemporaries (such as M.E. Francis).[44]

Lynch's more bohemian and vagabond persona in her travel writing and fiction differs from, but also intersects with, earlier writers like Kathleen O'Meara and especially Kavanagh, whose interests in women's subjectivity and observations about European life at times offer inflected readings of Irish women's lives.[45] 'As a Catholic Irish woman who had lived most of her life in France before living and writing in England, Kavanagh may have considered herself an outsider in mid-nineteenth century London.'[46] Kavanagh and her family moved to London from Tipperary and then to Paris, 'where they stayed for twenty years, after which they returned in 1844 to London where Julia was to begin her writing career'.[47]

In many ways, she was just as much an outsider in Ireland as in London, although her writing did find an Irish readership. It was noted in the *Irish Monthly* in a long obituary that:

> The name of Julia Kavanagh is, we think, not so well known in Ireland as it deserves to be, and a few words to remind the readers of this Magazine that a Catholic Irishwoman, who was an accomplished and singularly graceful and pure novelist, as well as a skilled writer of biography, has recently passed away, will not be found amiss in the these pages.[48]

Reclaimed as an Irish writer by the *Irish Monthly*, Kavanagh had made clear her Irish affiliations much earlier to Gavan Duffy, editor of the nationalist newspaper, *The Nation*, in 1849: 'I am Irish by origin, birth, and feeling, though not by education; but if I have lived far from Ireland she has still been as the faith and religion of my youth.'[49] Kavanagh was the author of numerous works including fiction (*Natalie, Daisy, Grace Lee* and *Sybil's Second Love*, to name a few), non-fiction, with a particular focus on women's writing and achievements over 200 years (*French Women of Letters*, 2 volumes, 1862 and *English Women of Letters*, 1862, for example), as well as a travel book on Sicily. Like her predecessors in Ireland, Lady Blessington and Lady Morgan, who also wrote about Italy, Kavanagh pays special attention in *A Summer and Winter in the Two Sicilies* (2 volumes, 1858) to particular female characters she meets on her journey and the domestic more generally.[50] For example, the travelogue begins in Sorrento with an introduction to Carmela: 'Since Carmela has thus come across me, I cannot do better than describe her, her mode of life, and at the same time give the reader some knowledge of the way of an Italian farm, or masseria.'[51] Later,

Donna Anunziata is introduced: 'a pretty Sorrento girl, of eighteen, has given me on the important subject of marriages here, such precise information, that I shall give it in her own words, as the best illustration of Italian manners and habits, which differ so essentially from ours'.[52]

The focus on the feminine and the domestic is a distinctive feature of women travel writers in Italy and elsewhere during this period:

> a construction of domesticity is constantly present in their travel journals, and also in other writings produced by women abroad. Women's texts show the continuing importance that domesticity had, even for those who were deeply involved in political issues.[53]

Kavanagh's careful observations of the delicate position of the female traveller in foreign climes in her book would have elicited more approval in Father Matthew's *Irish Monthly* than Lynch's travel pieces. However, her perspectives on the sexual politics she encounters during her sojourn in Sicily, despite being channelled and therefore softened through descriptions of attractive female figures encountered along the way, are sharp and even bitter. In her discussion with Donna Anunziata about marriage in Italy, she discovers 'that Italian wives are not very happy. Their husbands rarely trust or honour them, they treat them like children, and are jealous as Turks.'[54] On the subject of single women in Italy, often destined for the convent, Kavanagh is even more vocal:

> It is rather a pitiable case that single women should be considered and should consider themselves as only fit to be locked up for life; but setting aside the immorality of doing from worldly reasons what should never be done save from the highest and purest motives, it should not be forgotten by those who condemn this system that these Italian nuns are at least provided for. The poor girls who hunt for husbands for the sake of a position until great writers proclaim to the world in bitter and eloquent pages their misery and their degradation; the wide and unhappy class of gently matured and educated women, who are flattered in the bloom of their youth, sneered at in its decline, made the butt of jests, more or less good natured, in their old age, who are handed about all their lives, the bore and burden of a family, who teach your children for the sake of a home, who daily fill the columns of newspapers with their sad advertisements, and who are a living reproach to the society that gives them liberty and denies them its privileges, are here, either of them, unknown as a class.[55]

While Kavanagh's ostensible subject here is the life of the single woman in Italy, her observations become a targeted critique of the much harsher social conditions for the single woman in Victorian society generally, and the plight of the quintessential spinster figure, the governess, in particular.[56]

Kavanagh's broader critique of the status of women in the nineteenth century through considerations of the lives of women abroad as wives, as spinsters and in terms of education again anticipates and offers a clear model for Lynch's travel writing at the end of the century. And like Lynch, who worked her own travel experiences into her fiction, the earlier O'Meara and Kavanagh's lives in France and also their European travels become part of the fabric of the subject and setting of their fiction.[57] Several of O'Meara's novels are set in France (*A Woman's Trials*, 1867, for example) and others are set in Eastern Europe or Russia (*Iza: A Story of Life in Russian-Poland*, 1869). Just as the often impetuous journeys across Europe by Jinny Blake and Rosni Harvey in Lynch's novels can be read in some ways as a supplement to her travel writing (or vice versa), many of Kavanagh's novels are also set in France where she grew up, or feature travel. These settings not only give an insight into what shaped Kavanagh as a writer, but how they enabled her to express often critical ideas about gender formation and the role of women.

Kavanagh's *Grace Lee* (1855) is perhaps closest to Lynch's novels in its evocation and celebration of a woman who can travel. Grace Lee is a young woman who finds herself suddenly an heiress and takes flight to Europe and the East: 'Miss Lee travelled alone; she was twenty-three, wealthy and fearless.'[58] After returning from her travels and becoming a celebrated *salonnière* in London, Grace renounces her inheritance and retreats to a simple life in Wales, the setting for the rest of the romance plot.[59] The interlude of transnational travel for the heroine, although occupying only one chapter in a very long and convoluted three-decker novel, is especially interesting for several reasons. In her evocation of the immensely wealthy Grace's travels and sojourn in Rome, Kavanagh utilises her own travel experience in a mix of fantasy and romance, social and political critique:[60]

Who would not travel? Who would not feel strange suns; behold new skies; hear the greeting of foreign speech, and pass a wanderer among the scenes beautiful and still; amongst nations living and moving, yet left behind with their passions, their contests, their hopes and sorrows, like the images of a dream.[61]

Kavanagh's celebration of foreign travel and invocation of the trope of
the wanderer in the narrator's declaration is a prelude to the description of Grace's journey that is clearly indebted to the author's own
visits to Italy and her reading of descriptions of female travellers in
the East (Grace spends time in Egypt and Jerusalem).[62] The trope of
the wanderer as a female observer who nonetheless remains detached
recalls Kavanagh's observations about being a tourist in her *Summer and
Winter in the Two Sicilies*: 'Tourists', she notes, 'are, or ought to be, external
observers.'[63] The trope also anticipates Lynch's more liberated vagabond
figures, but both writers, in the context of elsewhere, imagine a different
position for women. The figure of the wanderer also takes on a further
resonance for the Irish female writer who, by choice or circumstance,
experienced displacement in terms of gender and nation.[64]

Grace's ability to wander, without censure, is of course possible because
she is rich:

> Then, indeed, spreading her wings like a long captive bird, she had taken
> her flight towards the burning East. Gold smoothed a path else too rough,
> and charmed away peril. She travelled in the style, with the suite, and with all
> the privileges of a princess. The world might have reproved this adventurous
> spirit in a poorer woman, but it admired and extolled it in the wealthy lady.[65]

Neither Lynch nor Kavanagh or many of their counterparts had this
luxury, and Kavanagh was careful to refer to the company of her mother
in her Sicily travelogue, while Lynch often turned the necessity of
propriety into a subject of satire, at the same time assuring the reader
of her own adherence to these conventions. But in this single chapter,
Kavanagh simultaneously celebrates the possibility of freedom for
women while highlighting their restrictions, and also 'bears witness to
the element of difference afforded to both gender and class in Victorian
England'.[66] Voicing her critique of distorted social values, particularly in
relation to the position of women, through narratives in foreign settings
is a strategy Kavanagh uses often. For example, in this same chapter,
Grace muses aloud on an offer of marriage that will give her:

> Une position politique, and in Paris, too, the most charming of
> charming cities? In France, where women once reigned – where they
> still rule; where, with position, and mind, and skill, one of our poor
> despised sex can still have her say in the world's story.[67]

Finally, Grace might be seen as a prototype for a character such as Lynch's Jinny Blake, idealistic in her desires to improve society, especially women's lives, wealthy enough to travel unimpeded and independent enough to reject a range of suitable, even desirable, marriages. Grace, after all, rejects a Polish count but offers to support his cause against Russia, and Jinny rejects an attractive and wealthy Spanish nobleman. In addition, Jinny's encounters with suitors from different nations and across Europe embody an often overt critique of the relationship between England and Ireland. Kavanagh offers a more implicit critique through Grace's encounter with the Polish count:

> The Polish exile was one of the remarkable men of Europe; but he had no country, no true sphere of action; all his energy, all his talent, were wasted on a hopeless cause … he never spoke of Poland, very rarely of Russia, but his life was devoted to raise one and wound the other. If he failed, it was because the task was superhuman.[68]

It is possible to read an implicit parallel with England and Ireland here. Murphy describes this kind of reading as the 'hidden Irish dimension school of reading', and there are several other examples to be found throughout her novels, including her best known and most popular, *Natalie*.[69]

This novel is one of several set in France, allowing Kavanagh to draw on personal experience and knowledge for the setting and observation of character, as well as to stage a strikingly sharp analysis of the less than ideal conditions of marriage for women. By staging the debate about marriage and other female-centred issues in France rather than England or Ireland (though there are several Irish characters in her fiction, including the Kennedys who preside over an estate in northern France in *Sybil's Second Love*), Kavanagh practises a similar technique used in her travel writing, as well as in her other European set fiction. In her travelogue on Sicily, Kavanagh attacks the precarious position of women in Italy, and she implies at the same time that similar difficulties are evident in England, and by extension Ireland. Likewise, in *Natalie*, the interrogation of various assumptions about femininity and the institution of marriage are safely set in France. Natalie Montolieu, the eponymous heroine, is from the south of France, teaching in a school in provincial Normandy run by the pedantic and prim Mademoiselle Dantin: 'They were anti-pathetic by nature, temperament, and birth; theirs was the old quarrel of the northern and southern races.'[70] The novel draws attention to the question of feminine behaviour and codes of conduct in the opening pages, where Mademoiselle Dantin quarrels with the young woman, who she perceives as 'some young and half-wild thing', and dismisses her unjustly: 'Because your behaviour has been improper, unwomanly, immodest.'[71] In addition, the north/south divide between the temperaments of the two women provides, as Murphy highlights, another 'prime candidate for the hidden Irish dimension school of criticism. Set in France, the novel continually contrasts the cold, rational – one could say Anglo-Saxon – northern French, with the irresponsible, emotional – one could say Celtic – southern French.'[72] In the novel, this scrutiny of gender and regional identity shifts, as Natalie leaves the school for the Saineville Chateau and the sanctuary offered by Madame Marceau after her dismissal, to a focus on love, passion and marriage.

Marriage as plot and topic was central to many of the novels published by women in the mid-nineteenth century and Kavanagh's novels participated in and contributed to the debate carried out through the domestic novel.[73] In her reading of *Natalie* alongside Charlotte Brontë's *Jane Eyre*, Fauset observes that '[w]hile the two novels contain elements of patterned romance in which Kavanagh adheres to commercial demands, she consciously exposes the double standards required to maintain patriarchal hegemony.'[74] The novel does this in part by setting up a vehement attack on marriage through Aunt Radegonde who describes it as 'most fatal to women',[75] and through Natalie herself who at first declares that 'I submit to and obey no man'[76] Natalie succumbs in the end to the demands of M. de Sainville that she be obedient before they marry, but not before a prolonged debate about relations between husband and wife:

'A woman's husband ought to have all the authority of a father,' gravely replied Monsieur de Sainville.

'And of a master, it would seem,' bitterly exclaimed Natalie, who on this subject had all the rebellious feelings of her sex.[77]

Significantly, M. de Sainville goes on to compare notions of obedience from wives with his dismissal of his faithful gardener, which Natalie had so strongly opposed earlier in the narrative. His perception that both servants and wives should be subject to their 'masters' is not dwelt on in the novel, but this conversation sharpens Kavanagh's interrogation of the social expectations and the role of women in French life, depicted here and implicitly elsewhere too. That this interrogation takes place in a French setting is significant, giving a glimpse into French life but also generating a protective distance for Kavanagh's critique of the ideologies about femininity and marriage dear to Irish Catholicism as well Victorian England.[78]

Hannah Lynch's travels and residence in France provided similarly important landscapes and contexts for shaping her 'Europeanized perspective' and for channelling her cultural and feminist critique. As has been argued elsewhere, '[a] key element of Lynch's engagement with France and with French culture was the opportunity it presented for subversive, even rebellious explorations of national and gendered selves – both at the level of content and in terms of genre, perspective and narration.'[79] Lynch spent part of her schooling in a French convent and many of the last years of her life in Paris. She wrote novels and short fiction with French settings and offered cultural commentary on French life and letters in her regular 'Paris Letter' for the London *Academy* as well as in articles for other London-based journals, and in her book *French Life in Town and Country*. In addition to offering an insider/outsider perspective on French life for her mainly English readers, Lynch's cultural commentary often concealed an even more stinging critique of the position of women in nineteenth-century society than Kavanagh's. Like her observations on the lives of Spanish women, portraying the social fabric of life for French women – education, religion, marriage are all of interest for Lynch – became an opportunity to offer broader critical commentary in both fiction and non-fiction. Refracting her critique of Catholicism, education for girls and the lives of women, for example, through the lens of a specifically French setting 'at once distances the author from the critical commentary and liberates her to make it'.[80] There are numerous examples of this strategy, from attacking the repressive regimes of French convents in her article 'The Young French Girl Interviewed', to foregrounding the double standards inherent in French life that overshadowed the lives of men and women in her novel, *Denys d'Auvrillac: A Story of French Life*.

Irish Literary Legacies: Owenson and Edgeworth

Shaped by their experiences of life abroad, an intellectual and literary lineage can be traced from Kavanagh and other contemporaries to *fin-de-siècle* writers such as Lynch. This lineage can also be traced further back. In fact, Lynch's exploration of literal and intellectual vagabondage in *Jinny Blake*, as well as in other novels and numerous travel pieces, might seem to share more with Sydney Owenson and Lady Blessington, publishing at the beginning of the nineteenth century, than the more conservative mid-century novelists and travel writers Julia Kavanagh and Kathleen O'Meara.[81] In *Jinny Blake*, Lynch alerts the reader to a distinct Irish national and feminist literary lineage through her invocation of 'the wild Irish girl', clearly alluding to Lady Sydney Morgan's perhaps best-known work not only through this epithet, but also through Jinny's biography, which shares certain parallels with those of Sydney Morgan.[82] If Jinny Blake is an Irish New Woman figure, Lynch clearly indicates her origins.[83] Many of Lynch's 'Europeanised' mid-century precursors, as well as her contemporaries such as Somerville and Ross and Emily Lawless, also acknowledge their debts as readers and writers to the cosmopolitan, well-travelled and innovative female writers Owenson and Edgeworth, either implicitly or more directly.[84] Somerville and Ross, for example, identify their indebtedness to Edgeworth, whom they describe as 'the brilliant pioneer of Irish novelists' in *Irish Memories*.[85] Emily Lawless wrote a full biography of Edgeworth, aiming 'to establish Maria Edgeworth's central role in Irish literature'.[86] Her project of naming and celebrating Edgeworth as an important Irish female literary precursor also has an antecedent in the work of Julia Kavanagh.[87]

Kavanagh includes both Edgeworth and Morgan in her *English Women of Letters: Biographical Sketches* (in volume 2). This volume, along with her *French Women of Letters: Biographical Sketches*, was intended, she explains in her preface, 'To the Reader', 'to show how far, for the last two centuries and more, women have contributed to the formation of the modern novel in the two great literatures of modern times – the French and the English'.[88] As well as demonstrating the 'importance of the woman's voice' and her major contribution to literature, Kavanagh's biographies give an insight into her own continental reading practices and those of her subjects.[89] Including Edgeworth and Morgan in her canon of significant French and English female writers, Kavanagh touches on their European travels and specifically their engagement with French culture and writing, as well as their vital contribution to Irish writing.[90] It is, in fact, in her consideration of Owenson's *Wild Irish Girl*, that she extols 'the splendid chances of exile' and the opportunities afforded by continental Europe:

> The claims to ancient and novel descent of the great Irish families have received their true test in three of the most aristocratic countries of the Continent – Spain, Austria, and France. There we find that the O's and the Macs – so barren an inheritance in their own land – have done their owners good service.[91]

For Kavanagh, Edgeworth was 'very Irish in temper', despite her English background, and:

> Had she written nothing else, *Castle Rackrent* and *Belinda* would have sufficed to establish Miss Edgeworth's reputation. They show us the double aspect her genius took – Irish life and Fashionable Society. All her tales owe their attractions either to the introduction of Irish character or to their close delineation of the great world.[92]

While Sydney Owenson did not have the genius of Edgeworth, according to Kavanagh, her significance lies in her devotion to her subject:

> If Miss Owenson had not the merit of being, in date and in ability, the first of Irish writers who have made their country the theme of their writings; if Miss Edgeworth came before her, and showed a higher power; yet to none did she yield in ardour for the cause of Ireland, in enthusiasm and generous desire to serve it, or to avenge its unmerited obloquy.[93]

By noting that Owenson's Irish heroines, such as Miss O'Hallaran, Florence Macarthy and Beavoin O'Flaherty, were 'clever, intriguing women', Kavanagh gives an outline of model female characters as well as a model woman writer.[94] Owenson and Edgeworth, who 'in different ways espoused the right of women to literature and engaged with the emerging feminist writings',[95] left an important legacy for later Irish female novelists. Kavanagh identifies aspects of this rich legacy of earlier Irish women writers who chose to focus on women's lives, often in broader European contexts as well as with a specific Irish focus. Traces of this inheritance can be seen in her own work as well as later writers like Lynch and many others.

As Kavanagh herself noted at the end her recuperative study of key French and English women's writing:

> We cannot open a novel of today on which these past and faded novelists have not left their trace. And whilst the human mind, its toils, its pleasures, are worth noting, that trace, however fine and often invisible, is worthy of attention and record.[96]

Attending to these traces provides one way in which to gain insight into the shaping of the intellectual and writing lives of later nineteenth-century female Irish novelists. Attending to other traces of European cultural encounter and transfer, through travel, residence and reading, among the contours of the complex map of the literary terrain of Ireland during the Victorian period, further develops an understanding of particular writing lives.

Finally, mapping Lynch and selected other writers of the period in these contexts also offers new ways in which to read their work outside established categories and across class, economic and religious boundaries. For example, Julie Anne Stevens has highlighted how the 'preoccupation with Ireland's colonial inheritance may lead to neglect the influence of Europe in Somerville and Ross's writing'.[97] The same might be said of other female writers of this period, some of whom were Anglo-Irish and whose travels abroad were cultural, and some middle-class Catholic Irish, who either had the leisure and finance to travel or, more likely, were obliged to travel or live abroad through marriage or for economic reasons. Reading across class and religion and through other contexts, such as transnational and cosmopolitan experiences, offers the possibility of further enriching perspectives on the intellectual life of Irish women and, more broadly, on that 'fertile seedbed of nineteenth-century Irish writing'.[98]

Acknowledgements: My thanks to Maureen O'Connor and Patricia Moran for their helpful comments and suggestions. I am grateful for financial assistance towards research on Hannah Lynch from the MIC Research Seed Funding Scheme.

4

General Practice?
Victorian Irish Women and
United Kingdom Medicine

MARGARET Ó HÓGARTAIGH

Women entered the medical profession after the passing of the 1876 Medical Act. At that time Ireland was part of the United Kingdom. This chapter will assess their impact on the medical profession in the first quarter of a century after their qualification, through biographical studies of some of the more prominent members of that pioneering generation. Hence it will discuss a selection of the first generation of Irish medical women, who qualified to practise medicine between 1876 and 1901. Some of these doctors spent their professional careers in Britain. British medical women in Ireland, such as, famously, Sophia Jex-Blake, received their licentiates from the Royal College of Physicians of Ireland as it was the first institution in the UK to allow women to sit for their professional licence.

Ethel Bentham

Dr Ethel Bentham was the first female doctor to sit in the House of Commons. Although born in London, in about 1861, she grew up in Ireland. Her father, William Bentham, a Quaker, was a Justice of the Peace for Dublin County. She was educated at Alexandra School and College, an important progressive school for middle-class Protestants, though some Catholics would also have attended. In keeping with the welfare interests of so many female doctors, she began to study medicine and was

particularly anxious to cater for the poor; a desire fostered by her involvement in the 'Sunday club for shop girls' while at Alexandra. Bentham
studied at the London School of Medicine, but had to obtain a statutory
qualification from Scotland, qualifying, in 1894, with the Licentiate of the
Royal College of Physicians and Surgeons in Edinburgh. The previous
year she sat the licentiate in midwifery at the Rotunda Hospital in Dublin.
In 1895, Bentham received an MD from Brussels, where many early
female medics received their qualifications. Her medical career was spent
in England. Bentham worked in the Blackfriars Provident Dispensary
for women and children, and was a clinical assistant at the New Hospital
for Women. Furthermore, she spent fifteen years in general practice in
Newcastle upon Tyne. In 1906, Bentham became a general practitioner in
Kensington, London. Her interest in social conditions, particularly work
and wages, led her to establish a baby clinic in Kensington, in 1911. Later
an antenatal clinic was added, then a mothers' dental clinic and, finally,
a small hospital for children.[1]

Her public life was intertwined with her professional interests.
Bentham was chair of a court which dealt with non-attendance at
school, and she was also a member of the Metropolitan Asylums
Board. In 1929, after three unsuccessful attempts, she was elected as
a Labour MP for East Islington. Her contemporary, Dr E. Honor
Bone, argued that Dr Bentham's

> most important contributions to the social welfare of her time was the
> inception of the baby clinic ... [Dr Bentham] realised in the course of
> her practice that the start in preventive medicine should really be made
> in the earliest months of a child's life, and that it should therefore be
> possible for mothers to bring their children to some centre where they
> could get advice about diet and hygiene.

This practice was to be emulated in St Ultan's Hospital for Infants
in Dublin. Dr Honor Bone described Dr Bentham as one who had
little patience 'with palliatives. She wanted to get to the root of
all social troubles.' Her Dublin childhood was vital in this respect.
As a child, she had been sent on an 'errand of mercy' to a Dublin
tenement house.[2] While there, she met an impoverished group of
children standing around a child's coffin. Dr Bentham's pragmatism
motivated her to seek preventative cures for ills, especially those of
children. The baby clubs were her legacy.

Emily Campbell

Although a licentiate of the Royal Colleges of Physicians, and the Royal College of Surgeons in Edinburgh in 1896, Emily Campbell was born in Kerry, the daughter of Revd William Chestnut of Tralee. Campbell was attracted to medicine through her first husband's (Dr Fitzsimons) missionary work. After being abroad for several years, she returned, after his death, to study medicine. She practised in Antrim Road, Belfast for three years before marrying the well-known gynaecological surgeon, John Campbell. Emily Campbell may have had connections there, as she had been educated in Victoria College, Belfast. She worked with her husband as an anaesthetist, and took a 'deep interest in the welfare of the Samaritan and other Belfast Hospitals'. Her tenderness and compassion, as well as her 'good works and her interest in everything pertaining to the medical profession in Belfast', made her a popular figure.[3] One of her two sons also became a doctor. Lady Campbell died at 'Culloden', Craigavad, County Down in 1937. She left a personal estate of £5,544.

Ann Elizabeth Clark

A contemporary of Dr Ethel Bentham was Dr Ann Elizabeth Clark (1844–1924). Her professional career was spent primarily in Birmingham, where she worked for over twenty years in the Children's Hospital. Like Dr Bentham, she built up a private practice, particularly among the poor. Dr Clark was especially noted for her willingness to share ideas with younger members of staff, which was valued, as she was considered a leading authority on children's diseases. On her retirement, she was still giving advice at the local baby clinic. Like Dr Ethel Bentham, Clark was a Quaker.

Emily Winifred Dickson-Martin

Dr Dickson-Martin was one of the earliest medical graduates and the first female fellow of the Royal College of Surgeons. After being educated at Victoria College, Belfast, she decided, with her father's encouragement (Thomas Dickson, MP for Dublin), to study medicine. She received her licentiate from the Royal Colleges of Physicians and Surgeons in 1891. A fellowship followed in 1893. In the same year, she graduated with a first class honours medical degree from the Royal University of Ireland (RUI). In 1896, Dickson-Martin obtained her MD and MAO. She was turned down for a post, in the 1890s, at the famous Rotunda Lying-in Hospital, because of her sex.

After study on a travelling studentship in Vienna and Berlin, Dr Dickson-Martin established a private practice in Dublin. She was later appointed gynaecologist to the Richmond Hospital and Assistant Master to the Coombe. It seems her appointment as an examiner in midwifery in the Royal College of Surgeons created consternation. None the less, the decision was not overturned. She married in 1899, and decided that she could not practise due to family commitments. But Dr Dickson returned to her profession in 1915, when her husband was on service and her children were at school. She was an assistant at Rainhill Mental Hospital in England, as well as being the local Medical Officer of Health at Ellesmere, Salop. Later, Dr Dickson-Martin worked in a South Wales mining community, 'for whose womenfolk she had the greatest sympathy'. Noted for her strong personality, she had particular views on the role of women in medicine. In 1895 she presented a paper on the need for women as poor law guardians to the State Medicine section of the Royal Academy of Medicine. She believed that women were suited to this kind of work as it was like 'household management'.[4] In a speech on 'Medicine as a Profession for Women' to Alexandra College students, in 1899, she declared that women should retire on marriage, though she did not strictly adhere to her own philosophy.

Elizabeth Gould-Bell

Elizabeth Gould-Bell graduated from Queen's College, Belfast, in 1893. She became honorary physician to the Women's Maternity Home and Baby Home in Belfast, and was heavily involved in the Babies' Club Welfare Scheme in Belfast. From a well-to-do family, she was the daughter of Joseph Bell of Killeavey Castle, Newry, County Down. Dr Gould-Bell built up an extensive practice in Belfast, particularly among women. As one of the medical officers of the Belfast Corporation's 'Baby Club' scheme, she was a well-known medical figure in the city. Her personal life was marred by tragedy. She married Dr Hugh Fisher, who predeceased her. Their only son, a medical student, died in a German hospital after being wounded in France during the First World War. During this war, Dr Gould-Bell was in charge of a ward in Malta. She was described as 'a strong supporter of the women's franchise movement, and a close friend of Mrs Pankhurst', the women's suffrage leader. Like many female doctors, she was 'keenly interested in social welfare work'.[5]

Sara Gray

Dr Sara Gray from Roscrea, County Tipperary, qualified in 1888, and was a consulting surgeon at the Nottingham Hospital for Women. However, she had to overcome opposition from the local general practitioners. In 1891, she became the first woman to undertake general practice in Nottingham. Dr Gray was medical examiner to the Board of Education and the Nottingham Education Committee. Her interests included temperance, foreign missions, rescue work and social reform. The *British Medical Journal* alluded to her 'warm sympathy ... volcanic energy [and] Irish brogue' and the fact that she 'even mastered the motor-car'.[6]

Amelia Grogan

Dr Amelia Grogan, the daughter of Revd John Grogan, MA, grew up in Wicklow. Educated mainly at home, and later at Alexandra College, she graduated with a BA in Experimental Science and a medical degree, in 1895, from the RUI, after taking various courses in the Royal College of Science. Just as the pioneering female physician Elizabeth Garrett had taken scientific courses at the Royal Institute, so Dublin's Royal College of Science was useful for women preparing for a medical degree. Her interests were primarily in psychiatry, and she was assistant medical officer at Mullingar Asylum, in charge of the women's wing. Later, Dr Grogan worked at Fulborne Asylum in Cambridge. She had a general practice in north London, and also did part-time medical work at the General Post Office. A pioneer in child welfare work, Grogan was noted for her voluntary service. By 1930, she was medical officer to infant welfare clinics in Brixton, St Pancras and St Luke's Day Nursery, Holloway. Described as an 'ardent supporter' of the St John Ambulance Association, she lectured for twenty years to the Northampton Polytechnic Institute on first aid, home nursing and hygiene.[7] An obituary in *The Lancet* paid tribute to her 'Irish wit and ready invention', and to her popularity among mothers at the welfare clinics. Apparently, Dr Grogan was always patient and, like Dr Ada

English, who also worked in psychiatry, she kept in touch with some of her asylum patients. 'Innumerable were the small kindnesses that she did' was the epitaph of the *British Medical Journal*. Grogan died, unmarried, in 1930.[8]

Kathleen Lynn

Kathleen Lynn was probably the most famous of the pre-1900 medical graduates. The daughter of a Church of Ireland rector, Revd Robert Young Lynn, she was born in 1874 near Cong, County Mayo. Kathleen's maternal grandfather was Revd Richard Wynne of Drumcliffe, Sligo while Revd Wynne's wife, Catherine, was the daughter of Colonel Richard Beaver Brown. Kathleen Lynn's grandfather was a younger son of Owen Wynne, MP for Hazelwood, and Anne Maxwell, the Earl of Farnham's sister. Despite these aristocratic connections, she never associated herself with the privileged, and her later career was primarily concerned with the less well-off. The Mayo of Lynn's childhood was characterised by extreme poverty. The suffering wrought by the bad harvests of the late 1870s stimulated intense political activity, particularly by the Land League, which sought to improve the lot of tenants. These two strands, the poverty of so many people and political activity which sought to eliminate the causes of that poverty, were to be continually intertwined in Dr Lynn's professional career. After education in Manchester and Dusseldorf, she attended Alexandra College. Lynn graduated in 1899 from Cecilia Street, the Catholic University Medical School, since as a female she could not attend Trinity College Dublin; and became a fellow of the Royal College of Surgeons in 1909. Additionally, she did postgraduate work in the United States. Like many Irish doctors, she joined the British Medical Association.

Dr Lynn was refused a position in the Adelaide Hospital; male colleagues objecting to a female appointment, even though she had been elected as a resident doctor. It was not until May 1913 that the medical board allowed female students to apply for residence at the hospital. Lynn eventually joined the staff of Sir Patrick Dun's Hospital, and she also worked at the Rotunda between 1902 and 1916, according to an obituary of her friend Madeleine ffrench-Mullen. Between 1910 and 1916, she was a clinical assistant in the Royal Victoria Eye and Ear Hospital, but was not allowed to return after the 1916 Rising. Another female doctor, Dr Georgina Prosser, was appointed to replace her. It has been suggested that Dr Lynn was the first female resident doctor at the Eye and Ear Hospital. Her private practice, at 9 Belgrave Road, Rathmines, was her home for over fifty years. An active suffragist and an enthusiastic nationalist, Lynn was a friend of James Connolly, the labour activist who established the Irish Transport and General Workers' Union.[9]

When the Irish Citizen Army (ICA) was set up in 1913, in order to defend striking workers, Dr Lynn was asked by Connolly to teach first-aid. Dr Lynn went on to become a captain and chief medical officer in the ICA. This would bring her into close contact with the families of unemployed or poorly paid workers in Dublin. She worked with Countess Markievicz, Constance Gore-Booth (they were distantly related, as a Wynne had married a Gore-Booth), in the soup kitchens which were established during the 1913 Lockout. Markievicz, like Lynn, was a Protestant republican who would fight in the 1916 Rising against British rule in Ireland. A photograph of women involved in the 1916 Rising indicates the importance of Dr Kathleen Lynn and Madeleine ffrench-Mullen, as they are prominent in the foreground of the photograph. During the 1916 Rising, Lynn's medical training was vital. From her post in City Hall, in the centre of Dublin beside Dublin Castle, the administrative centre of British rule in Ireland, Lynn organised the medical needs of the ICA. She also established a temporary surgery. After the Rising, Lynn, like many women, was imprisoned, and her diaries include interesting comments on conditions in Kilmainham and Mountjoy prisons. She mentioned receiving gifts of fruit and flowers, but the lice in Kilmainham were not to her liking. One officer was 'quite civil', and he cleaned out the lavatory.[10] Dr Lynn was later Surgeon-General to Sinn Féin and a member of the Sinn Féin executive in 1917. She was 'on the run' between May and October 1918. When arrested, she was sent to Arbour Hill Detention Barracks. The Lord Mayor of Dublin, Laurence O'Neill, 'made representations to the authorities with a view to having her professional services made available during the influenza epidemic'.[11] The authorities agreed to release her but because of her republican activities, Lynn was still monitored carefully. When she visited the Red Cross in Switzerland in 1923, her house was searched. In the same year, Lynn was elected to Dáil Éireann on the anti-Treaty side, but did not take her seat. Her nationalist/socialist principles remained undimmed. In 1925, she wrote in her diary: 'Hogan's [Patrick Hogan, Minister for Agriculture] new Land Bill in, all landlords must sell, good.'[12] She was also a very religious woman and a regular attendee

at Holy Trinity Church, Rathmines. However, she was not afraid to
be critical. When her relative, Canon Wynne, who was to establish the
Samaritans in Ireland, asked her, 'Why is the Church not pacifist?', she
replied, 'Because it is not Christian.' Dr Lynn is remembered, primarily,
for her work in St Ultan's.[13]

Katherine Maguire

Dr Katherine Maguire was the youngest daughter of Revd John
Truelock Maguire, a rector at Boyle, County Roscommon. One of the
first two female students admitted to the Adelaide Hospital, along with
Isabella Harper, Maguire won the Hudson scholarship at the Adelaide
(the first woman to do so) in 1891, after studying at Alexandra College
and the RUI. She graduated in first place in her final medical examinations. In 1878, twenty-eight Adelaide students had complained that
they would not study certain subjects with females present. Hence
the decision to admit two females was unexpected. Maguire had
already obtained first place, first class honours and an exhibition in
the BA examination in biological science, the first woman in the RUI
to do so. She was noted for her interest in social medicine. In 1898,
her paper to the Alexandra Guild on 'Social Conditions of the Dublin
Poor' motivated the guild to establish model tenement houses.

Dr Maguire's work in St Ultan's Hospital exerted a powerful
influence on Dr Dorothy Stopford-Price, a 1921 graduate.
Dr Stopford-Price noted:

It was from Dr. Katherine Maguire that I learnt to take an interest in
clinical observations; or rather renewed an interest inculcated in my
student days by Professor William Boxwell ... For about nine years
I had imbibed wisdom from her in St. Ultan's Hospital, making a
point of doing her round with her, and she would pause at the last
cot, with the baby clutching her fingers whilst she drifted off into a
very interesting discourse, drawing on her great experience and her
wealth of reading. She was a very clever woman and Sister Mulligan
and I enjoyed these bedside talks, when she would range far and
wide ... Dr. Maguire encouraged any never-so-feeble evidences of an
enquiring mind, and urged one to take trouble to find things out and
to read and publish. During her last illness in 1930–1, I carried on her
extensive practice for her which indeed she left in my hands in the

end. She wrote me frequent and almost indecipherable letters about her patients up to the end. She was very indignant when I said some lady was suffering from *Anno Domini*.[14]

It is clear from Dr Stopford-Price's later career that she heeded Dr Maguire's advice to read and publish.

Dr Maguire had a private practice in Mount Street and later in Merrion Square in Dublin. She also opened a Free Dispensary at Harold's Cross. As part of her interest in alleviating the causes of ill-health, she bought four tenement houses in Tyrone Street and let them at a minimum rent. As a lecturer on hygiene at Alexandra College (her lectures on health began in 1893), she was described as an 'exceptionally gifted teacher'. She was a member of the Royal Academy of Medicine, but her 'self-effacing disposition did not permit her to speak or to show cases'. Enthusiastic about women's rights, she was described, somewhat oxymoronically, as a 'non-militant suffragette'. After her death in 1931, a 'bronze tablet' was erected in her memory at 27 Grenville Street.[15]

Margaret Smith-Bell

The sister of Elizabeth Gould-Bell, Margaret Smith-Bell received her licentiate from the Royal College of Physicians and Surgeons in 1894. Like her sister, she married a medical practitioner, Dr Douglas Boyd of Oldham. Smith-Bell worked in the Ulster Hospital for Children and in the Eye, Ear and Throat Hospital, Belfast. However, most of her short professional career was spent in Manchester, where she 'acquired a large practice, chiefly among women'.[16] She was not the first female to practise in the city but, according to the *British Medical Journal*, 'she, perhaps, did more than anyone to modify the prejudice which at one time in that, as in other cities, militated against the work of women in this department'.[17] She was co-opted as a member of the midwives' supervisory committee and was medical officer both of Ancoats Day Industrial School and 'The Grove', Retreat, Fallowfield. Unfortunately, Dr Smith-Bell became ill while on holiday in Portrush and, despite the medical assistance of her sister, she died in 1906 aged 42, leaving an infant son.

Elizabeth Tennant

Dr Elizabeth Tennant received her licentiate from the Royal College of Physicians and Surgeons in 1894, and practised in Harrington Street, Dublin between 1894 and 1937. She was an honorary visiting physician to St Ultan's Infants' Hospital, where she was a 'valued member' of staff, and was also medical officer to St Catherine's School and Orphanage in Dublin. Her large general practice in Dublin specialised in midwifery. As a student in the Meath Hospital, she made lifelong friends, including Sir John Moore, MD. In an obituary, *The Irish Times* wrote that 'her devotion to her work and to the hospital [St Ultan's] is acknowledged by all those connected with it to have been one of the biggest factors in the success of the institution'.[18] She never married, dying in 1938 at her niece's home in London.

Ella Webb

Dr Isabella Webb was the eldest daughter of the Dean of St Patrick's Cathedral. Like many female doctors, she was educated at Alexandra College, though she also studied at Queen's College, Harley Street, London and at Gottingen, Germany. Although Ella Webb wanted to study medicine, she first graduated with a natural science degree from the RUI. In 1904, she graduated with first place in her medical degree from Cecilia Street, to the delight of 'Speranza', a pen name of a female contributor to *St Stephen's*. The University College Dublin students' magazine pointed out that it 'was a record to gain it over the heads of so many competitors of the sterner sex, which, until recent years, regarded medicine as exclusively its own ground'.[19] Webb was awarded her MD in 1906. Like Dr Katherine Maguire, she won the prestigious travelling scholarship and went to Vienna. After her marriage to George Webb, a fellow of Trinity College Dublin, she combined rearing a family (she had a son and a daughter) with private practice and a free evening dispensary in Kevin Street. Her busy professional life also included working as a demonstrator of physiology in the Women's Department of the Trinity Medical School, as well as election to the visiting staff of the Adelaide Hospital, as assistant physician to the children's department. In 1918, she was appointed as anaesthetist to the Adelaide, a position she resigned due to other work commitments in 1927, although she continued to run a children's dispensary.

Her work in the Women's National Health Association and St Ultan's are discussed in the current author's biography of Kathleen Lynn. Given her interest in paediatrics, it is not surprising that she worked in the Stillorgan Children's Sunshine Home. In 1924, Dr Webb had written a paper on 'Sunshine and Health' for the Alexandra Guild Conference. This interest coincided with her research on rickets. Subsequently, a committee of women 'interested in child welfare had been formed to provide an open-air convalescent home'.[20] Ultimately, this led to the development of the Sunshine Home. Her work with Drs Lynn and Stopford-Price further enhanced the reputation of female doctors in the prevention of diseases, particularly those which were exacerbated by socio-economic deprivation. Dr Webb did not lose her Alexandra links and was an honorary commandant in the Alexandra College St John's Ambulance Brigade Nursing Division, where she taught first-aid. Her friend, Letitia Overend, was commandant in the brigade. Like Dr Lynn, Webb saw action during the 1916 Rising, as the brigade was on duty at the Emergency Hospital at 14 Merrion Square (the St John's headquarters). Dr Webb 'cycled continuously through the front line to visit hospitals. She was later made a Lady Grace of the Order of St John of Jerusalem in recognition of her services'. She was also awarded a medal for gallantry.[21] In 1918, Dr Webb was awarded an MBE. Noted for her 'strong personality' and her toughness, she had, according to Mitchell, 'a rugged sense of humour, a charming smile and a deep contralto laugh'. An obituary in the *The Irish Times* commented on her great energy, her plain speaking and her love of sacred music.[22] She died in 1946, at the age of 68.

All of these medical women had studied medicine in the Victorian era. They were part of a generation of professional women whose careers transformed the lives of others. The barrier-breaker, Sophia Jex-Blake, was grateful to the Royal College of Physicians of Ireland for their professional innovation in allowing women to sit their licentiate from 1876. She could scarcely have imagined the impact of that decision.

5

Intellectual Women: Irish Women at Cambridge, 1875–1904

SUSAN M. PARKES

In the nineteenth century, prior to the development of university education for women in Ireland, a number of female Irish students attended the women's colleges in Oxford and Cambridge. These pioneer residential academic colleges were regarded as ideal model institutions for the higher education for women and served as examples for others to follow. At Cambridge, Girton College for women was founded by Emily Davies in 1869, and Newnham College in 1871 by Professor Henry Sidgwick, with Anne Clough as first principal. At Oxford, Somerville College for women was founded in 1879 and Lady Margaret Hall in the same year. While the number of Irish women who had the privilege of attending the Oxbridge colleges remained small, they were an influential pioneer group who gave leadership and became role models for younger women. This chapter is concerned with Irish women who went to two of the Cambridge women's colleges, Girton and Newnham, in the years between 1875 and 1904, before Trinity College Dublin opened its doors to women.

Development of Higher Education of Women in Ireland

In Ireland the opportunities for the higher education of women in the 1880s and 1890s were still limited. The three Queen's Colleges in Belfast, Cork and Galway, founded in 1845, had begun to admit women from 1882 but the numbers remained small. The degrees of the

Royal University of Ireland (RUI), established in 1879, were open to women but the lack of suitable girls' academic secondary schools and of a university college open to women hindered the growth of higher education. The oldest university in Ireland, Trinity College Dublin, University of Dublin, founded in 1592, did not admit women until 1904, but the new National University of Ireland, founded under the Irish Universities Act of 1908, consisted of three constituent colleges, University College Dublin, University College Cork and University College Galway, all of which admitted women from the outset.[1]

The first major breakthrough in girls' academic education came with the founding of the Ladies' Collegiate School (later called Victoria College) in Belfast in 1859 and of Alexandra College in Dublin in 1866. Both these colleges offered girls an academic education similar to that of boys. The curriculum included subjects such as mathematics, Latin and science along with the customary 'ladies education'. Mrs Margaret Byers, who founded Victoria College,[2] and Mrs Anne Jellicoe, who founded Alexandra College, were both well-to-do widows who had the financial resources and the social concern to promote middle-class girls' education.[3] Another leading advocate was Isabella Tod, also of Belfast, who was a founder member of the Belfast Ladies' Institute in 1867, which organised academic lectures 'to provide advanced classes for ladies of a higher class than hitherto had been attempted'.[4]

Another pioneer institution for the education of women in Dublin was the Queen's Institute, founded in 1861 by Mrs Jellicoe and Miss Ada Barbara Corlett. It was modelled on the Society for Promoting the Employment of Women, founded by a group of women in London in 1859. At their offices in Langham Place, this society had established an employment register for women and offered courses in practical and commercial subjects for women seeking work. The Queen's Institute at Molesworth Street, Dublin, offered courses in subjects like law writing, telegraphy, book-keeping, woodwork and porcelain painting; it has been called 'the first technical college for women in the British Isles'.[5] However, after a time, Mrs Jellicoe left the institute and founded Alexandra College as a college of higher education in 1866. She believed that girls needed a solid secondary education before embarking on technical training.[6]

In 1869 there was another small breakthrough – both Trinity College Dublin and Queen's University Belfast introduced 'Examinations for Women'. These examinations were organised by the universities to encourage girls to undertake academic study. A standard examination syllabus was laid down but the universities provided no teaching. The obligatory subjects that were examined were English, arithmetic, history and geography, while the optional subjects included the classics, French, German, Italian and Spanish with mathematics, the sciences and theory of music. Although the numbers sitting these examinations remained small, they did show how female students were well able to undertake study of and master academic knowledge.[7]

In 1878 the introduction of the Intermediate Board public examinations system, which was open to girls' secondary schools, provided the opportunity for girls to show their academic ability. The standard of the curriculum in girls' schools was raised by the public examinations and the schools competed against each other to gain the best examination results and win the most prizes. There was a strong rivalry between the Protestant schools like Alexandra and Victoria College and the Catholic convent schools of the Loreto and Dominican orders. Success in these examinations encouraged girls to aspire to a university education but the opportunities still remained limited.[8]

The founding of the RUI created a new avenue for women's higher education. Founded in 1879, following the example of London University, which had been established the previous year, RUI degrees were open to women. However, it was an examining university only and there was as yet no university college open to women where they could study. Therefore, to provide more access to university education, the leading girls' schools developed university classes. Alexandra College and Victoria College both had university classes, as did the Loreto Convent in St Stephen's Green and the Dominican Convent in Eccles Street. Although the numbers graduating were small, they were influential in persuading young women to aspire to higher education. However, the women were deprived of the experience of a university campus and had to make do with what was available to them.[9] In 1892, when Trinity College Dublin was celebrating its tercentenary, a petition signed by 10,000 Irish women was presented to the board of the college requesting the admission of women to degrees. However, after lengthy consideration, Trinity refused to agree to this request, arguing that the presence of female students on a residential male campus would be 'a danger to the men' and 'a risk' not to be taken.[10] The campaign for admission had been led by Alice Oldham, one of the early female graduates of the RUI and a lecturer in Alexandra College.

As secretary of the Central Association of Irish Schoolmistresses, she was bitterly disappointed when the petition failed.[11] It was to take another ten years for the women to be admitted.

The link between so called 'ancient universities' of Oxford, Cambridge and Trinity College Dublin had been strong, so Trinity used the occasion of the admission of women to offer to successful students from the Oxbridge women's colleges Dublin University degrees under the historic practice of '*ad eundem gradum*'.[12] The offer was to last for three years only. Because of the close connections between the Cambridge women's colleges and Trinity, large numbers of Girton and Newnham past students came to Dublin to take BA and MA degrees, including quite a number of the Irish women who had gone to the Oxbridge colleges. Trinity had lost these talented young Irish women and it may be said that the offer made in 1904 of '*ad eundem*' degrees to Oxbridge women was an attempt to make amends for the refusal to award degrees to women earlier. Nearly 700 women, nicknamed 'the Steamboat Ladies', because they arrived overnight on the Holyhead steamer and returned the next day, came to Dublin to make use of the '*ad eundem*' privilege between 1904 and 1907.

Irishwomen Attending Oxbridge Women's Colleges

Therefore, prior to 1904, one attractive alternative for an intellectual girl was to go to one of the women's residential colleges in Oxford or Cambridge. This opportunity was open only to those who could afford to go or who could obtain a scholarship. In Londonderry there were university scholarships for women, funded by the Irish Society of London. The Londonderry Branch of the Association of Irish Schoolmistresses had requested these scholarships in 1884. They were awarded on the results of the Intermediate Board senior grade examinations. The candidates had to have 'studied continuously, for at least two years immediately before competing, at a school in the city of Londonderry or in the town of Coleraine'.[13] These scholarships could be held at Girton College, Cambridge and so quite a number of the Irishwomen went there from Londonderry. In addition the Drapers' Company, London had established a university scholarship for women, also based on the results of the senior grade Intermediate examination. Miss McKillip, head of Victoria High School in Londonderry, handled the applications for these scholarships and able pupils were encouraged to apply.

Why would these Irish girls wish to travel to one of these Oxbridge women's colleges? What did they have to offer? Not, as yet, the award of a formal degree of the universities of Cambridge or Oxford. However from 1881, their female students were allowed to sit the university examinations and, if successful, received university certificates. Girton College, in particular, insisted on its students taking the full university degree courses and sitting the final year degree examinations, which were known as the 'Tripos', so that they could prove their academic equality and be ready to graduate, if and when the university would admit women.[14] Newnham College adopted a different policy – the women were encouraged to choose what courses they wished to study and to tailor their choice to subjects of their interest rather than attempting the Tripos examinations. The lack of a formal qualification did little to diminish the students' desire for academic learning, though as the years went on more Newnham students began to study for the degree examinations. Quite a number of Scottish women continued to enrol at Cambridge, although the Scottish universities were now open to women.[15]

What these women's colleges offered to students was the experience of living in an academic community. Each student had a room of her own in which to sleep, work and entertain other women. This privilege was not always open to young women at home where they often had to share a room and did not have much privacy to study. The residential aspect of the college life was a major feature. The students mingled with the female academic staff on a daily basis and dined formally in the Hall. The colleges were built at a discreet distance from the university to provide protection for young women, yet near enough to allow the students to attend university lectures in the town.[16] The regular routine of study and recreation under supervision appealed to parents, provided they were in a position to cover the costs of fees, travel and maintenance. The majority of students, therefore, came from professional classes who were prepared to allow their daughters the freedom of an education before entering into marriage. These women were out of the ordinary and were challenging the middle-class conventions of the day, where women were expected to enter marriage early and to spend their time and talents in the domestic sphere. Many of the women were to use their higher education to lead independent lives as principals and teachers in the growing number of girls' secondary schools and some were to return to Cambridge to educate the next

generation of women. The founding of the Girls' Public Day School
Trust (GPDST) in England in 1872 had led to the development of a
network of girls' academic high schools which prepared their pupils
for university education and which in turn provided opportunities
of employment to the new graduate women teachers.[17] Many of
the Irishwomen made use of the *entrée* that the Cambridge colleges
offered to these new high schools and made their careers in them.
In addition, under the Balfour Education Act of 1902, local authorities were empowered to provide secondary schools for the first time,
so many new county and municipal schools were opened, which
offered challenging headships to the new graduate female teachers.

Early Irish Women at Cambridge

The majority of Irish women who attended the Cambridge colleges
were from Protestant northern middle-class families, including
the daughters of clergymen. The first Irish woman to go to Girton
College was one of the pioneer group who attended the college when
it was first founded by Emily Davies in Hitchin in Hertfordshire in
1869, before it moved to the spacious premises built in Girton village
in the outskirts of Cambridge. Presided over by Davies, the college
pioneered the higher education of women, encouraging them to
study for the Cambridge University Tripos examinations and set high
academic standards. More than fifty Irish students attended the two
Cambridge colleges between the 1870s and 1904, the year that Trinity
College Dublin opened its doors to women. In this essay, however,
it is proposed to examine only a select number of students who had
professional careers, both inside and out of marriage. A full list of the
Irish students attending both colleges is given in Appendix 1. Both
Girton and Newnham kept detailed registers of their students and
of their subsequent careers, so biographical data used in this essay is
drawn from these published registers. The date of entry to each college
is given in a bracket.[18]

The first Irishwoman to go to Girton College as a student was
Isabella Frances Vere Townsend, who entered Girton in 1869. She was
born in 1847 into an Anglo-Irish family. She gained a scholarship for
essay writing and sat the Cambridge entry examination known as
'Previous', in which she gained a first class result. She later became
an artist and settled in Rome; she very much admired the work of

William Morris and the Pre-Raphaelites. Sadly, she died in 1882, aged 35, of typhoid fever in Italy. Townsend is pictured in the Hitchin photograph with the other first Girton students, namely, Sarah Woodhead, Emily Gibson, Rachel Cook and Louisa Lumsden.[19] Of these, Emily Gibson, daughter of John Gibson, shipbuilder, was to marry, in 1873, Isabella's brother, Chambrey Corker Townsend, an architect. Emily Gibson kept a diary of her time at Girton and recorded how she was nearly removed from Hitchin as her family did not approve; however, she was determined to continue, and she wrote: 'I have announced my determination to take teaching as the occupation of my life, secondly to be a student at the College, and thirdly to set about preparing myself for it without delay … '.[20] She added that she wanted to avoid a 'life of long, listless, idleness'. She later became a member of the council of St Felix School, Southwold and was active in public life, including the women's suffrage movement and membership of the Fabian Society.[21]

In 1882 two Irish women came to Girton, both of whom were to have successful careers in education. Amy Barrington (1882) was the daughter of Edward Barrington, of Fasseroe, Bray, Co Wicklow. She sat the Classical Tripos in 1885 and became a teacher, making use of the opportunities offered by the expanding British Empire, including five years in Australia at the Girls' Grammar School, Brisbane (1888–93) and three years (1888–91) in a school in Vancouver. In 1906 she became a lecturer in Bedford College Training Department in London (1907–19), working in teacher education. She also did pioneer work (1906–19) in eugenics at the Francis Galton Laboratory at University College London, and she published in the field of human inheritance.[22]

The other Irish student who entered in 1882 was Charlotte Young, daughter of William Young of Londonderry. She was an Irish Society Scholar and took the Natural Science Tripos, Part I. She first taught science at Leeds High School from 1885 to 1892 and in 1893 she married (Sir) Benjamin Robertson of the Indian Civil Service. She spent much time working with her husband in India in the Central Provinces, where Benjamin was Chief Commissioner. She was awarded the Kaisar-i-Hind Gold Medal for her services there. During the First World War she worked in Mesopotamia and was awarded a CBE in 1918. Young was an example of the new educated woman who made an equal career for herself within a professional marriage.[23]

The following year, 1883, another girl from the north of Ireland, Anna Grace Hogben, came to Girton. Her father was a divisional inspector in the Royal Irish Constabulary in Londonderry and she was also an Irish Society Scholar. She took the Classical Tripos and began her teaching career as an assistant mistress in Croxteth Road Girls' School in Liverpool from 1886 to 1889. She then became headmistress of Baxter Ladies' College in Cupar, Fife, in Scotland from 1889 to 1907 and of Clarendon House School, Southport, from 1907 to 1920. Eventually, she founded her own school, Brentwood, in Southport. She remained a classical scholar and in 1904 she was one of the first women to take a University of Dublin MA when these degrees were opened to women who had studied at one of the Oxbridge colleges.[24]

In 1884, Mary Sybil Raymond, a clergyman's daughter, entered Girton to read mathematics. She was from Blennerville, County Kerry, where her father was rector of Ballyheigue. She had attended the Clergy Daughters' School in Bristol and won a Drapers' Scholarship to Girton; she is an example of an able girl who, supported by the scholarship, established a career. She became a notable teacher of mathematics, teaching in prestigious girls' schools – the Perse School for Girls in Cambridge, Howell's School in Llandaff, James Allen's Girls' School in Dulwich and, finally, at Sydenham High School, for over twenty years from 1902. Like other young female teachers, she took advantage of the opportunities offered by the British Empire, teaching in Brisbane from 1893 to 1898.[25]

Georgina Tarleton Young (1884)[26] was also to have a long career in girls' education, becoming a distinguished headmistress. She was born in 1865 in Northern Ireland, daughter of James Young, an agent. She attended Alexandra College in Dublin and Hohere Tochterschule in Hanover. She took the Medieval and Modern Languages Tripos and taught in Merchant Taylors' School, Great Crosby. She was appointed head of Huyton Girls' School in 1894, when she was only 29. In 1899 she was appointed head of Edgbaston High School, where she became one of the leading headmistresses in girls' education. She came to Dublin in 1907 to take a MA from Dublin University under the 'ad eundem' privilege for Oxbridge female students.[27]

In the following year Mary Kennedy (1885), daughter of a farmer, John Cochrane Kennedy of Coleraine, County Derry, entered to read science; she also had a distinguished career in education, entering the school inspectorate. She had been educated at the Ladies' Collegiate

School in Derry and was an Irish Society Scholar. She was one of the first Irish women to gain a first class grade in the Science Tripos, Part I. She taught in a number of schools and was headmistress of the Secondary School, Birkenhead from 1906 to 1914. In 1914 she was appointed as one of His Majesty's Inspectors; she was one of the earliest women selected to serve in this office, which provided a senior career opportunity for female teachers.[28]

Future Mistresses of Girton

There were two able young Irish women who were destined to become mistresses of Girton College: Elizabeth Welsh from 1885 to 1903 and Edith Major thirty years later, from 1925 to 1931. From the beginning, when Emily Davies founded the college, the principal at Girton was known as the 'Mistress', emphasising the femininity and pastoral responsibility of the role.

Elizabeth Welsh (1871), born in 1843 in Portaferry, County Down, was one of the earliest students at Girton College when it was still at Hitchin. She had been educated privately and came to Hitchin in 1871, studying for a Mathematical Tripos in 1875. After a short teaching career she returned to Girton as a lecturer and soon rose to a position of authority – she served as vice-mistress and garden steward, eventually becoming mistress in 1885. She steered the college through the difficult years following the refusal of Cambridge University in 1897 to award degrees to women. The campaigners were very disappointed with the decision and were affronted by the strong negative reaction of the Cambridge male lobby. The male graduates and students organised an angry campaign and the vote was defeated amidst a large public demonstration outside the Senate House in Cambridge.[29]

The other Northern Irish mistress of Girton was Edith Helen Major (1885), a student of the next generation.[30] She was born in Lisburn in 1867, daughter of Henry Major, and attended Methodist College, Belfast, the leading Wesleyan school founded in 1843. She came to Girton in 1885 to read for a History Tripos. She began a distinguished teaching career at Blackheath High School, one of the leading GPDST girls' schools in London.[31] She was appointed headmistress of Putney High School for Girls for ten years from 1900 to 1910, moving to the headship of King Edward VI School for Girls in Birmingham. She became mistress of Girton in 1925, a somewhat surprise appointment as she had had a career in school teaching rather than as an academic lecturer. (She had served as president of the Headmistresses' Association from 1919 to 1921.)[32] She proved a very capable and popular head of the college, encouraging more participation in the wider world of Cambridge, 'both town and gown'. She was awarded a CBE for her work in education in 1931 and the following year an honorary LLD degree from Queen's University Belfast was conferred on her. Her obituary stated:

> She was an inspiring leader and wise counsellor, because her advice was based on ungrudging readiness to understand the factors of the situation and a swift perception of its essentials. Wise, gay, courageous, she was the best of company at all times. She had the rare gift of being always witty and never unkind. Her salt never lost its savour.[33]

Two Pioneer Astronomers

Two Girton Irish students were destined to become leaders in a new profession for women. Alice Everett and Annie Russell (Maunder), who both entered Girton in 1886, became pioneer female astronomers, renowned in their field.[34] The older of the two, Alice Everett, had already studied at Queen's College, Belfast, where her father, John David Everett, was professor of natural philosophy. Born in Glasgow in 1865, she had been first educated at Methodist College, Belfast. She took the Mathematical Tripos at Cambridge and became the first female computer at the Royal Observatory, Greenwich, in 1890. (A team of computers did the difficult numerical calculations and assisted with recording star crossings with the telescope for astronomical time keeping.) Everett then became an assistant at the Royal Astrophysics Observatory in Berlin for five years from 1895 to 1900, after which she spent a year at the observatory at Vassar College, the first women's university college in America. When Everett returned to Britain she became an expert in optics, collaborating with her father in work on lenses. During the First World War, she worked at the National Physical Laboratory and on retirement continued to do research work, moving into the pioneering technology field of the new medium of television, and she was one of the first women to view a television screen.[35] She was a founder member of the Television Society.

Annie Scott Dill Russell (Maunder) (1886), on the other hand, worked in astronomy alongside her husband, Walter Maunder, who was a distinguished British astronomer. She was born in 1868 in Strabane, County Tyrone, daughter of Revd William Andrew Russell, a Presbyterian minister. She was educated at Victoria College, Belfast and entered Girton with a scholarship in 1886, taking a Mathematical Tripos in the same year as Everett. She taught for a year at Jersey Ladies' College and then became a computer at the Royal Observatory, Greenwich from 1891 to 1895. In 1895 she married Professor Walter Maunder, under whom she had been working. She had to resign her post but she continued to work with her husband in solar research.

Photography was used to study sunspots and eclipses and the two travelled widely. They went to India to view the total eclipse of the sun in 1898 and Everett designed her own camera. The Maunder partnership become best known in astronomy for 'the butterfly diagram' – photographs of sunspots taken over an eleven-year cycle. In 1910 they published a popular book, *The Heavens and their Story*, which was mostly written by Maunder herself. She continued to work together with her husband but it was not until 1915 that the ban on female members in the Royal Astronomical Society was lifted and she could be made a fellow. After her husband's death in 1928 she continued to do research and her name is honoured among astronomers.[36]

1880s – Other Irish Women at Girton

For the remainder of the 1880s Irish female students continued to go to Girton. Schools were encouraging girls to take the Intermediate senior grade examinations and although from 1882 women were admitted to the Queen's Colleges in Ireland, the attraction of an all-women academic residential college was still strong. There were increasing opportunities for graduate female teachers as the number of girls' high schools grew, and Irish schools like Londonderry High School, Methodist College, Belfast and Alexandra College, Dublin encouraged their most able pupils to apply to the Oxbridge colleges. The majority of them read languages as their main subject and a number of them who were intent on teaching began to follow their degree with a professional education course. In 1879 the Cambridge Teachers' Syndicate had been established to offer professional certification in education, both theoretical and practical. It was led by Oscar Browning and Elizabeth Hughes of the

Cambridge Training College for Women, which Hughes founded in 1885. Secondary teacher training for graduates was still in its infancy but women teachers were supportive of formal certification as it gave status to the profession.[37] The lack of a formal degree at times made it difficult for Cambridge women to compete for posts against women holding degrees from London University and the Scottish universities.

Annie McClure Warnock (1888) was one of the small number of students who returned to teach in Ireland. She was born in 1870, daughter of William Warnock, clerk of sessions. She attended Londonderry High School and took a Classical Tripos at Girton. She was one of the first Irish graduates to undertake a professional training course for teachers. She went to St George's Training College in Edinburgh and was awarded the Cambridge Teachers' Diploma with distinction. She took a Dublin University degree in 1906. She returned to teach in Belfast and became well known in literary circles – she wrote plays and became a member of the Belfast branch of the PEN Club and of the Irish Literary society.[38] The PEN club (Poets, Essayists, Novelists) was founded in London in 1921 as a worldwide organisation to promote friendship and intellectual co-operation among writers.

Another student who undertook professional training after studying at Girton was Jane Rankin Pollock (1889), who attended the Cambridge Women's Training College from 1892 to 1893.[39] Pollock, who was born in Londonderry in 1869, daughter of John James Pollock, a draper, had come through the established elite network of Victoria High School, Londonderry, and North London Collegiate School. She took the Classics Tripos in 1892 and first taught at Sheffield High School, before emigrating to South Africa where she had a successful teaching career, thus making use of the opportunities offered in colonial education. She was vice-principal of the Collegiate School for Girls in Port Elizabeth and classics teacher at the Girls' High School, Bloemfontein, 1905–15 and, thirdly, at the High School, Pretoria. She remained in South Africa and died in Capetown in 1941.[40]

The 1890s

In the 1890s the number of Irish students going to Cambridge became smaller, partly because access to the degrees of the Royal University of Ireland (RUI) became more readily available through the Queen's Colleges as well as the university classes offered in the girls' high schools.

One of the most distinguished Irish students of the 1890s was Elizabeth Margaret Cunningham, who played a major role in the introduction of female students into Trinity College Dublin after 1904. She became the first warden of Trinity Hall, the women's university residence established in 1908, and she brought with her ideas of what a women's university residence should offer to students, based on her own experience at Girton. Thus, the structure and life of Girton College were influential in the development of subsequent women's university colleges. Although Trinity Hall in Dublin was a women's residence only and not an academic college (the women attended lectures on the Trinity campus), Cunningham sought, as warden of Trinity Hall, to create an intellectual and creative atmosphere for the resident female students. As warden from 1908 to 1940 she imprinted a lasting stamp on the life of Trinity Hall, which has continued long after her death.[41]

Cunningham was born in Buncrana, County Donegal in 1872, daughter of John Cunningham, Irish Land Commissioner. She was educated at Victoria College, Belfast and was awarded an Irish Society scholarship. She read for the Medieval and Modern Languages Tripos and obtained a first class grade in the university examinations. She embarked on a teaching career at Withington Girls' School, Manchester, from 1894 to 1896, and then returned to Victoria College, Belfast as a lecturer in French and German for four years, 1896–1900. She became a senior lecturer in German at Royal Holloway College, London in 1900, but returned to Victoria College as vice-principal in 1906. She took a Dublin MA degree in that year.

In 1907 she was appointed to be the first warden of Trinity Hall, the new residence for female students attending Trinity College Dublin, which was opened in 1908 at Dartry, a suburb of south Dublin. This was (like Girton) near enough to the university for the women to travel to attend lectures either by bicycle or tram, but far enough away to avoid 'mixed' social life on the Trinity main campus. Trinity placed much importance on the residential aspect of university education and therefore it was considered essential that the women should be offered this opportunity. Miss Cunningham, affectionately known 'Cun' by generations of 'Hall' students, created a 'country house' lifestyle – students had their own study rooms, changed for a formal dinner in the evening, and were required to return to Hall in the evening before 'lights out'. Cunningham invited a constant flow of distinguished guests to dine with her at 'high table' and encouraged the students to enjoy the arts and music. However, she herself, despite her previous academic experience, did not lecture in the university, and her role was confined to supervising the residence. She was active in public life, an Irish nationalist and supporter of women's suffrage.[42]

Another able student of 1896, who also had a long career in education, was Katherine Sara Howard McCutcheon (1896). She was born in 1875 in Donaghdee, County Down, daughter of a clergyman, Revd Oliver McCutcheon, LLD, who taught theology at Methodist College, Belfast. She was educated at Methodist College and later studied at Queen's College, Belfast, where she was awarded a degree in 1900. She entered Girton in 1896 with a scholarship and studied classics and philosophy, obtaining a first class grade. She became a member of staff at St Leonard's in Aberdeen from 1910 to 1922 and then went as a tutor to Lady Margaret Hall, one of the women's colleges at Oxford; she returned to become head-mistress at St Leonard's from 1922 to 1938. She co-edited a history of St Leonard's, published in 1927. As a leading educationalist, she became a governor of Girton, and served on the Board of Bedford College, London, a women's college which had been founded in 1849. She was also a governor of the Furzedown, a London County Council Training College for female teachers.[43]

Jessie Gertrude Deed (1894), daughter of Alfred Deed, leather manufacturer of Blackheath, was an example of a student who made an Irish professional marriage – she married William Woods Haslett, who was the first headmaster of St Andrews College, a Presbyterian school founded in 1894 in Dublin. Haslett was very successful as first head of the school. He was a graduate of Queen's College, Belfast and had continued his studies at Oxford. In 1900 he was appointed as the first head of St Andrew's College, a post that he held until his untimely death in 1906. He was regarded as 'the Beau Ideal of a head'. One of his staff wrote: 'under his guidance the College flourished. Discipline was excellent and the staff did their work quietly and efficiently. The college was Billy's child and he guided its early steps in the proper path.'[44] In widowhood, Jessie Deed was fortunate to be able to use her qualifications to have a career in education and she became a teacher of mathematics at Northampton and Huddersfield High Schools.

Irish Women at Newnham College, 1872–1900

The links between Newnham College and Irish women were less strong than those between Girton College and Irish women. The number who went to Newnham College was smaller and fewer Newnham students came to Dublin to take the Dublin University '*ad eundem*' degrees between 1904 and 1907. This was partly due to the fact that, whereas Girton encouraged their students to take the university examinations in order to be qualified for a degree whenever Cambridge University would eventually grant the privilege, Newnham had a different, more flexible, approach of encouraging their students to select courses which suited them without being pressurised into taking the degree qualification. However, once the university Tripos examinations became open to women from 1881, more students began to study for the degree courses.

Newnham College dated from 1871, when a series of lectures for women was organised at Cambridge University under the leadership of Professor Henry Sidgwick, later professor of moral philosophy. An Association for Promoting the Higher Education of Women in Cambridge was founded in 1873 to develop the scheme and Newnham Hall was purchased to serve as a residence for women attending these lectures. In 1880 the Newnham College Association was formed to become a women's university college. The first principal, Anna Jemima Clough, who had been a pioneer of women's higher education in the north of England, was invited in 1875 by Professor Sidgwick to preside over the new residence for female students in Cambridge. Miss Clough was principal until 1892, and Mrs Eleanor Sidgwick, wife of Professor Henry Sidgwick, succeeded her; they lived in Newnham until her retirement in 1910. Newnham differed from Girton in that it consisted of a number of separate halls, which were built over the years around an open garden space, giving it a more domestic, homely atmosphere, which was less institutional than the Girton buildings.[45]

There were two Irish women among the early members of staff at Newnham. Mary Jane Martin, daughter of Revd Henry Martin, a congregational minister from Armagh, was to spend most of her life in Cambridge. Educated at home, she came to Newnham in 1876 and studied for the Moral Science Tripos in 1879. She became a lecturer at Newnham until her marriage to Professor James Ward of Trinity College, Cambridge in 1884, but continued her connection with Newnham as a member of the council. She later became an active leader in the Cambridge Association for Women's Suffrage. A former student recalled: '... Miss Martin was a perfectly delightful Irish woman, delicate and swift in both wit and humour, and so kindly to me, the young intruder, I never felt in the way, or not clever enough'.[46]

The other young Irish woman on the Newnham staff was Jane Lee, who was a daughter of Archdeacon William Lee, DD, professor of ecclesiastical history at Trinity College Dublin. Born in 1850, she was educated at Alexandra College, Dublin, and Gottingen University before coming to Newnham in 1882. She became a lecturer in modern languages, from 1882 to 1895, and later a vice-principal of the college. She died young in 1895. She was remembered as a lively, clever lecturer who went boating:

> I remember once getting Miss Lee, a don in South Hall, to come with us as 'chap' (chaperon) on the Backs. Miss Lee was *not* an oarsman in any sense of the word; she steered. I always liked Miss Lee; I believe she knew sixteen languages, one of them Sanskrit (she said she would teach me Sanskrit if I would learn the alphabet first).[47]

Three other young Irishwomen made their way to Newnham in the early days of 1875. Two Townsend sisters from Wilton, Cork, Alice Maud and Mary Hungerford, had both attended University College, Bristol before coming to Newnham in the Easter term of 1875. Mary Hutton, on the other hand, came for two years from 1875 to 1877. Hutton came from an intellectual background, being a niece of Anne Swanwick, one of the founders of Bedford College, London. She did not stay long at Newnham. Hutton was to marry William Wilkins, who was headmaster of the High School, Dublin, and was to spend much of her life in Ireland. Wilkins, a graduate of Trinity College Dublin, was a member of an intellectual Dublin family and was a successful, if controversial, head of the High School, which had been founded in 1870 by the Governors of Erasmus Smith as a grammar and commercial high school for boys. Their grandson, Maurice Wilkins, a professor at King's College London, was to be the 'third man' in the discovery of DNA in 1962, for which he was awarded the Nobel Prize.[48]

Later in the 1870s, four more pioneer Irish students came to Newnham – all from differing backgrounds. Elizabeth Finlay, who was born in Belfast in 1853, had been educated in England and came from 1878 to 1881 to read for the Moral Science Tripos; later she took an MA from Dublin University. Alice Mary Lloyd, who was born in New Zealand in 1859, was the granddaughter of Bartholomew Lloyd, provost of Trinity College Dublin. She spent two years at Newnham but did not sit for the Tripos examinations. She married Albert Dew Smith and became a journalist and writer. The third student, Lucie Anne Earl, had been educated in Ireland at the D'Israeli School, Rathvilly, County Carlow. This was an unusual endowed school founded by the local landlord, who was cousin of the prime minister, Benjamin D'Israeli.[49] Earl came to Newnham for a year in 1879 but did not study for the Tripos. Nevertheless, she had a subsequent active career, teaching for ten years at King Edward VII High School, Birmingham and then becoming headmistress of Tadcaster Girls' Grammar School and later of Allerton School, Sutton Coldfield, thus making good use of the expanding opportunities in girls' academic education, despite not having a formal qualification.

The 1880s

In the next decade the number of Irish students at Newnham increased as the confidence of young women grew. One of the most talented students of 1880s was Frances Ralph Gray (1880) who was to be the first high mistress of St Paul's School for Girls in Hammersmith, London. Gray was born in Roscrea, County Tipperary in 1861, daughter of James Gray, who was clerk to the Roscrea Board of Guardians, in charge of the workhouse for the poor in the town. She was educated at home and sat the entrance examination for Plymouth High School, where she was made aware of her Irish background and differences in speech and style. She entered Newnham to read for the Classics Tripos, where she became very friendly with another Irish girl, Anne Wakefield Richardson (1881), who was a Quaker and a member of the Richardson family who had founded the factory and temperance village of Bessbrook, County Armagh. In 1883 Richardson was invited by another pioneer of women's higher education, Constance Maynard, who the previous year had founded Westfield College in London, to transfer to the new college as a student. Richardson studied for a

London BA degree and became a member of staff there. Gray followed Richardson to Westfield as a lecturer in classics and the three women formed a strong trio of leadership at the new college. Maynard, who had been an early student at Girton (1872), was deeply religious and wished to create a university college like Girton but on a firm religious basis.[50] She much admired the pioneering American women's college, Mount Holyoke in Massachusetts, founded by Mary Lyon in 1837. Mary Lyon had been a devout Christian and strong believer in the higher education of women; Maynard modelled Westfield on this famous New England college.[51]

Gray, however, left Westfield in 1893 to become headmistress of St Katherine's School, which was a junior school for St Leonard's School at St Andrews. She then moved to be the high mistress of the new St Paul's School for Girls, Hammersmith, where she served from 1903 from 1927. In 1907 she came to Dublin to take her 'ad eundem' MA degree. An outstanding principal and a leader in women's education, she was president of the Association of Women Teachers from 1921 to 1923 and of the Headmistresses' Association from 1923 to 1924. In 1927 she was awarded an OBE for her services to education and in 1931 she published her lively autobiography entitled 'And Gladly Wolde he Lerne and Gladly Teche'.[52]

Anne Richardson, on the other hand, remained at Westfield College with Maynard for the rest of her career, becoming vice-principal in 1918. Westfield, as a college of London University, was able to offer degrees to its students from the outset and it became one of the leading colleges for women in London.[53]

Another student of the 1880s was an outstanding Irish headmistress, Henrietta White (1882), who was principal of Alexandra College, Dublin from 1890 to 1931. White was born in Charleville, Roscrea, County Tipperary, educated at Alexandra College, Dublin, and went to Newnham from 1882 to 1885; she did not sit for Tripos but brought back to Ireland her deep appreciation of the education she had received at Newnham and which she tried to emulate at Alexandra College. She believed strongly in the value of separate education for women and she hoped that the college would one day become a university women's college like Newnham.[54] From the 1880s, Alexandra College had been offering university courses for degrees of the RUI, which were open to women, and it was hoped that eventually it would become a recognised college of Dublin University. Sadly for White, this did not happen, as in 1904 Trinity College Dublin chose to admit women onto the main university campus rather than recognise Alexandra as a women's college; thus it became a senior secondary school, albeit one with high academic standards.[55] White was a keen horticulturist and created a beautiful garden at the college, shared by students and staff alike, and she gave inspired leadership to her students in the responsible feminine role to be played by educated women.

While most students who came to Newnham in the 1880s were to follow an academic or teaching life, others were to enjoy professional marriages to successful men in public life. One such was Constance Maud de La Cherois Crommelin (1885), born in Cushendun, County Antrim in 1867, daughter of Nicholas de la Cherois Crommelin, a member of the Huguenot family who had been one of the founders of the linen industry in Ulster. Constance was educated at Alexandra College, Dublin before entering Newnham in 1885. She obtained a Mathematical Tripos in 1888 and spent a number of years teaching mathematics in Roedean School in Brighton.[56] In 1902 she married the poet John Masefield, who was ten years her junior. They shared an interesting marriage, Masefield being appointed Poet Laureate in 1930. Crommelin's broad education at Newnham had prepared her well for life among English literary circles.

Another student who participated in an intellectual marriage was Blanche Vernon (1888), born in County Dublin in 1863, the third daughter of John Edward Vernon of Mount Merrion House, who was agent for the wealthy Pembroke estate in Dublin. The Vernons were well known for the philanthropic work of the Pembroke estate in providing housing and supporting education in Dublin. Blanche entered Newnham in 1888, at the age of 25, but did not sit for the Tripos examinations, leaving after two years. In 1895 she married Professor Grenville A.J. Cole, professor of geology at the Royal College of Science in Dublin, and director of the Geological Survey of Ireland. Like Crommelin, Blanche shared her husband's successful career and they both were keen cyclists and travellers on the Continent. Cole was a petrologist and mineralogist, who particularly encouraged practical fieldwork in geology and made a major contribution to its study in Ireland. He organised field visits for his students, travelling across the countryside by bicycle. He published a large number of articles and some popular textbooks on Irish geology.[57] Blanche co-wrote a book with him entitled *As We Ride* (1902), a lively account of their cycling visits to Austria, Germany and Poland. They shared the chapters between them and the text reveals Blanche as a strong and articulate person.[58] She was active in social work in Dublin and was secretary of the Children's Sunshine Home, Stillorgan, which was founded in 1925 by Dr Ella Webb, a pioneer doctor who had made a study of the disease of rickets and the detrimental effect of lack of sunlight on the health of city children.[59]

Two daughters of another distinguished Irish geologist, William Johnson Sollas, also attended Newnham – Hertha Beatrice Coryn Johnson, as a student in 1897, and Igerna Brunhild Johnson, as a member of staff in 1903. Sollas was professor of geology and zoology at Bristol University (1879–83), then professor of geology and mineralogy at Trinity College Dublin (1881–97) and finally at Oxford University (1897–1936). When in Ireland he did pioneer work on fossils and on the origins of marbles. He also worked with the Irish botanist Robert Lloyd Praeger on glacial deposits of the Dublin district.[60] His elder daughter, Hertha, born in Cambridge in 1875, was educated at Alexandra College, Dublin, while her father was at Trinity College Dublin. In 1897 she went to Newnham to read for the Medieval and Modern Languages Tripos. She obtained a first class degree and went to Heidelberg to study for her PhD. She worked as a linguist and published a number of books translated from German, including the influential geological study by the Austrian geologist Eduard Suess *Das Antitz der Erde* (The Face of the Earth), which ran to five volumes.

Her younger sister, Igerna, born in 1877, was also educated at Alexandra College, and in 1897 she went to Newnham to study for the Natural Sciences Tripos, obtaining a first class degree. She was a lecturer in zoology at Newnham from 1903 to 1904 and from 1906 to 1913, and became an associate academic. She published papers on fossils and on crossbreeding in guinea pigs and moths. These two intellectual women gained much from being members of an academic family, which supported and encouraged their innate intellectual ability.

Mary Pakenham Walsh (1888) was to have a long career as principal of St George's School, Ascot, from 1905 to 1922. She came from Dublin, where she was born in 1862, the daughter of Revd William Pakenham-Walsh, later bishop of Ossory, Ferns and Leighlin (1878–97). She attended the French School, Bray, which had been founded in 1864 by Heloise de Mailly, a French widow; it had a strong academic record and an emphasis on the French language. It was later to send a number of girls to Trinity College Dublin, when the university admitted women after 1904.[61] The Pakenham-Walshs were a Church of Ireland clerical family with a strong sense of duty and service and Mary had two brothers who became missionaries in India and China.[62] She did not pursue the Tripos examinations at Newnham but moved to the Cambridge Training College for Women in 1891 to train as a teacher. She taught first at Blackheath School, one of the leading GPDST schools, and then moved in 1902 to St George's, Ascot, to become its first principal. The school had been founded in 1877 as a boys' preparatory school but was refounded in 1902 by Pakenham-Walsh as a finishing school for girls, to encourage them to aspire to higher education.

The 1890s

The 1890s brought another group of young women to Newnham, one of whom was Margaret Elizabeth Gardner (1892), who had long career in education. Born in 1873 in Downpatrick, County Down, she was the daughter of Edward Gardner, a solicitor and sub-sheriff of County Down. Her mother was a school teacher and she was educated first at her mother's school in Downpatrick and then at Tunbridge Wells High School. She entered Newnham in 1892 and read for the Medieval and Modern Languages Tripos. In 1895 she was appointed to Croydon High School and the following year moved to South Hampstead High School, one of the GPDST flagship schools. In 1905 she was appointed headmistress of Blackburn High School, one of the new civic schools for girls, where she presided for twenty-eight years. In 1905 she came to Dublin to take her Dublin University MA, which would prove useful to her when competing for headships. Gardner also found time for active social work, serving with the London County Council's Children's Care Committee from 1934 to 1939, as a server of the Blind League from 1934 to 1954, and as a teacher of Jewish refugees from 1934 to 1942.

Her contemporary at Newnham was a student from the south of Ireland who also had a successful career in women's education. Maria Hamilton Meade (1895), born in Tralee, County Kerry in 1876, was the daughter of a clergyman, Revd Gerald de Courcy, and attended the new Dublin girls' school St Margaret's Hall, where a former

Newnham student, Edith Badham (1885), was an assistant mistress from 1888 and became headmistress in 1895. Badham would have encouraged Maria Meade to aspire to attend her own college at Cambridge. Meade went to Cheltenham Ladies' College and entered Newnham to read for the Moral Science Tripos in 1895. She was an exhibitioner and kept in contact with the college throughout her life, becoming an associate fellow from 1933 to 1949 and serving as both president and vice-president of the Newnham Roll of past students. She had a challenging career, first taking her London Teachers' Certificate before going out to Egypt as a tutor to His Majesty Maharani of Baroda from 1902 to 1905, and later serving under the Egyptian Ministry of Education, as principal of Saniel Training College, Cairo, where she stayed from 1906 to 1916. In 1907 she took her 'ad eundem' MA degree in absentia from Dublin University. On returning to England she continued in teacher education, becoming principal of Dartford College of Physical Education (for women)[63] and later serving on the appointments board of Manchester University. In 1919, at the age of 43, she was appointed headmistress of Bolton High School, where she presided for nineteen years. In retirement she continued to teach, lecturing to HM Forces during the Second World War and to the Workers' Education Association and the Women's Institute.

Access to University Education, 1900–08

In the four years from 1900 to 1904 Irish students continued to go to Cambridge, despite improvements in women's access to university education in Ireland. In 1901 a Royal Commission on University Education in Ireland was set up, the purpose of which was to find a solution to the long-running 'Irish University Question'. An acceptable structure of higher education needed be found which would satisfy the demands of the Catholic Church hierarchy.[64] The government was not prepared to endow a Catholic university but the Catholic Church had forbidden young Catholics to attend Trinity College Dublin, a Protestant foundation, or the non-denominational Queen's Colleges. University College in St Stephen's Green, under the auspices of the Jesuit order, was attended by Catholic men but was not open to women.[65] The increase in secondary education had created a demand for higher education among both young Catholic men and women and the RUI, founded in 1879 as a non-denominational examining university, was regarded as a 'stop-gap' measure only, as it provided no stimulating collegiate life for students.

The controversy over the higher education of women was one issue reviewed by the Robertson Commission. In 1902, the RUI women graduates formed the Irish Association of Women Graduates, the purpose of which was to publicise their case and to make submissions to the royal commission. However, the women were divided among themselves as to whether they should support co-education and seek entry to the male colleges or whether they should argue for single-sex women's colleges as at Cambridge and Oxford. Those like Alice Oldham and Mary Hayden, both RUI graduates, favoured co-education, as they wanted women to have equal opportunities with men and did not 'want to be shut up in women's colleges'.[66] On the other hand, the Catholic religious orders of the Loreto and the Dominicans sought support for separate women's colleges, as did Henrietta White, the influential principal of Alexandra College, Dublin. They considered that women needed the support of a community of female scholars and to have their particular needs catered for.[67] St Mary's College had been opened by the Dominicans in 1893 to provide university teaching for young Catholic women and Loreto College on St Stephen's Green had done the same. In Cork, St Angela's College had been opened by the Ursulines.[68] White, having attended Newnham from 1882 to 1883, had the Newnham ideal of an academic community in mind and, since the 1880s, Alexandra had been providing university-level classes for the RUI degrees. The colleges of the Catholic religious orders likewise supported the arguments in favour of women's colleges. Other headmistresses who argued the case for single-sex education and gave evidence to the commission were Margaret Byers of Victoria College, Belfast, Margaret McKillip of Victoria College, Londonderry, and Margaret Deane of Strand House School, Londonderry, which had been sending girls to Cambridge.[69]

However, when the final report of the Robertson Commission was published in 1903, it recommended a co-educational structure for higher education and stated that women should have equal access to the university colleges.[70] The report itself failed to agree on a future structure for Irish higher education and it was to be another five years before a compromise solution was found – the National University of Ireland was established by the 1908 Irish Universities Act. It consisted of the Queen's Colleges in Cork and Galway and University College in Dublin, which were all to become constituent colleges of the

National University, while Queen's College, Belfast was raised to full university status. Women were to be admitted on an equal basis to men at all these colleges.[71]

Meanwhile, in 1904, by then under considerable public pressure, Trinity College Dublin decided to admit women to the university campus to attend lectures and examinations, although not to reside. Alexandra College and the Loreto and Dominican colleges were very disappointed not to achieve university status for their institutions under these new arrangements.[72] Irish women now had full rights to higher education and there was no longer any need to travel to the women's colleges in England. Ironically, just as the close links with the Oxbridge women's colleges were beginning to weaken, a large number of Oxbridge women came to Trinity College Dublin to take Dublin University degrees under the 'ad eundem gradum' privilege which was introduced in 1904. This privilege had long existed between the 'ancient universities' of Oxford, Cambridge and Dublin, whereby they recognised each other's examinations for the award of a degree. More than 700 women who had successfully passed the degree examinations at either Oxford or Cambridge came to Dublin in the three years between 1904, and 1907. The Oxbridge colleges encouraged their students, particularly those pursuing professional careers, to make use of the Trinity privilege, as it seemed that Oxford and Cambridge universities were unlikely to grant degrees to women in the immediate future.[73]

The decision by the Trinity Board to offer Dublin University 'ad eundem' degrees to the Oxbridge women was partly the initiative of an Irish student who had attended Girton College from 1900 to 1903. Leota Kathleen Bennet came from Belfast, the daughter of a bank manager, James Bennet. Educated in a private school in Knock, Leota had been awarded a scholarship at Girton and had read for the History Tripos. When it was announced that Trinity would be admitting women to degrees, Leota's father wrote to the Board requesting that his daughter, who recently had qualified for a Cambridge degree, could be awarded a Dublin University degree under the old 'ad eundem gradum' privilege. After due consideration, the Board decided to agree to this request, assuming that only a small number of other Irish women might apply. However, the Oxbridge women, many of whom were in public life or were teachers or college lecturers, applied for degrees in considerable numbers. The older graduates could be awarded a University of Dublin BA and MA degree on the same day, as Trinity awarded the MA degree to all its graduates a number of years after graduation.

In June 1904, Leota Bennet was conferred at the first University of Dublin commencements ceremony to admit female graduates. There were two other Girton women conferred that day, Helen Bartram (1891) and Sophia Nicholls (1892), as well as three older women from Newnham College: Agnes Amy Bulley (1873), one of the first students, and two Irish women, Edith Anne Stoney (1890) and Edith Badham (1885). In addition, the university, in order to celebrate the occasion, offered honorary degrees to three distinguished Irish women: Sophie Bryant, headmistress of North London Collegiate School; Isabella Mulvany, head of Alexandra College, Dublin; and chairperson of the Irish Association of Women Graduates, and Jane Barlow, the popular authoress.[74]

Leota Bennet was to make full use of her Dublin University degree, becoming a lecturer in teacher education. She became a lecturer in history first at Homerton Training College, Cambridge, then at Southlands College, London (1916–21), and finally at the Home and Colonial Training College (1921–29). Sophia Nicholls, born in Watford in 1872, also had a notable career, this time in the field of geography. She travelled abroad lecturing and became a fellow of the Royal Geographical Society, a member of the Ladies' Alpine Club, and author of a number of geography books. Helen Bartram became headmistress of the County Secondary School, St Pancras, London in 1907 and later head of the County Secondary School, Plumstead, for twenty years from 1913 to 1933. These two county schools were examples of the pioneering work in girls' education being carried out by the local education authorities to provide secondary schooling. Bartram herself had been born in London in 1873 and was educated at North London Collegiate School. She had read mathematics at Girton and undertaken the teacher professional training course at Bedford College, and she was awarded the Cambridge Certificate in Education in 1896. She returned to teach at North London Collegiate School for ten years, before becoming headmistress of a new county secondary school.

The two notable Irish women who were awarded Dublin University degrees that day in June 1904 – Edith Anne Stoney (1890) and Edith Badham (1885) – had both attended Newnham at a time when few Irish women were venturing to Cambridge. Edith Stoney was the daughter of George Johnstone Stoney, a pioneer Irish scientist, who studied the electron and the calculation of the power of electricity.[75] Edith taught physics at the London School of Medicine for Women and later at King's College Household and Domestic Science Department. Along with her sister, Dr Florence Stoney, she served with distinction in the First World War as a pioneer radiologist in France and Serbia and was awarded the Croix de Guerre. In 1904 she wrote an article in the *Newnham College Letter* encouraging her fellow students to apply for the Dublin degrees, and praising Trinity College Dublin for its generosity to Oxbridge women. However, she regretted that Dublin could not offer the residential experience of a women's college like Newnham, writing that:

> ... those of us who have a life-long joy in the memory of the worth and the keenness of work and play in such a residential College as Newnham, with its student friendships, its utter freedom from trouble, and an almost selfish isolation from contact with helplessness, age, or suffering, will acknowledge that Dublin as yet offers nothing comparable.[76]

Edith Badham had gone to Newnham in the 1880s from a rather different background. She was the clever daughter of Revd Leslie Badham, rector of Fenagh, County Carlow, and she returned to Ireland to teach in St Margaret's Hall in Dublin. She became headmistress of the school in 1895, a position she was to hold until her death in 1939. She was to become a leading figure in girls' education in Dublin and gave much support to the new female graduates of Trinity College Dublin and to the Dublin University Women Graduates' Association. Later, she was the first woman to be awarded a degree of LLD from the University of Dublin.[77]

Trinity College Dublin Commencements, December 1904

More Oxbridge graduates appeared at the December commencements in 1904 as news of the Dublin 'ad eundem' privilege became more widely known. Most of the women who came were already in established careers in education, where the formal title of MA and the wearing of a graduate gown were a marked asset. There were some Irish women among them, including Anna Hogben (Girton, 1883), who was now head of a school in Fife, and Rosa Paterson (Newnham, 1891), who was now head of North Manchester High

School.[78] Paterson came from County Down and had attended Victoria College, Belfast and Cheltenham Ladies' College before entering Newnham to read mathematics.[79] The following year there were two more Irish women who had been students at Newnham, namely Elizabeth Lyster (1890), who was now head of her own school, Crofton Grange in Orpington, and Mary Gardner (1892), who was the new head of Blackburn High School. Lyster had been educated at Alexandra College and had already obtained an RUI degree before going to Newnham to read classics.[80]

In 1907 the 'ad eundem' privilege was ended by Trinity, but the example of these successful professional graduate women was important to the new young women students of the university, showing what female graduates could achieve. In addition, the commencements fees of the 'steamboat ladies' were used to finance the opening of Trinity Hall, a residence for Trinity women students opened in 1908.[81]

When Trinity announced that the 'ad eundem' privilege was to end, a large number of Oxbridge women came to take Dublin University degrees. Despite requests from both Girton and Newnham to continue the practice, as there was no sign that either Oxford or Cambridge universities intended to grant degrees to women in the near future, Trinity refused, and there were to be no further under-graduate 'steamboat ladies' coming to commencements. From 1906 Trinity had begun to award degrees to its own female undergraduates. The example of Dublin University undoubtedly had an influence on the Oxbridge stance concerning degrees for women, but Oxford waited until 1919 to grant degrees and Cambridge until 1948.

Irishwomen at Cambridge, 1900–04

In the meantime, the ideals and the prestige of single-sex women's colleges remained high at Oxbridge, despite the fact that their students could not yet be awarded university degrees. Irish students continued to go to Cambridge while awaiting the outcome of the reform of higher education in Ireland. With the opening of more training colleges for female teachers, there were increased opportunities for female graduates to lecture at university level, and two Irish Girton women, in particular, made use of these opportunities. Sara Robinson Beatty Smiley (1900), who came from Limavady, County Derry, was the daughter of a Methodist minister. Born in 1882, she had been educated at Methodist College and at Queen's College, Belfast. She held a scholarship at Girton and read classics. She eventually came to Dublin to take her MA and became a lecturer at Southlands Training College in London.[82] Elizabeth Archer McCallum (1901), daughter of John McCallum, financial secretary to the Commissioners of National Education, was educated at Victoria College, Belfast. She read modern languages and later did her teaching certificate at Bedford College, London. Her decision to go to Cambridge rather than Queen's may have been due to family connections, although her two brothers were Queen's graduates. From 1905 to 1912, McCallum had the distinction of being the first female assistant lecturer at Queen's University Belfast, which was not an easy position for a young woman in an all-male staff. Her cousin Helen Waddell, the Belfast poet and literary scholar, who followed her to Queen's, had much difficulty in obtaining an academic appointment there.[83] In 1907 McCallum took her MA degree from Dublin University and later reverted to school teaching, becoming a member of staff at various schools including Roedean and Thoresby School, Leeds.

Margaret Willis (1904) was another Irish student who was to have a long and distinguished career in education, but in this case she returned to Ireland, to become headmistress of Sligo High School for thirty-six years, from 1911 to 1947. Born in 1881 in Belfast, she was the daughter of Robert Willis, a house and land agent, and was educated at Brookfield Collegiate School, Belfast. She then studied for an RUI degree at Queen's College, Belfast and was awarded an RUI BA in 1902 and an MA in 1904. Thus highly qualified, she went to Girton for three years to read for a further degree in classics. In 1908 she obtained a Cambridge Teachers' Certificate and taught in England before returning to become headmistress at the Sligo High School, then a small provincial school which, under her leadership, became a well-known institution with a strong academic record.[84]

One of the last Irish students to attend Newnham in this period was Annie Cecilia Aimers. Born in Dublin in 1885, she was educated at Alexandra College and read for the Medieval and Modern Languages Tripos at Newnham. She took her Dublin University degree in 1907, one of the last Cambridge students to benefit from this privilege. She became a teacher at Fulham Secondary School for Girls for five years, from 1908 to 1913, and then spent a year in Boston. In 1915 she married Henry Albert Wheeler and returned to Dublin, where she continued her teaching career at Alexandra for six years, from 1924 to 1930, and also at Rathgar Junior School. She later became an actress, known particularly for her radio work.[85]

There were also the three talented Dodd sisters, whose father was Rt Hon. William Huston Dodd, a judge of the High Court in Dublin. The eldest, Helen Letitia Dodd, born in 1878, attended Miss McCutcheon School in Dublin and entered Newnham in 1899 to read for the Medieval and Modern Languages Tripos. Her younger sister, Edith Stuart Dodd, came to Newnham in 1905. Born in 1884, she had been educated at Alexandra College and also read for the Medieval and Modern Languages Tripos. She returned to Dublin to become an actress with the Abbey Theatre, the new Irish national theatre, which had been founded by Lady Gregory and W.B. Yeats. The third sister, Isobel Dodd, who had also been to Alexandra College, came to Newnham at the age of 30 to read for the Economics Tripos – an unusual subject for women. She had an active career in the First World War, serving first as a welfare officer at the Woolwich Arsenal and later as superintendent of the gunpowder factory at Waltham Abbey, where women were beginning to undertake new work. Isobel Dodd later served as secretary of the National Council of Women in Dublin. The differing careers of the three Dodd sisters showed how women were now using their education to find wider opportunities for their talents.

Conclusion

With the growth of opportunities for women to study for university degrees in Ireland, the numbers attending the Cambridge colleges declined. The network of girls' schools in Ireland had provided access to the degrees of the RUI through their university classes at the top of the school. In addition, more women had been attending the Queen's Colleges, particularly in Belfast. In the decade from 1890 to 1900, a total of 216 women graduated in Ireland, the largest number of whom were ninety-five students from Victoria College, Belfast. From its rival, Alexandra College, Dublin, there had been eighty-four graduates and from Victoria High School, Derry, there had been twenty, while seventeen came from St Mary's Dominican College, Eccles Street, and twenty from Loreto College, St Stephen's Green. Queen's College, Belfast had nineteen female graduates; Queen's

College, Cork had one; Queen's College, Galway had two; Magee College in Londonderry, a Presbyterian college founded in 1865, had seventeen.[86]

The success of these institutions in providing university education for women had led to a heated debate among the female graduates themselves as to whether they should seek support for co-education, whereby the women would enter the existing male colleges, or for the separate women's colleges which were so successful at Oxbridge. The experience of those graduates who had been fortunate enough to attend one of the Oxbridge colleges led them to emphasise the value of residential student life, the opportunities for and leadership of female academics and the encouragement of academic excellence. However, there was as yet insufficient demand from the educated young women of Ireland to create a viable argument for a discrete female college, particularly if Catholic and Protestant women had to be catered for separately. Despite the marked achievements of both the Protestant colleges, Alexandra and Victoria, and of the colleges of the Dominican and Loreto orders, it was feared that small women's colleges would be underfunded and ill-equipped in comparison with the existing men's universities. The opening of Trinity College Dublin to women in 1904, despite the restrictions placed on female students, emphasised the value of co-education on a shared campus where women had equal access to academic teaching and a broader university life.[87]

The Irish women's colleges undoubtedly lost out in the new higher education structure. Alexandra College was very disappointed not to become a recognised college of the University of Dublin; the two Catholic women's colleges also failed to gain recognition within the new National University of Ireland and so became residences for women attending University College Dublin.[88] The attendance of Irish women at the Cambridge women's colleges, though small in number, had an important long-term effect on women's higher education in Ireland. Many of the students became leaders of girls' education both in England and Ireland, and figures like Henrietta White at Alexandra College, Edith Badham at St Margaret's Hall and Margaret Cunningham at Trinity Hall brought back to Dublin experience of the high standards of academic achievement and the value of the residential community life offered in a women's college. Others, like Edith Stoney at the London School of Medicine for

Women, Alice Everett and Annie Maunder, the pioneer astronomers, and Igerna Sollas, the geologist, served as role models of
what could be achieved by educated women who had secured a
higher education. For intellectual girls, prior to the development
of higher education in Ireland, the Cambridge colleges offered a
valuable opportunity to create an independent and professional life
in education and to contribute to the quality of teaching in girls'
academic high schools. Leading girls' Protestant schools in Ireland,
particularly Victoria College, Belfast and Alexandra College, Dublin,
had played an important part in encouraging their pupils to aspire
to higher education. The senior grade of the Intermediate examinations was also effective in providing a high standard of attainment for
Irish secondary schools, and it became a recognised certification for
entry to university study.[89]

Though the Robertson Commission recommended the admission
of women to all Irish university colleges, the success of the women's
Oxbridge colleges had undoubtedly already shown that women were
fully capable of advanced academic study. In addition, the prestigious
women's colleges in America such as Vassar (1865), Wellesley (1875) and
Bryn Mawr (1885) were examples of female residential communities
where women staff were the leaders of academic life.[90]

However, it was the RUI women graduates who led the campaign
for the admission of women to universities in Ireland, and not the
women who had been to Cambridge. Most of the Cambridge
graduates did not return to Ireland but sought employment in the
English and Scottish network of schools, many of them succeeding
to headships. The opening of Trinity College Dublin to women in
1904 was influenced by the academic success of these Irish women
and, indeed, the experience of the Cambridge students was used by
the campaigners to argue that the presence of women at university
lectures had not proved too 'disruptive'. It could be argued that
if Trinity had opened its doors to women earlier or had given recognition to women's colleges such as Alexandra College and Victoria
College, the emergence of a viable single-sex college might have
taken place. The long delay in settling the 'Irish University Question'
also delayed the emergence of the Catholic women's colleges.
The irony was that, having successfully won the right to higher
education, Irish women found themselves as a minority in male-
dominated colleges, in which female academics had to struggle to

compete for lectureships and did not gain equal opportunities until the 1960s. Even as late as the 1990s, only 20 per cent of Irish university staff were women. Would they have fared better with single-sex women's colleges or not?[91]

6

A Woman's Reply:
Women and Divorce Law
Reform in Victorian Ireland

DIANE URQUHART

When incompatibility, infidelity, domestic violence or desertion inter-rupted the supposed idyll of Victorian domesticity, the reaction was often to rally to the defence of the institution of marriage. For example, in published transcripts of criminal conversation trials, the legal action whereby a husband, and less frequently a father, could claim monetary damages from a wife or daughter's alleged lover, romanticism loomed large. Charles Phillips, one of the most acclaimed and verbose Irish barristers of the Victorian era, 'raved about embers of decayed lust, beacon-lights to warn innocence, fair flowers trampelled [*sic*] on by the accursed hoofs [*sic*] of ruffian sensuality soiled and blasted for ever [*sic*]'.[1] Fear of a moral decline was another common theme. As the anonymous compiler of the *Annals of fashionable gallantry* noted in 1883, 'During the latter part of the last century conjugal infidelity had become so general that it was hardly considered criminal, espe-cially in the fashionable world.'[2] These publications therefore served to titillate and moralise in equal measure, though unsurprisingly the former effect was never referred to: 'it is only by the public circulation of the transactions of the adulterer and the adulteress that others will be preserved from the like crimes, not only through the fear of shame but the punishment that awaits them in the end.'[3] The sexual double standard also ensured that a woman's fall from grace was regarded very differently to that of an errant husband:

If an unfortunate woman commits a *faux pas*, she is immediately stig-
matised as an adulteress, and her name echoed with approbation by all
guilty villains and villainesses who are only more fortunate than she is
by keeping their sins a secret. If a married man stumbles, he is kindly
dealt with, and it would be treason to call him an adulterer ...[4]

By comparison, a woman's seducer was widely vilified, often portrayed
as a predatory 'villain, who destroys the peace of mind of respectable
families, and who irreparably injures unsuspecting females, [with] ...
the desertion of his unoffending offspring – a cruelty to which inferior
animals are often strangers'.[5]

Marriage in Victorian Ireland

Victoria's reign from 1837 to 1901 coincided with a consistent fall in
the number of marriages in Ireland. Without any compulsory registration of marriage, births or deaths until 1864, census commissioners
estimated the figures and veered towards the conservative. Marriage was
certainly an increasingly popular option in the pre-1840 period, with
41,840 and 46,751 marriages recorded in 1830 and 1835 respectively,
but by 1840 the annual number had fallen to 40,004. The Famine years
intensified this decline, with the number of annual marriages below
30,000 for the first time since 1830, with 25,906 marriages recorded
in 1847. This decrease continued: the number of marriages rarely
exceeded an annual rate of 30,000 in the post-Famine period. Indeed,
the nineteenth-century reports of the registrar only cite 1865 and 1866
as years when marriages exceeded this number and even then it was
marginal: 30,803 marriages were recorded, representing 5.51 per 1,000
of the population, in 1865 and 30,121, representing 5.45 per 1,000 of
the population, in 1865. By 1880 the annual marriage rate was 20,363
(3.29 per 1,000 population) and this number only increased slowly: in
1900 21,330 marriages were recorded (5.05 per 1,000 population).[6]
    Death rather than any legal solution continued to end the majority
of Irish marriages well into the twentieth century, and this was
particularly true for women. Gender breakdowns of marriage figures
recorded in the census from 1841 to 1901 reveal a consistently higher
number of widows than widowers, with the female rate often over
twice that of the male. In 1841, for example, 7.5 per cent of the
female population was widowed, compared to 2.77 per cent of men.

This pattern continued throughout the remainder of Victoria's reign: in 1861 9.56 per cent of women were widowed compared to 3.4 per cent of men and in 1901 9.34 per cent of women compared to 4 per cent of men.[7]

The options for ending a legally valid but unhappy marital union were limited to separation or divorce, but the former offered no recourse for remarriage.[8] Thus, for barrister Francis Plowden, separations provided only limited relief to 'the injured appellant, inasmuch as they fall short of the permission to re-marry'.[9] Indeed, with the exception of death, divorce was the only permanent legal solution. Yet the combination of stigma, cost and the publicity associated with divorce proceedings, especially when heard in parliament as was the case in England and Wales from 1669 to 1857 and in Ireland until 1922, was undoubtedly an effective deterrent.[10] The result was that many boasted of Ireland's purity in the Victorian era. As Judge Baron Dowse in Dublin's Court of Exchequer remarked in 1880, 'he was happy to say, they had little necessity for any Divorce Act' in Ireland.[11] However, divorce was not completely unknown in Victorian Ireland. From the time of Ireland's exclusion from the Divorce and Matrimonial Causes Act of 1857, which moved the proceeding from parliament to court for England and Wales, until 1907, thirty-five Irish divorce acts were passed by Westminster. Numbers also augmented: two Irish divorce acts were passed from 1857 to 1867; three from 1867 to 1877; five from 1877 to 1887; ten from 1887 to 1897 and fifteen from 1897 to 1907.[12]

The aforementioned sexual double standard not only shaped reactions to infidelity but also underpinned the whole premise of divorce. Adultery on the part of the wife provided adequate evidence of a husband's need to end the marital union. A wife, however, had to prove aggravated adultery, sometimes referred to as double offences, on the part of her husband: incestuous adultery; adultery with bigamy; adultery with cruelty to the extent that the latter would have alone entitled her to a separation; rape or unnatural offences, a term veiling sodomy and bestiality.[13] Given this situation, it is perhaps unsurprising that only four women had divorced by 1857 and it was nearly another three decades before the first Irish woman divorced: Louisa Westropp's 1886 case was therefore both pioneering and precedent-making. Her case proved that the widening grounds for divorce established by case law in the divorce court could also be applied in parliament. Subsequent decades saw the number of Irish women seeking a parliamentary divorce rise considerably: five Irishwomen followed Westropp to divorce in parliament by 1900, a figure which represents more female divorce acts than had been passed in the preceding 150 years.[14]

Divorce law reform was never a popular cause in Ireland or elsewhere in the nineteenth and early twentieth centuries. As Lord Donoughmore remarked to the Lords in 1859, 'the House would ... have to wait a long time ... until they received many petitions on the subject'.[15] The resultant lack of debate provided a scapegoat for those in the anti-divorce camp who could assert that Irish citizens neither sought access to the cheaper divorce court in London nor the establishment of an indigenous court. Only a few ventured to counter these claims: barristers like William Brooke and Arthur Samuels and parliamentarians such as the Earl of Wicklow and the aforementioned Lord Donoughmore.[16] Women were excluded from parliament until the Representation of the People Act of 1918 and from the legal profession until the Sex Disqualification Act of 1919. Therefore, the only alternative to bringing a test case to parliament was for women to publicise their own marital woes in an effort to convince legislators and the public more generally of the righteousness of their cause.

Marital Strife

In 1857, the 213-page *Narrative of the case of the Marchioness of Westmeath* was published in London to coincide with the debates on divorce law reform which resulted in the Divorce and Matrimonial Causes Act of the same year.[17] Lawrence Stone has considered the Westmeath case in detail, deeming the author and subject of the *Narrative*, Emily, First Marchioness of Westmeath, 'obstinate, petty, vindictive and fanatical about the injustices done to married women'.[18] The Westmeath case was undoubtedly one of the most protracted and highly publicised marital wrangles of the nineteenth century, but a reading of the marchioness's tract as a feminist lambasting of the realities of the sexual double standard and its bearing on the reform of divorce law in 1857 suggests that an alternative portrait can be drawn.

Lady Emily Cecil, second daughter of the First Marquess of Salisbury, married George Nugent, Lord Devlin and son and heir to the Seventh Earl of Westmeath, in her family's private chapel at Hatfield House in Herefordshire in 1812. The Nugent family seat was Clonyn Castle in County Westmeath and George also had a residence at Blackrock in Dublin, but the estates were in debt and much of this related to his father's divorce from his wife on the grounds of her adultery in 1796. Marriage into the Cecil family was certainly advantageous for the Nugents: the marriage settlement epitomised the difference in the families' financial and social standing – Emily received a £15,000 portion settled on any younger children resulting from the marriage and pin money of £500 per annum. A jointure of £3,000 per annum to be paid from the Nugent estates was also settled and quickly proved to be financially testing. Stone rightly suggests that the disparity between the families' status indicates that this marriage was grounded in mutual affection, but Emily's mother may also have favoured an Irish match. As the daughter of Irish peer, Lord Hillsborough, later the Marquess of Downshire, she regarded herself as Irish.[19] The match, however, was soon troubled, and not just on financial grounds. At the time of their marriage, George already had an illegitimate child by an Irish mistress and, although Emily was alerted to this by her brother, the financial support which he provided to this second family was a constant source of strife. A daughter, Rosa, was born in 1814 but George's mistress also bore another illegitimate child, and his decision to support them financially whilst refusing to hire a wet nurse for his legitimate daughter was an additional cause of conjugal conflict.[20] As Emily wrote in 1815:

> if you do not entirely get rid of the whole of that infamous gang … it is impossible for us to live together without making ourselves miserable … I cannot endure such a want of sincerity towards me. I must have all or nothing. You know my opinion in regard to your conduct before marriage; and God knows that that discovery was sufficiently afflicting to me, without having further to discover all that has since passed in that respect; but let us make an end to it; you have been the dupe of two wretches, the very dregs of mankind, and you and I have very nearly become the victims of our enemies, high and low, and this ought to be a lesson for us never to disguise anything.[21]

Violence also featured in this marriage, but a reconciliation was brokered in 1815 by a neighbour and friend, Henry Wood, who sided with Emily in this and future legal challenges.[22] Under the terms of this agreement, financial support for George's mistress was limited, but this only held for a few years. Emily was denied money from 1816 to 1817, writing: 'You took possession of my pin-money, would turn me out of doors if I dared to insist upon having it. You beat me … and all this time, when I was undergoing all the privations I mentioned for want of money, you could find money for a prostitute.' Irish residency was also difficult for her; she hankered to return to the social niceties of aristocratic life in England and accused her husband of removing her from 'all my friends, [and] as good as shut me up in an obscure corner of the world'.[23]

By 1817 a deed was drawn up in which Emily essentially took control. Determining the grounds for any future separation from her spouse, this is one of several occasions where her sense of social superiority came to the fore. She agreed to continue cohabitation if George gave up his mistress and if a separate annual sum for Emily's use was raised from the Irish estates. She also specified that their daughter should reside with her and be under her sole control if they separated but be maintained and her education provided for by her father. George did not hold his side of the bargain: in the summer of 1817 Emily left him, taking Rosa to London.

George freely admitted that he was at fault and considered suicide in the wake of her departure:

I brought everything on myself by a bad outset: I changed you … under your contempt and disregard I cannot live … All I dare hope for, and what I only value in the world, is your regard, that the person … whose soul has given over to the loving friend of wretched, wretched me, should not fling me from her mind … I have not now an object on earth, and I only wish and pray to die when I have secured my impoverished Estate, in the way you wished it, to little Rosa, your flesh and blood … *Thank God, Emily, I did not commit a last act of brutality and madness by taking her away from you, who suffered twice what most mothers suffer, all through mind as well as body* … I have gone through my repentance, but bitterly, bitterly as I have suffered … pardon for much *brutality* I have shown you …[24]

He also apologised for threatening to disinherit his daughter in favour of his half-brother and throw his wife out, but commented less on his attempts to hide his encumbered estates whilst continuing to support a second family financially.

Further mediation from Wood and pressure from Emily's parents, exerted as they were anxious to avoid the public scandal that a formal separation or divorce would cause, led to another deed being executed in 1818. Custody rights and Emily's separation allowance were again to the fore. She was to be allowed to live where and with whom she wanted and her spouse agreed not to bring a case for the restitution of conjugal rights in the ecclesiastical courts, although he did not abide by this.[25] Her portion of £15,000 was reversed to Rosa, along with much of the Nugent estate if they failed to produce a surviving male heir. This was certainly 'a very unusual arrangement, since it potentially separated the descent of the property from that of the title, and cut out of the inheritance George's half-brother by his father's second marriage'. The deed also 'differed from all the deeds of the same nature' that the Attorney General had seen, as Lord Westmeath was not protected from his wife's debts[26] and, as William Sheldon, a Bencher of Gray's Inn and George's legal adviser, later averred, 'he would rather cut off his right hand than put it to such a deed'.

Emily was essentially pre-empting a reform in matrimonial law, but she was arguably too confident of being able to dictate the terms of her marriage. Her boast, 'I now have George completely in my power',[27] deterred him from signing the document until mid-1818, and even then he claimed it was 'got from him by surprise, and by ... misrepresentation'. In addition, his wife was pregnant for a second time: 'her life and that of the child she was carrying, would be in danger if he would not execute the deed'.[28] The Westmeaths subsequently lived together for twelve months and a son was born in November 1818. According to Emily's counsel and her own later claim, they did not cohabit as husband and wife from 1820. Instead, this was a pretence so 'that the separation might not be known to the world'.[29] Whatever the motivation, this condonation barred Emily from pursuing a divorce and affected her chance of having the deed enacted.[30] As the Attorney General noted, 'it did away with the effects of the deed ... if fresh cohabitation took place that was the end of the suit'. He also branded the deed 'viscous', allowing separation at the will of one of the parties.[31] Others agreed, fearing such deeds were in effect 'private divorces' and arguing that if the Westmeath deeds were allowed to stand then 'it would tend to encourage private divorces of the same kind'.[32] Despite claims to the contrary from Emily's side, both the Court of Exchequer test case in 1819 and the House of Lords

in 1831 decreed the separation deeds worthless as a result of the pair's
reconciliation. The publicity which enveloped the Westmeaths was
not, therefore, generated solely out of curiosity; these were test cases to
ascertain the validity of private deeds of separation.

Lord Westmeath, however, was at least partially responsible for
giving the case wider resonance. He claimed that to accede to his
wife's demands would not only injure him emotionally and financially, but, as his legal adviser averred, also endanger 'public policy and
morality' by making separation attainable by mutual consent rather
than by a ruling of the ecclesiastical courts.[33] The *Freeman's Journal*
certainly took the bait. Under the headline 'Separation in High Life',
it covered Lord Westmeath's attempted injunction in the Irish Court
of Chancery to prevent £1,300 being raised on Irish lands as an
annuity for his wife's maintenance, over the course of three days in
March 1820. In contrast, the Attorney General wanted this case, based
on 'differences of a private nature', to be heard privately, advising 'that
it was the interest of the parties to bury their disputes in oblivion'.
He also over-optimistically predicted that 'the public could be in no
way interested'. His attempts in this direction, however, were resisted
by the Countess of Westmeath and thus she must be held partially
accountable for publicising the case. As a result, the Attorney General
decided to skirt around the details of the case, querying whether the
Westmeaths' private correspondence needed to be read in public.
He only agreed to this on the basis of both parties' consent.[34]
The countess's defence argued that Lord Westmeath's charges against
her were 'of such an infamous and horrible nature … that no Judge …
would order the woman so abused to again cohabit with a man who
was infamous enough to make them'. They depicted Westmeath as a
'slanderer and abuser' who subjected his wife to 'the greatest cruelty,
violence, and ill-usage … [he] struck, [and] beat [her] … she could
not, consistent with her personal safety, suffer herself to be under his
protection again'.[35]

The deed of 1817 was ruled null and void except in relation to the
children's maintenance and education but the 1818 deed remained
'in place for a year to enable the parties to try the effect of it at
law'.[36] The marquess, however, successfully appealed to the London
Consistory Court in 1821 for restitution of conjugal rights which,
although at odds with the 1818 deed, forced his wife to return to
the marital home.[37] Emily then sought a separation on the basis of

thirty-three charges of cruelty in 1821, and twenty-five charges
of adultery with five women were levied a year later, although
these were later dropped due to questionable witnesses' evidence.[38]
The Westmeaths' litany of legal challenges and counter suits had
thus begun; five attempts at reconciliation would fail and litigation
continued for another twenty-five years. Between 1819 and 1834 suits
were brought in equity and the common law courts concerning the
1817 and 1818 deeds and from 1821 to 1834 in the ecclesiastical courts.
There were also numerous appeals to the higher courts and thus 'at
least seventeen law suits before eleven or more different tribunals,
embracing all three legal systems' were brought.[39]

Custody and alimony, which had featured prominently in the earlier
deeds, were the main bones of contention. Emily tried to secure custody
in chancery but, despite the earlier deeds granting her custody, this was
unsuccessful. She was also unsupported in this endeavour by her mother
who, when asked by Lord Chancellor Eldon to care for the children
whilst he considered the case, refused, stating she 'would not be a party in
keeping children from their father'.[40] The children were taken to Clonyn
and, although George agreed to give Rosa back if he could approve
her governess, this arrangement collapsed, as he became convinced
his wife was turning their daughter against him. In March 1820, after
the death of their infant son in the previous year, he refused to return
Rosa and denied his wife access. Emily immediately brought a writ of
habeas corpus to the Court of Common Pleas but Lord Chief Justice
Dallas ruled 'The father, in point of law, was entitled to the custody of
the child', underscoring the far reach of paternal property rights at this
juncture.[41] Emily smuggled letters to her daughter but only saw her
once, by stealth, in 1825. Later in the same year she tried to see her again
but the child rejected her, and in an 1832 letter she alleged that her
daughter was 'brought up to detest her'.[42] This was the bitterest part of
the case for Emily and the earlier deeds indicated the importance of her
maintaining custody. Those deeds also show that she refused to meekly
accept the law as it stood regarding custody rights.

Both the ecclesiastical courts and chancery ordered George to pay
maintenance, yet Emily only received her £500 per annum pin money
and even that was unpaid from 1823 to 1826. Emily consequently ran
up debts and arranged for one of her creditors to sue George in King's
Bench for repayment and won. George refused to pay; he spent May
to August 1822 in debtor's prison.

One of the most significant suits was in the ecclesiastical Court of Arches in 1827 when Emily was granted a legal separation on the basis of her spouse's cruelty, alimony and partial costs.[43] Correctly branded as her 'greatest victory', Stone also suggests it was won 'on very narrow, and indeed dubious, grounds'.[44] There were, however, witnesses to the abuse she suffered. The evidence of her personal maid suggested that Emily was 'literally without money for months' and 'as poor as any poor person'. Verbal abuse was also documented; she was called 'a damned bitch, and ... he would kick her to hell' and Westmeath was described as 'more like a madman than a reasonable being'.[45] Physical abuse was also witnessed from 1814, including beatings, to the extent that 'she carried the marks for a long time' and required medical treatment.[46] This violence continued whilst she was heavily pregnant. Judge Nicholl commented on this forcefully in the 1827 trial: 'it requires no definition of cruelty to pronounce this to be an act of aggravated cruelty ... No provocation could justify it or palliate it.'[47] He also interpreted her effort to conceal the physical abuse, pretending 'that she had fallen', as indicative of a desire 'to bear her wrongs secretly and in silence'.[48] Lord Westmeath also admitted to slapping her and placing a pillow over her face; apprehension of more violence affected her health by 1815.[49]

The question of provocation on the part of a wife was of central importance in cases of both separation and divorce. In the Court of Arches, Emily's father, Lord Salisbury, noted she would display a 'violence of temper', but only under provocation, and Nicholl confirmed that her correspondence showed no evidence of the 'fretful, peevish, ... perverse and malicious disposition, that took delight in initiating and provoking a husband without cause', as alleged. Rather she possessed sufficient 'spirit to remonstrate upon maltreatment, and when it was aggravated by repetition she had firmness and resolution to insist upon redress and protection'.[50]

Granting Emily a separation on the grounds of cruelty and discounting her renewed cohabitation with her spouse from 1818–19 as 'continued condonation', Nicholl's judgement ran counter to the English and Irish chancery, the House of Lords and the London Consistory Court rulings. It was also significant in helping to widen the legal definition of marital cruelty beyond violence which endangered life to include abuse of a non-physical nature that could threaten health.[51] The question of how the upper classes might tolerate such abuse was also central to Nicholl's decision, and he was not alone in holding such a view. To the Marchioness of Westmeath, writing in 1857, 'superior rank not only is no protection, but an aggravation of the offence, and brings "his order" into disrepute'.[52] And just two years later, Dublin solicitor James Byrne noted, 'A blow of the fist, which in the humbler classes is followed by reprisals and instantly forgotten, will ... in a higher station, prove ever fatal to conjugal repose.'[53]

Courting Publicity

Although there was blame on both sides in making their affairs public, Lord Westmeath's 1828 pamphlet, *A Sketch of Lord Westmeath's Case*, broke new ground.[54] Written after eleven years of marital litigation, the *Sketch* aimed to vindicate its author. Westmeath's inspiration came from the more voluminous case evidence presented by his wife, running to fifty-three pages compared to his ten, presented to the House of Lords, and more particularly an overruling on appeal which allowed much of her evidence to be heard even though it had not been previously presented to a court below that of the Lords. To Westmeath this 'disingenuous compilation' had the 'scandalous purpose' of humiliating him and providing 'gossip to the tea-table of every lady who had a lord a member of that House ... and to make the Table of the House of Lords the medium of introducing it'.[55]

Westmeath maintained that his wife's printed evidence amounted to a pamphlet and as such he was justified in answering in print. This line of argument would have been more convincing had he simply disseminated his printed case notes submitted to the Lords. By comparison, his forty-seven-page 'answer' was compiled without having to comply with the stricture of the Lords' rules for evidence and was four times longer than that evidence.

Westmeath denied keeping a mistress and two illegitimate children, but the claim that he was violent towards his wife rankled with him most. This was common to many faced with such a charge, as it was at odds with the notion of the husband as a wife's protector which grew in import as the century drew on and notions of companionate marriage grew. Westmeath admitted to giving his wife 'a *fillip* on the cheek' but professed he was an 'innocent man' who only wanted to provide a 'decent existence for those children both born before my marriage'. He thus portrayed himself as a victim of 'vermin in action … venom … malice [and] pure fabrication'.[56] He also used Emily's concealment of marital violence as evidence of fabrication. The idea that his wife, like so many victims of domestic violence, may have been ashamed of being treated in such a way or feared reprisals if she spoke out was not entertained.[57]

The fact that he had not maintained his wife rested more easily with Westmeath; he did not consider her worthy of financial support.[58] Claiming to be the victim of an attempt 'to degrade me from my caste', he presented a 'conspiracy … by agents, some powerful, some ingenious, and others the very dregs of society in Ireland'.[59] The fact that evidence of his cruelty towards his wife had been levied by a gardener, housekeeper and two ladies' maids, all rewarded for their testimony by Lady Westmeath, which was not unusual in such cases, was also used to undermine their credibility.[60]

Westmeath also suggested that his wife's behaviour ran counter to the strictures of not only her class but also her gender, having 'entirely forgotten her rank and sex'.[61] Her stance was, however, more likely to have derived both from the social superiority she felt over her spouse and from indignation. He also attempted to dehumanise her, citing her departure from Ireland before their infant son was buried in 1819, but not noting that the child was dead by the time she travelled to Clonyn with her brother and trustee, Lord Cranborne. Her refusal to reconcile with her mother, even following her father's death, was also given as evidence of her cold nature:'unmoved by this second death bed scene, as she was at the former one, even at those of a child and a father!'[62] The suggestion that she did not desire to live 'with any husband' or bear any more children because 'it spoilt the shape'[63] provided Westmeath with further evidence of her abhorring natural maternal and wifely functions. He labelled her behaviour as 'supercilious selfishness … dictated by caprice [and] … audacious … a married woman ruining her husband's *de gaité de coeur* as a passport to a footing of *respectable independence*'.[64]

A sense of his emasculation also emerges as his wife exerted more control: 'She wished to leave me, and I wished her not. She had laid her plan, and employed every species of insulting and unworthy device to induce me to leave my house and abandon my children – *to make it appear as my act*. My own servants were taught to insult me.'[65] Westmeath also admitted that he had written letters 'in terms of humiliation and self abasement' which his wife had appended in 'wanton publication' to her Lords' evidence, but claimed that they were part of a wider correspondence which he had destroyed and 'if they proved there had been differences, they evidenced also the strongest affection for the person for whose confidence they were written'.[66] Nor did this deter Westmeath from the same act: he included an 1817 letter from his wife in the *Sketch* in which she stated:

> Frankly speaking, I will never live with a man as his wife, who thought any other woman and her children, had the slightest claim upon him. You and I are not intended for each other, and cannot understand each other.[67]

A Female Divorce Law Reformer

Emily made no public response to her husband's 1828 *Sketch*. Although she considered publishing in the mid-1840s, she kept her counsel until 1857 when she sought to help reform the 'barbarous' laws relating both to divorce and married women's property. Though 'in shattered health', she determined that it was her duty to publicise her case, which although 'not unexampled … has few parallels in the sad history of the wrongs of women'.[68] She also deigned to follow the 'recipe'[69] of English reformer Caroline Norton, who proclaimed herself 'tormented and restless … suffering from every one' of the law's 'defects of protection'. Westmeath and Norton were acquainted, co-operating over Thomas Talfourd's unsuccessful 1837 bill to give custody of young children to mothers; the Custody of Children Act enshrining this was passed in 1839.

In 1855 Norton published *A Letter to the Queen* on the divorce bill then before parliament. She appealed for married women to have a separate legal identity from that of their spouses, rather than the 'fiction' which absorbed her into the legal identity of a husband, even if he had deserted her. Norton also suggested that women were naturally inferior to men and therefore needed the law's protection, and that the only function of condonation as a bar to a wife's divorce proceeding was to prove female forbearance: 'she endured as long as endurance was possible'. Like the Marchioness of Westmeath, Norton was writing from personal experience: both were barred from divorcing their husbands as they were considered to have condoned their misdemeanours, and Norton cited her own and the Westmeath case as examples of legal bias against women.[70] Although Norton claimed that her husband's advertisement stating that he would not cover her debts was the first of its kind, Lady Westmeath disputed this: 'It was advertised by Lord Westmeath in the newspapers very early in the business.' She also averred that her own well-publicised treatment had 'served as a sort of programme for the course pursued' against Caroline Norton.[71]

Lady Westmeath dedicated her tract to the later Lord Chancellors Lyndhurst and Brougham, who 'disinterestedly making to obtain justice for a suffering class, may be further stimulated, by this Narrative, published with a view to the exposure of such cruelties, legal and personal … may, I trust, lead to mitigation of persecution against others, by providing a remedy for all'; she hoped they would help to reform the law surrounding married women, custody rights and marital breakdown.[72] The opening quote from *Othello*, 'Nothing extenuate, Nor set down aught in malice', further highlights the political purpose of her writing. However, her husband's new mistress's use of her former title, Lady Devlin, in the 1840s and his unsuccessful attempt to present her at the viceregal court in Dublin, coupled with the birth of three further illegitimate children, whom Westmeath maintained were legitimate, can only have strengthened her zeal.[73] Westmeath also referred to this woman as Lady Westmeath, and Emily was referred to in *The Times* as the Marchioness Dowager of Westmeath, as if she was widowed.[74]

The *Narrative* highlighted that marital difficulties would not necessarily lead a woman's family to rally to her cause. In Lady Westmeath's case, none of her family supported her wish for a private separation and her mother urged her to be 'more conciliatory', criticising her for speaking 'as if she hated' her spouse in court.[75] Her mother also gave evidence in support of Lord Westmeath. Although the judgement did not attach too much significance to this, as a consequence of Lady Westmeath seeking to hide much 'of her unhappiness' from her family, her mother's fear of 'the affair becoming town talk' led to what the judge depicted as 'almost a morbid sensibility upon the subject, and … she became … highly offended at her daughter'.[76] Emily also blamed her brother for failing to secure her alimony and averred that advice given by her mother and some of her trustees amounted to a 'system of intimidation'. In consequence, she had to take more of an interest in her legal concerns.[77] Her father also felt constrained by familial

pressure in what help he could proffer her; he did not cut her out of
his will and showed rare sympathy towards her predicament:

> they wish me to cut off poor Emily with a shilling, and for the sake of
> a quiet life it has been impossible for me to show how much I feel for
> her ... my wish was to pay her separate maintenance, and pitch him to
> the ____ ... she has always been a good an affectionate child to me.[78]

Emily clearly resented her reputation as 'vindictive ... bearing
malice ... radical ... I radical, forsooth ... because I will not justify by
my countenance, and apparent approbation, the ill-usage and aban-
donment of a wife and sister'. She also reproduced correspondence in
the *Narrative*, some by her own hand, earlier presented as evidence in
the 1827 Court of Arches case which granted her a separation. Here
her aim, like that of Norton, was to underscore the error of enforcing
condonation too rigidly in matrimonial disputes. She concluded that
it was her 'evil destiny to experience, and suffer for years, and to the
end of my days, to prove, the fallacy and the dangers' of tolerating
men's infidelity and castigating women for condoning their actions:
'An English wife is absolutely nothing but a slave, and a most helpless
and oppressed one; ... who ever heard before of condonation *to* its
master, *by* the slave, except now in the relations between man and
wife.' Even if she could divorce her spouse, she believed her reputation
would be destroyed, she would be disgraced and 'turned adrift' and the
divorce, by allowing her husband to remarry, would cast her 'children
to the mercy of a step-mother'.[79]

Unsurprisingly, given the earlier emphasis on maintaining custody
in the separation, the trial of being separated from her surviving child
featured in the *Narrative*. She was unsuccessful in an 1821 case to
recover custody of her daughter in the Court of Common Pleas and
her health subsequently declined: she claimed that she was confined
to bed, suffering from erysipelas, a skin infection causing blisters
and lesions. She also declared herself financially bereft. She received
no alimony from 1819 to 1827, when she separated, and only
£315 per annum thereafter: 'I am supposed to have lived upon air ...
I was too poor to procure a bit of meat for myself. ... [and] lived for
three months ... upon bread, cheese and barley-water ... I paid my
servants' wages and board wages from my [£250] allowance as Lady of
the Bedchamber' (to the Duchess of Clarence, from 1818).[80]

Emily certainly faced monetary difficulties, yet she still financed the publication of the *Narrative*. She was also not wholly lacking in supporters. The Duke of Wellington, a second cousin of Emily's mother and brother-in-law of her sister, mediated on her behalf, with the result that Westmeath challenged him to a duel and considered bringing a criminal conversation case against him in 1818.[81] In 1826 she was given a rent-free apartment at St James's Palace and, when the Duchess of Clarence became queen in 1830, she appointed Emily an extra lady of the bedchamber at £275 per annum in a largely sinecurial post.[82] The heir to the throne, the Duke of Clarence, also successfully approached Wellington to secure a controversial Irish pension of £385 per annum for her, as an 'injured lady … [and] excellent and ill-used friend' who was 'much in want' in 1829.[83]

Believing that they were on the cusp of divorce law reform, Emily overstated the popularity of this cause, referring to it as 'a measure so loudly called for by the voice of the public, for the liberation of her sex from cruelty and oppression'.[84] If she could procure no improvement in her own situation, she hoped that her *Narrative* would assist those bringing the reform forward. Of course, one can question the sincerity of the avowed motive, but by the time of writing, she was a woman not only with little left to lose but also little to gain. She was clearly disillusioned, writing: 'I am not sanguine as to any *real* justice being intended' by proposed reforms regarding married women, 'but at any rate, I hope the married women separated from their husbands may have the means secured to them of defending themselves and punishing libels, and may be freed from further interference in business matters'. Nor was she impressed by the proposed divorce reform, which would fail to equalise access to divorce amongst the classes or the grounds for divorce between the sexes. It was, consequently, a breach of 'any principle of justice'.[85] She concluded her 'sad scene' thus: 'if I shall have assisted the spirit of inquiry now aroused, as to the dreadful state of the laws, respecting married women in this country in any degree, my object is answered'.[86]

Conclusion

To Stone the *Narrative* was vengeful, a 'diatribe against all her enemies, real and imagined, including her husband, her daughter, the members of her own family, and the judges who had sided with her husband. She once more dredged up all the sordid details of her version of the story of her sufferings during her marriage some forty years back, and the injustices she had met with in the lengthy litigation.'[87] Lord Westmeath's reaction was similar and was made public during the committee stage of debates on the Divorce and Matrimonial Causes Bill in 1857. Moving a controversial amendment proposing that any husband or wife separated for twenty years or more could remarry if they had legally separated 'without Condonation or subsequent Cohabitation', this provided the first opportunity to vent his feelings on his wife's *Narrative*. This was all the more striking as Westmeath, although a regular attender of the Lords, seldom contributed to its proceedings, especially at length:[88]

> it was in the power of any woman who was separated from her husband … to make her husband's life totally unendurable. This Bill was no sooner bruited … than a book was put forth of 200 pages, which was surreptitiously published – that is to say no printer's name was affixed to it – but bearing the name of the lady who did him the honour to call herself by his … name. It was sent to all the clubs; and within the last fortnight a severe, and, as he thought, libellous attack had been made upon him in consequence in the columns of a most respectable newspaper, naming him and connecting him with the Bill that was now before their Lordships … From first to last this book contained the grossest perversion of matters where they related to fact, and some of the most unjustifiable untruths that could be put together to blast and ruin the reputation of the man who was the subject of it. … Their Lordships might think it a very serious thing for a man sitting in his place to be the subject of accusations which if true, would make him unfit to move in any respectable circle of society, and disqualified to take his seat in their Lordships' House.

The Lords were indeed unimpressed, if not unmoved, by Westmeath's protest. He was called to order by chair of the committee, Lord Redesdale, who 'could well believe their Lordships would, on a proper occasion, afford the noble Marquis an opportunity, if he wished it, of putting his own conduct in the light in which he desired it to be held', but stated that it was not permitted to introduce into committee deliberations 'matters in which he was personally concerned'.

Westmeath tried to continue, only to be censured by the Earl of Derby: 'the subject he [Westmeath] was introducing was exceedingly

painful to the House, and one which he … thought must be not less
painful to the feelings of his noble Friend himself'. Still Westmeath
persevered: 'The Marchioness of Westmeath had named him at full
length. He was told that the law was open, but he defied any lawyer
to show how he had any means of redress.'[89] A solution, was, however,
quickly found, as in June of the same year he published a ninety-seven-
page *Reply*, but he did not remind either his readers or the Lords that
he himself had fired the opening shot, in publicly airing his marital
woes some three decades earlier.

Rather, Westmeath felt vindicated by his wife's publication in airing
his version 'of the history of our lives', publishing their correspondence and that of other family members, much of it extant, from 1819
onwards. He denied the authority of the 'valueless' deeds of 1817
and 1818, extracted 'as the price of cohabitation', and the charges of
cruelty levelled against him: 'There was not a scintilla of evidence of
cruelty on my part'.[90] He refuted, 'with good reason' according to
Stone, the countess's proclaimed reforming zeal in publicising their
affairs, asking whether her pamphlet 'was not rather prompted by the
pent-up malice of years':

> gladly seizing hold of the first opportunity to discharge itself, in defiance
> of all rules and feelings of shame and delicacy, and in disregard of the
> anxious desire of relations and friends, that events now almost forgotten,
> except by those immediately connected with them, should not again be
> obtruded on public notice … It is so unusual and so alien to the habits
> of this country for a woman to interfere, or come forward actively in
> the promotion if any measure of legislation, that one is inclined closely
> to scrutinize the motives of any lady whom does so distinguish herself.[91]

Westmeath alleged that his wife's real object was to be rid of him, citing
her reproach when she left him in 1819: she had 'a right to live where
I think proper, unmolested by you'.[92] Although by 1846 he referred
to himself as her '*quasi* husband', he still felt he was 'the injured and
oppressed party' and criticised Wellington's mediation as countering
one of 'the rights which belong to me as a husband'.[93]

George claimed the legal proceedings cost him £30,000; Emily
maintained that she had spent £12,000 in litigation up to 1831. But,
as Stone acknowledges, the costs were not only financial. Emily's health
was permanently damaged and by the 1840s she was 'chronically sick'.[94]

She could never totally be free of her marriage and felt that her family failed her. The separation and estrangement from her surviving child was, however, undoubtedly the bitterest blow. Emily died in 1858; George remarried a month later, aged 73. He experienced further marital difficulties four years later, seeking a divorce on the grounds of his new wife's adultery. Claiming English residency, this case passed in the divorce court. In 1864 he married again and this marriage lasted until his death in 1871. Neither of these unions produced a child so his legitimate heir was Rosa, his daughter with Emily.

The Westmeath's marital saga underscores the emotional and financial costs of not being able to divorce in the Victorian era. Emily was not adulterous and thus, even if her spouse had been willing to be rid of her, divorce was not an option. Condonation barred her from taking that route. The Westmeaths' penchant for self-publicity allowed this case to provide a lens through which the reality of the law of divorce and the need for reform becomes clear. Some of their multiple legal challenges, particularly the 1827 Court of Arches separation granted to Emily on the basis of her husband's cruelty, were significant: Nicholl's emphasis on verbal as well as physical cruelty which, although not endangering Emily's life, made her live in fear and affected her health was indicative of the legal shift which was occurring and may have further hastened this change.[95] The much-disputed separation deeds also attracted considerable attention: 'they made legal history'.[96] The inability of the ecclesiastical courts to overrule decrees passed by parliament was also brought to the fore by this case and this, alongside with a desire to force Westmeath to pay his wife's legal costs and alimony, prompted Lord Brougham to introduce the Ecclesiastical Court Powers Bill in 1832. Therefore, the parallels which Lady Westmeath drew between her role in affecting change and Norton's part in reforming custody law in 1839 were perhaps not so ill-founded.

Stone assigns Emily equal responsibility for the breakdown of her marriage and, whilst he concurs that the law failed to offer protection to married women in her position, he depicts her as frigid and in possession of 'an iron will ... extremely obstinate, and never forgot or forgave an injury ... self-righteousness ... almost unendurable'.[97] She was certainly determined to exert control over her situation, a desire which was reinforced when the failings of the law towards married women became all too apparent. This attracted some criticism in the mid-1820s; during the 1825 suit George's counsel noted that his client had:

> a foolish notion that he should be master in his own house. The Marchioness, however, had her own notion of the interesting subject. She is a genuine descendent of the great Cecil, the minister and favourite of the glorious virgin queen [Elizabeth I], and inherited from her progenitor a natural propensity to petticoat government.[98]

Stone's claims that there is some evidence that she was 'a bully' who 'gave George plenty of provocation for his outbursts of uncontrolled fury' are harder to substantiate. Those relating to her 'sluggish libido', 'prudery', 'immaculate chastity' and what she was willing to tolerate sexually within the marriage are even harder to support. Beating her when she refused sexual demands is likely to have further alienated her from her spouse. This marriage was broken and trust was lost. As Emily wrote: 'You lived three years with me in constant deceit ... Last year you began again, and broke your most solemn word of honour, and now you dare to tell me that you never thought of anyone but me. Remember your oath to me, and then ask yourself if you are to be trusted.'[99] Stone also branded Emily's desire for fidelity within marriage as equating to 'unusual sexual possessiveness'. He also suggests that she 'was by far the stronger character of the two', but she was not stronger in terms of her legal position or her physical capacity to defend herself from abuse. Surely there can be little surprise that she 'no longer showed much affection' to her spouse after 1814, 'whereas George remained deeply attached to her until 1820'.[100] George, however, does not provoke much sympathy – his alleged deep attachment involved bouts of violence as well as fathering and financing another illegitimate child when he knew this would endanger his marriage. In many instances it is hard to countenance one side of the Westmeath story above the other. Emily Westmeath, however, stands as a forgotten voice in the cause of divorce law reform. Wealth and aristocratic standing provided no protection from a law which treated all married women as the property of their spouses and punished those who endured cruelty and infidelity. It was perhaps unsurprising that she ultimately saw herself, like all married women, as a pauper.[101]

7

A Terrible Beauty?
Women, Modernity and Irish
Nationalism before the Easter Rising

MARGARET WARD

During the course of the long reign of Queen Victoria, a woman exco-
riated by Maud Gonne in her famous polemic as 'The Famine Queen',
Ireland experienced uprisings, a land war, famine, constant political
unrest and a significant nationalist cultural revival. Women were actors
in all of this, but often doing much more, as they struggled to develop
an agency informed by their own hopes for a more egalitarian future.
The Victorian era also witnessed significant improvements in women's
access to education and to public life and the opening up of some professions; all these reforms impacted on the ability of women to contribute
to political movements and, indeed, to shape aspects of the political
agenda, most notably with regard to land reform and the cultural revival.
When Victoria died in 1901 a new organisation for Irish nationalist
women was almost one year old and the campaign for women's right to
vote would soon erupt into a most unfeminine militancy in both Britain
and Ireland. The Easter Rising of 1916 would witness the Proclamation
of the Republic promising equal citizenship to Irish women, uniting
republican and feminist aspirations. This chapter explores the stages in
the journey made by Irish nationalist women as they sought entry to the
different movements working for an independent Ireland.

In the eighteenth century and much of the nineteenth century, nationalist endeavour had been conceived purely in terms of armed rebellion,
and few women considered joining male comrades on the battlefield,

although there is some evidence of women accompanying their men and joining them in battle. Betsy Gray, fighting in Ballynahinch in 1798 with her fiancée and brother, is a notable figure, while an estimated 200 women participated in the Battle of Vinegar Hill.[1] Intellectually, feminist political aspirations had also reached Ireland. Mary Ann McCracken, sister of Henry Joy, one of the leaders of the United Irishmen, was an admirer of Mary Wollstonecraft and had hoped that the revolutionaries would have shown 'an example of candour, generosity and justice superior to any that have gone before them'.[2] There was also a Society of United Irishwomen, which renamed young members in terms that revealed strong sympathies with the French Revolution – for example, 'Miss Liberty' and 'Miss Equality'.[3] There is, however, no evidence that the United Irishmen, any more than the French revolutionaries of 1789 had done, would have included women in their definition of citizen, despite the iconography of the liberty-capped woman of that revolutionary era.

In the next generation of revolutionaries, significant numbers of women wrote for the *Nation*, the journal of the Young Ireland movement of the 1840s. Jan Cannavan calculates that at least fifteen women made contributions (including 'Speranza', who was Jane Francesca Elgee, later to be the mother of Oscar Wilde).[4] Some made it clear that they believed women had a right to equality that included the right to take up arms. For example, 'Eva' (Mary Ann Kelly) wrote in her article 'To the Women of Ireland' that 'it is not unfeminine to take sword or gun, if sword or gun are required', finishing with a pledge that women would in future have greater power to determine events: 'Circumstances have hitherto moulded us. We shall now mould circumstances.'[5]

Unlike 1798, there was no large-scale insurrection in 1848, but women in Ballingarry, County Tipperary were part of a group of villagers consisting of many women and children, as well as men, who were routed by an armed police force, with at least one woman arrested in consequence.[6] In Cannavan's assessment, 'although women were certainly not treated as equals by the men of Young Ireland, the most politically radical male leaders began to take women's participation much more seriously over time'.[7] Again, however, it is highly unlikely that the Irish, if they had succeeded, would have gone further than full adult *male* suffrage, an aim shared by the European revolutionaries of 1848. Despite the defeat of revolutionary hopes, Speranza remained active, writing in her journal in 1850 that married women had the right to employment and economic independence.[8]

The impact of the Famine on Irish life has been attested to by many historians – mass starvation, death, disease and enforced emigration. The society that emerged from this catastrophe, deeply scarred and determined to avoid any recurrence, was changed irrevocably. Land consolidation rather than sub-division was the priority, leading to restricted opportunities for marriage, an increased emphasis on women's domestic role and greater gender differentiation regarding public space. The Irish Church was reformed and the authority of Rome was imposed. Catholic women were active but, as educators and healers of the sick, only in their capacity as nuns. The women who campaigned for girls' secondary and higher education and for the opening up of the professions to women – Anne Jellicoe, Anna Haslam, Isabella Tod and Margaret Byers – came from the Protestant side of the community.[9] The mid-nineteenth century in Ireland was not an easy place for politically aware women with nationalist inclinations.

Revolutionary nationalists in the 1860s were part of a conspiratorial, terrorist organisation that was entirely male – the Irish Republican Brotherhood, organisers of the Fenian Rebellion of 1867. Toby Joyce, in his discussion of 'Ireland's trained and marshalled manhood', emphasises the fact that 'there is a marked absence of female participation in Fenian activities in Ireland … Women are conspicuously missing from Fenian gatherings … Women were not allocated any auxiliary role such as intelligence-gathering, message-carrying, medical or commissary duties – roles traditionally filled by women in revolutionary movements.' He concludes that Fenianism 'appears to have been totally in the male sphere'.[10] It is significant that thirty years later, the best-known poem of Irish poet and political and cultural activist Alice Milligan, 'When I was a little girl', features 'one little rebel' who wanted to join the Fenians but '[w]ished she had been a boy' and '[a]ble to walk for miles/With a gun on her shoulder'.[11] Even Milligan, an activist in many spheres, and a woman who challenged many conventions, was unable to envisage a role for women in that revolutionary brotherhood.

'Respectability' was also important for the Fenians, who courted 'respectable young men' as members and frowned upon the tradition of rioting at election times – which was carried out by the poorest section of labourers, and in which women, with their shawls tightly wrapped round them, occasionally joined.[12] Joyce comments: 'This aim to develop discipline among their supporters, and help make respectable the country, bolstered a general Victorian trend.'[13] It also served to disadvantage women.

The defeat of Fenian hopes turned the political tide towards constitutionalism. The Irish Parliamentary Party, sitting in Westminster, developed formidable skills in the art of obstruction, particularly after the election of Charles Stewart Parnell. Parnell's sister Anna, living in London in order to pursue her art studies, followed the parliamentary sittings of 1877 while forcibly enclosed in the 'mean, dimly lit den' of the Ladies' Gallery, which was the only space in the Commons open to women.[14] She entitled her articles *Notes from the Ladies' Cage* and emphasised that she was confined to a gallery reserved for the 'unenfranchised portion of the population'.[15] Commentators assessing the acuity and power of Anna Parnell's writing agree on her 'analytical turn of mind ... fine appreciation of the intricacies of parliamentary rules and procedure, and ... well-developed sense of the comic and of the absurd'.[16] Roy Foster, while admiring her abilities, concludes more ambiguously with the comment that her articles 'as well as giving a good history of the obstructionist debates, show clearly where Anna's own sympathies lie; and they portray somebody with a keen interest in political agitation, and the tendency to élitism which so often characterises a dedicated revolutionary'.[17]

Comparisons have been made between Anna and her older sister Fanny.[18] Fanny, the 'poetess' of the Land League, exemplified the 'traditional philanthropic middle class woman', while Anna, 'prepared to challenge authority, break down barriers between male and female spheres of public life, and pave the way for radical change', represents the modernity of the 'new woman' of the late nineteenth century.[19] While Fanny Parnell was an organiser and fundraiser for the Land League and established branches of the Ladies' Land League in America for that purpose, C.L. Innes persuasively concludes that in her best-known poem 'Hold the Harvest' (famously described as 'the Marseillaise of the Irish peasantry' by Michael Davitt) Fanny sees herself as 'the muse who inspires men to fight; she cannot envision herself as part of that action – perhaps because her class as well as her gender mark her difference from the "pallid serfs" she appeals to'.[20] In the same year she published another poem, 'Ireland, Mother', where she made her sense of helplessness explicit: 'I am a woman, I can do naught for thee, Ireland, mother!'[21]

The Land League had been formed in 1879 in response to a renewed threat of widespread famine. It was a 'New Departure'[22] in Irish political life, bringing together as it did the Parliamentarian

and Fenian traditions in a fight for Irish tenant rights. While this was
hardly promising in terms of female involvement, the existence of the
Parnell women (including also Delia, the American mother of Charles
Stewart) and the urgent need for funds provided the initial impetus
for limited involvement. The situation was to change dramatically in
1880, as the land war gathered momentum and the British government retaliated with the introduction of a Coercion Act, intended to
decimate the Land League through the mass jailing of its leaders and
members. Michael Davitt, recognising the abilities of Anna Parnell,
persuaded the leadership to what they termed 'a most dangerous
experiment', allowing him to invite Anna Parnell to set up a Ladies'
Land League in Ireland.[23]

While the men did not believe that the women would be capable
of providing more than a 'semblance' of organisation,[24] concentrating
their activities on providing relief to evicted tenants, they reckoned
without the formidable talents of Anna Parnell, who was the right
woman in the right place and at the right time in Irish history to
demonstrate the hitherto untapped capabilities of women. And she
was not alone. The Ladies' Land League, formed on 31 January 1881,
succeeded in gathering together a group of women who worked in the
field as organisers, encouraging tenants to defy their landlords – even
when that meant eviction – and who succeeded in developing what
had been a fairly ramshackle organisation into a highly disciplined and
well-organised administration. Anna Parnell was described as one of
four honorary secretaries, but she was the effective leader from the
outset. The other organisers came from the small Irish middle class,
while members of the country branches came mainly from farming
backgrounds. By the start of 1882 there were 500 branches, a huge
increase in evictions and almost 1,000 prisoners to be looked after.[25]
When issues of the Land League paper *United Ireland* were seized by
the government, the women arranged for secret printing and used their
voluminous skirts to smuggle out copies for distribution. They were
denounced by Archbishop McCabe of Dublin, who accused them of
'degrading the women of Ireland', in parading themselves 'before the
public gaze'.[26] Thirteen women went to jail, but were convicted under
laws relating to prostitution; unlike the men, they were not regarded
by the State as political prisoners. Hanna Reynolds, one of the most
active of the organisers, advised Ladies' Land League members to 'put
out of their heads all hopes of being arrested as (political) suspects'.

They would come under the Act of Edward III, as interpreted by the Chief Justice.[27] The nationalist paper, the *Nation*, was horrified to see that a magistrate had 'designated the members of the Ladies' Land League by the worst name that can be applied to a woman'.[28] The gendered double standard regarding women's involvement in public life was starkly revealed.

Throughout all of this, Anna Parnell continued to give leadership, determined to make what she believed had been no more than a 'sham' resistance into a movement capable of achieving the abolition of the landlord system in Ireland. She addressed meetings throughout the country, travelled to England to muster funds and support, enlisted the help of Helen Taylor (stepdaughter of J.S. Mill and a well-known radical and suffragist) as chair of the Political Prisoners' Aid Society, maintained long working hours in the Land League office and wrote countless letters to the press describing the brutalities perpetrated by government and landlords and appealing for aid. One letter to her sister Fanny asked for more women in America to come forward as organisers, stressing the need for 'intelligence, physical strength, reliability, and a certain amount of education and refinement, besides not being too young'.[29] This was then translated by Fanny as a call for 'any ladies willing to undertake this most sacred service, this work of relief and consolation amongst their suffering countrymen'.[30] The emphasis upon 'women' by Anna and 'ladies' by Fanny is highly revealing regarding the differences they perceived women could make as political activists. As Beverly Schneller demonstrates in her analysis of the newspaper coverage of the time, 'the Anna Parnell of the newspapers was a strong, clear headed and well-spoken woman who was courageous and contemptuous of the impositions of the government on the Irish tenantry'.[31] At the height of the Land War she accosted the Lord Lieutenant while his entourage was driving past her in Dublin, seizing the bridle of his horse and berating him for forbidding the erection of Land League huts which was being organised by the women to shelter 500 people evicted in Limerick.[32] Henry George, an American radical who accompanied Anna Parnell on several tours of the country while he was working as a special correspondent for the *Irish World*, believed that the women had done 'a great deal better than the men would have done'.[33] Nevertheless, the men, on their release from jail, had the power to dictate terms to the women: they would only remain in existence if they confined their activities to charitable relief and left the political arena to the male leadership. Charles Stewart Parnell and Prime Minister Gladstone had, in secret negotiations, revived the prospect of Home Rule for Ireland in an agreement dubbed the 'Kilmainham Treaty'. Voteless women were now irrelevant and utterly dispensable. The Ladies' Land League executive (without Anna Parnell, who was absent from public life for several weeks due to shock following the sudden death of Fanny on 20 July 1882) refused to accept these terms. Anna later denounced this prospect of becoming 'perpetual petticoat screens behind which [the men] could shelter not from the government but from the people'.[34] Henry George informed Helen Taylor that 'the women really feel bitter towards the Parliamentary men. They have been treated badly and their obligations have not been kept, and on several occasions the men got a very frank piece of their minds'.[35]

The outcome of eighteen months of dedicated and dangerous campaigning, which had ensured that the Land League had not crumbled in the face of government coercion but had instead brought the British government to the negotiating table, was now to be forgotten as quickly as possible. Many years later, when lecturing on the Ladies' Land League to Inghinidhe na hÉireann (Daughters of Erin), Anna Parnell was asked by Frank Sheehy Skeffington her opinion of the Kilmainham Treaty. The pain of that time was not forgotten, as she looked 'coldly' at Skeffington, replying, 'Oh, I just think my brother found himself in an uncomfortable position, and he did what men usually do – got out of it in the easiest possible way for himself, regardless of the consequences to others.'[36]

Women were no longer welcome in the political arena. A new campaigning organisation was formed, composed of male politicians. The Irish National League was described as 'an open organisation in which the ladies will not take part'.[37] The traditional gender order was restored and women's ability to participate in the political sphere was greatly restricted in the coming decades as the focus shifted back to Westminster. Senia Paseta, reflecting on the impact this period had for future relations between women and 'old nationalism', describes the Ladies' Land League being held up 'as a sort of totem by subsequent generations of nationalist Irish women'. The consequence of 'young female nationalists and older parliamentarians [learning] very different lessons from the experiences of the Ladies' Land League' helps to explain '"some of the antipathy" towards women's future involvement in nationalist politics'.[38]

Anna Parnell moved to England, where she continued to follow Irish politics while becoming increasingly embittered at the rewriting of history, as the male memoirs of those times began to appear. Several members of the Ladies' Land League moved to America. Only one member would maintain a prominent role in Irish life – the young Jennie O'Toole, who would make a reappearance as the redoubtable Jennie Wyse-Power of Inghinidhe na hÉireann, Sinn Féin and Cumann na mBan.

However, while women were excluded from mainstream nationalist and cultural organisations, they could attract an audience for their poems and plays. In the last years of the nineteenth century a number of women took this route. Catherine Morris has detailed how Alice Milligan, a northern Protestant, began to publish ballads in the national Parnellite papers from the time of Parnell's death in 1891, her verses appearing in the same space as those of Katherine Tynan, a former member of the Ladies' Land League and now an eminent writer, whom Milligan regarded as Ireland's 'Parnellite poetess'.[39] Morris adds that while Milligan had expressed awe for Yeats, Davitt and Parnell, after October 1891 'she stopped looking for great men to admire and emulate and started to envisage herself as an agent of political and cultural change'.[40] By 1892 the term 'Irish Literary Revival' was frequently used. The Gaelic League was founded in 1893 – with women welcome as members - and its 'democratic membership policy and branch system'[41] provided an invaluable outlet for those, like Milligan, looking for ways in which to participate in the cultural nationalist renaissance. Her story in this decade is, as Morris has summarised:

> the story of the forgotten women's movement in 1890s Ireland; it is the story of the Irish language and the Gaelic League's northern origins; it is the story of a radical Irish publishing venture that was achieved by two northern women whose religious and political background make such a union visionary.[42]

Alice Milligan and Anna Johnston (who wrote poetry under the name Ethne Carbery) were the first founding female members of the language class in the Belfast branch of the Gaelic League. Two years later, in 1894, Milligan set up the Irish Women's Association in Belfast, Portadown and Moneyreagh – all strongly unionist areas – as a cultural platform for women, enabling them, in her words, to 'do something towards breaking down the forces of intolerance, ignorance and bigotry, which kept Ulster apart from the rest of the country'.[43] Women who joined, like the feminist Quaker Mary Hobson (mother of republican activist Bulmer Hobson, who would, with Constance Markievicz, co-found the Fianna, the revolutionary nationalist boy scout movement), argued strongly against moves to insist that women should be attending to 'domestic duties' alone: 'it is the duty of every woman to take an interest in the country in which she lived, to know something of its history, past and present'.[44] By meeting in the same Unitarian church used one hundred years ago by the United Irishmen, the Irish Women's Association consciously sought to connect themselves with Belfast's revolutionary history; it was a 'subversive feminist alliance',[45] yet still not sufficient for Milligan who, in 1895, helped to set up a more public organisation – the Henry Joy McCracken Literary Society – which was open to men and women and which unambiguously declared its revolutionary nationalist allegiance. For a short time the society had its own journal, the *Northern Patriot*, which was jointly edited by Milligan and Johnston – the only female members. However, internal political feuding led to the sacking of the two editors and their formation of another, and more significant journal – the *Shan Van Vocht* (a phonetic spelling of the Irish for 'poor old woman'), which ran from 1896 to 1899 and which was much less regional than the former paper. Contributors included historians, language activists, poets, writers and political commentators, including James Connolly, invited by Milligan to explain his ideas on the programme of political and social reform put forward by his Socialist Republican party. It was his first time in print. Women were given prominence, as the journal revived the writings of Mary Ann McCracken and Speranza, as well as publishing essays on notable nationalist heroines, such as Anne Devlin. As Catherine Morris concludes, the poor old woman 'was speaking out and speaking back against colonial occupation, cultural Anglicization, and the factional unionist and nationalist misogyny Irish women encountered'.[46]

The *Shan Van Vocht* was a vital ingredient in the mix of organisations and events that helped women to the realisation that female political agency was essential if Ireland was ever to regain political and cultural autonomy. Nationalist politics was bedevilled with factionalism and Milligan was forthright in her insistence that women had an important role to play. Two years before the centenary celebrations commemorating the United Irish rising, she was appointed organising secretary for the centenary celebrations in Ulster, a role that included a lecture series around the North.[47] In her capacity as editor, she took the opportunity to argue for women's right to become involved, while also castigating the activities of the men:

> Is it too much to ask … that the women of Ireland who are not called on to have any opinion whatever as to who has the right to speak for Ireland in the British Parliament, should form that Union which a historic occasion demands? The existing committee, in Dublin … is threatened on every side from within and without, with forces which may mar and shatter it.[48]

In October 1897 she established the Irish Women's Centenary Union in Belfast. Members included some with direct family links to past rebellions, such as the great-granddaughter of Wolfe Tone, the 1798 leader, and the sister of John Mitchel, the revolutionary journalist who was part of the Young Ireland movement. In reviving the spirit of the United Irishmen, the Women's Union tracked down forgotten graves and ensured that all known graves were suitably decorated. Pilgrimages were organised to gravesites, orations delivered and nationalist souvenirs commissioned. All this work was intended to ensure that thousands would participate in the procession in Dublin to celebrate the laying of the foundation stone for the Wolfe Tone statue. Alice Milligan and her colleagues took part in the procession, carrying a rock from Cave Hill – site of the famous oath taken by Wolfe Tone and the other United Irishmen – which was intended to be part of the foundation stone. Most significantly, it had been Milligan's proposal to the '98 Executive to have a statue of Wolfe Tone erected that had stimulated so much of the activity of this period. Despite that, she was excluded from the speakers chosen by the Executive for the unveiling of the foundation stone in August 1898.[49] Once again, Irish women found themselves on the margins.

One woman was, however, to be found on the platform during these ceremonies – and that was Maud Gonne, the daughter of a British Army officer who had abandoned her privileged background in order to work for the Irish cause and who had, in a very short time, inspired undying love from W.B. Yeats while also gaining the respect of some of the most venerable figures in the revolutionary movement. We know from Gonne's memoirs that when a new generation of women tried to join the national movement, the legacy of the Ladies' Land League lived on in the memories of the men who had worked with women in the land movement. Gonne was refused membership of the Celtic Literary Society and, when she visited the offices of the National League, hoping to be welcomed as a new recruit, she was told 'There are no ladies in the National League'. When she pursued the issue she was informed by Tim Harrington, an Irish Party MP and chief organiser of the League, that in his view women in the past 'did too good work, and some of us found they could not be controlled'.[50]

For some time Gonne worked as a 'freelance' on behalf of evicted tenants in Donegal and for the release of political prisoners. In newspaper articles she often described the poverty-stricken state of the women she met in the far west of the country. She also made appeals to Irish women to become politically active:

> Oh, my sisters, women of Ireland, it is time we shake off our indifference and realise that we have duties of solidarity to each other. It is a slight to all of us that it would be possible to treat any Irish women as these helpless, complaining, starving peasant women of Erris are being treated.[51]

One of the campaigns she joined was the Amnesty Association, working for the release of Irish treason–felony prisoners involved in an ill-fated dynamiting campaign in the 1880s. It was while visiting Belfast during this time that Gonne came into contact with Alice Milligan and Anna Johnston, who thereafter covered her activities in their paper. Their admiration was mutual; Gonne later wrote of their 'daring little paper'[52] and began to plan for a paper in Dublin. When she met Arthur Griffith, she gave him financial support to set up the *United Irishman*. In April 1899 the *Shan Van Vocht* ceased production, handing its subscription list over to the new Dublin paper, which would soon give full coverage to a new women's organisation. The *United Irishman* also featured poems and plays written by women, contained weekly columns by female writers and demonstrated the growing strength of women's writing and activism.[53] It was a time of significant change for women. With the 1878 Intermediate Education Act and the 1879 Royal University Act, both Protestant and Catholic women from the middle class were able to access higher education, while legislation regarding the rights of married women to property was leading to increased economic autonomy. By the turn of the century, women were also able to sit on Poor Law Boards and in local government, strengthening their claims for full political participation. The 'sustained interest' in women in the pages of the *United Irishman* suggests, according to Karen Steele, 'that the values of emerging feminism – promoting women as equal, if sometimes separate, participants in political activism – were beginning to influence the broader nationalist movement'.[54]

The visit of Queen Victoria to Ireland in April 1900 was the catalyst that brought together a number of women; initially this was to organise a 'Patriotic Children's Treat' to reward those who boycotted the royal visitor but, following their triumph in treating an estimated 30,000 children, these women decided that they wanted to form a permanent organisation. Gonne said that she had found women who, like her, 'resented being excluded as women from national organisations'.[55] Ann Matthews refutes any suggestion that Gonne was the founder of Inghinidhe na hÉireann, arguing that she was simply one member of a founding committee whose ranks included women with strong nationalist connections, such as Jennie Wyse Power.[56] This is ungenerous, omitting the inspiration that Gonne provided and to which so many have attested. As Margaret Quinn, a founder member and treasurer of Inghinidhe, recalled: 'Her teaching and inspiration acted like magic on all of us. We would have done anything she wanted us to do.'[57] Gonne's significance is that she was able to convince young, politically untested women that they had the capabilities to develop an organisation that would rival their male counterpart. Matthews sees the significance of Inghinidhe as 'the first all-female cultural nationalist organisation', but this omits the heroic efforts of Alice Milligan in the North to stimulate women's cultural and political activity. However, Milligan's efforts remained confined to the area around Belfast while Inghinidhe na hÉireann sought to be the female equivalent of a group like the Celtic Literary Society. Efforts were made to set up branches not only in Ireland but also within the Irish community in England, so that women could engage in the work of 'national education' of children. Gonne wrote passionately of 'an old prophecy which says that Ireland will be saved by the women, and if Irish women will only realise the importance of this work of national education for children, I think this prophecy may come true'.[58]

Alice Milligan and Anna Johnston joined Inghinidhe na hÉireann, and Milligan's experience in staging *tableaux vivants* proved invaluable. She had developed these over a number of years in Belfast, illuminating key events and characters in Irish history and mythology, and the Inghinidhe would stage both *tableaux* and short plays written by Milligan. The imagery was powerful. Morris argues that the silence of the *tableau* was deeply political, developing a communal sense in a country 'where many women were denied votes, jobs and education, and Irish national history and language were outlawed'.[59] They were projections of 'a future beyond the moment of their production'.[60] The *tableau* 'Erin Fettered, Erin Free' was staged in 1901, depicting Ireland as a woman eventually liberated. Maud Gonne described, as the last curtain rose, the children witnessing 'Erin as a beautiful girl with broken chains falling from her and a drawn sword in her hand appeared.'[61] These were ambitious events – Molly Hyland, a founder member, remembered Gaelic *tableaux* organised by Milligan and Ethna Carbery for Easter 1901 containing a cast of more than 100, including such notable figures as Douglas Hyde.[62]

While Inghinidhe was primarily a cultural group, teaching young children of the Dublin slums Gaelic literature and language and taking part in dramatic events (most famously in *Cathleen ni Houlihan*, the collaboration between Lady Gregory and Yeats which starred Maud Gonne as the old woman with the walk of a queen who inspires men to leave everything behind and fight for Ireland), they also engaged in political activity, particularly against recruitment into the British Army. This involved the distribution of anti-recruiting leaflets to soldiers and the women who consorted with them, necessitating walking on the west side of O'Connell Street, which 'ordinary civilians' did not walk upon. Many rows ensued. Helena Molony, one of the women who took part in this work, put it into context: 'women and girls were still living in a semi-sheltered Victorianism. The hurly-burly of politics, particularly the kind which led to the risk of being involved in street rows, was certainly not thought "becoming".'[63] Molony had the distinction of a jail sentence as a consequence of throwing stones at a royal portrait during protests around the royal visit of 1911. She did not serve her sentence as her fine was paid anonymously by Anna Parnell, who did not want Molony distracted from the task of editing her account of the Ladies' Land League.[64]

For three years Inghinidhe also produced a paper, *Bean na hÉireann*, which leaves us an invaluable legacy of what nationalist women at the start of the twentieth century were thinking. At that time there was no paper expressing an unambiguously separatist view (Griffth's *Sinn Féin*, which followed the ending of *United Irishman*, was not republican, advocating as it did the repeal of the Act of Union and the restoration of the Irish parliament of 1782; the women's views were much more radical) and there was no women's paper in existence. Helena Molony, its editor, stated that they 'wanted it to be a women's paper, advocating militancy, separatism and feminism'.[65] She described it as 'an odd kind of woman's paper. It was a mixture of guns and chiffon … a funny hotch-potch of blood and thunder, high thinking and home-made bread.'[66] They were modern young women, scathing about Victorian attitudes towards women and very willing to regard themselves as part of the 'physical force' tradition within Irish nationalism. One member, Molly Hyland, wrote that all the paper's issues:

> preached militant action, devoting articles to the Art of Street Fighting and Physical Force … The concluding paragraph of the articles asked every Irish man and woman to learn to discipline and be disciplined, to learn to shoot, to learn to march, to learn to scout, to learn to give up all for Ireland.[67]

Inghinidhe women, with their relish for direct action and their advocacy of rebellion as the only way of achieving independence, were very much in the mould of Anna Parnell, although they were circumspect in how they phrased their determination to fight for female autonomy. They were not antagonistic to men, wanting only the opportunity to be accepted as political equals. An editorial in *Bean na hÉireann* declared:

> Our desire to have a voice in directing the affairs of Ireland is not based on the failure of men to do so properly, but is the inherent right of women as loyal citizens and intelligent human souls … It is not our intention to countenance any sex antagonism between Irish women and Irish men … We Irishwomen must learn to throw off our present diffidence and assume our natural position in Irish life and men will have to frankly admit that it is only by working hand in hand that we can hope to make Ireland free.[68]

Bean na hÉireann ceased production in 1911, by which time there existed *Irish Freedom*, the paper of the IRB, and also, by 1912, the suffrage paper *Irish Citizen*. Much of the focus, for politically active women, now centred upon the fight for the vote, but that was not a campaign endorsed by Inghinidhe women, who took the view that 'an agitation for votes for women in Ireland inferred claiming British citizenship, and consequently was inconsistent with Irish Republicanism and Separatism'.[69] The two groups were, however, united on the principle of 'Equal Rights' and 'worked in the most friendly way with the Irish "Suffragettes"'.[70] Helena Molony, who acted as a mentor to Constance Markievicz during the latter's early membership of Inghinidhe na hÉireann, confessed she had 'some difficulty in bringing [Markievicz] to this point of view'.[71] The situation was less clear-cut than that, as Jennie Wyse Power, a founder member of Inghinidhe, was also a member of the non-militant Irish Women's Suffrage and Local Government Association, at least until she resigned on political grounds, together with Hanna Sheehy Skeffington, in 1906.[72] What we can say is that the Inghinidhe were undoubtedly feminist in their outlook, and when they found the suffrage movement under attack, particularly from the Ancient Order of Hibernians and the Irish Parliamentary Party, members were quick to give support. Constance Markievicz was a frequent speaker at suffrage meetings.

With the demise of their paper, Inghinidhe lost much of its impetus. Maud Gonne was in exile in Paris and made rare trips back to Ireland, following her bitter divorce from John MacBride. Their split had had repercussions in the nationalist movement, leading to Inghinidhe na hÉireann leaving Cumann na nGaedheal.[73] People took sides, and this might have been when Wyse Power left the group, but Inghinidhe as a whole remained loyal to Gonne. However, the women who were visible on the streets were, increasingly, the women of the Irish Women's Franchise League, particularly after militancy began in 1912. Irish society was witnessing the spectacle of women confronting the male political establishment, claiming the right to citizenship, and enduring imprisonment and hunger strike for their beliefs.

As the Home Rule crisis escalated, with the threat of secession from the North given weight by the formation of the Ulster Volunteer Force in 1912, and retaliation by the formation of the Irish Volunteers in November 1913, unionist and nationalist women seized the opportunity to become involved. Women from the Ulster Unionist Women's Council began training as despatch riders and nurses, in support of the Ulster Volunteer Force. In both north and south, the emphasis was on Irish manhood. Women who attended the inaugural meeting of the Irish National Volunteers had to sit, not in the main body of the hall, but on a 'special platform reserved for the ladies'.[74] There are echoes of Anna Parnell's 'Ladies' Cage' in this, although no one pointed this out. It was announced that 'there will also be work for the women to do',[75] but the implication was that women would raise funds and learn first aid, without needing a specific organisation for this, and without being admitted to membership of the Volunteer movement. This retrograde situation was not accepted by all. It took five months from that meeting before a women's counterpart organisation came into existence, and there is strong evidence that disagreement concerning the future role of women within the nationalist movement was responsible for the delay.

Mary Colum, writing in September 1914, admitted 'At first a great many difficulties came in the way; when at last, after many meetings, the organisation was formed, it had no name but it had very definite aims.'[76] Aine O'Rahilly believed that 'Mrs Wyse Power with a group of women had already held small preliminary meetings to discuss the proposal made by Eoin MacNeill at the Rotunda in November 1913 that the women should form an organisation to co-operate with the Volunteers, as the Ulster Women's Council was organised to help the Ulster Volunteers.'[77] Agnes O'Farrelly stated that 'Four months ago we came together twice to discuss the formation of a Society and it did not seem to us then opportune. We feared to hamper whilst we were anxious to help. Events have occurred since which convince us that the necessity for action on our part is urgent and a duty we owe ourselves and our country.'[78] Nancy Wyse Power, daughter of Jennie, believed that 'The promoters may have had in mind an auxiliary association of women acting under the general instructions of the Volunteer Executive but the organisation immediately declared itself to be an independent organisation of women determined to make its own decisions.'[79] All this testimony confirms the suspicion that setting up a women's organisation to support the Volunteer movement was not a straightforward affair. Nor was that 'declaration of independence' as immediate as Nancy Wyse Power's comments would imply.

Mirroring the Volunteers' choice of Eoin MacNeill, professor of early and medieval history at University College Dublin, for their front man, his colleague Agnes O'Farrelly, a lecturer in Irish in University College Dublin, was chosen to preside over the inaugural meeting of Cumann na mBan at Wynn's Hotel on 2 April 1914. Both were connected with the Gaelic League, and both choices were deliberately aimed at reassuring the general public that those associated with republicanism were not driving the new initiatives. MacNeill would end up jeopardising the Rising through his countermanding orders when he realised what was planned. O'Farrelly did not remain with Cumann na mBan for more than a few months. While it is unclear when she left, it is very clear that her conservative views found little resonance with those who joined the organisation. Her presidential speech imagined political participation as an extension of women's domestic responsibilities, appalling some of the younger members:

> We shall do ourselves the honour of helping to arm and equip our National Volunteers. Each rifle we put in their hands will represent to us a bolt fastened behind the door of some Irish home to keep out the hostile stranger. Each cartridge will be a watchdog to fight for the sanctity of the hearth.[80]

Aine O'Rahilly, whose sister-in-law was a member of the first committee, attended that first meeting. In her account, O'Farrelly 'suggested we should start making puttees for the Volunteers. I was disgusted. I came away and told my sister-in-law I was not going there again.'[81] Louise Gavan Duffy, appointed along with Mary Colum as first secretary for the organisation, commented in relation to O'Farrelly 'we did not think her ideas advanced enough'.[82] The difference in opinion on what role was suitable for women was therefore reflected *within* the women's organisation as well as the wider nationalist movement during these early days.

It is interesting to compare different testimonies from those who later gave witness statements to the Bureau of Military History. For example, Aine Ceannt, wife of a leading figure in the Volunteer movement, made no reference to Cumann na mBan's early days, other than to remark that she was present at the inaugural meeting of the Volunteers and joined the central branch of Cumann na mBan.[83] Many gave factual accounts of the first-aid classes, signal drilling and firearm practise they undertook, without revealing any huge enthusiasm. Nancy Wyse Power joined, not at first but in 1915, 'somewhat doubtfully. At that time their programme did not appeal to me, but from the trend of events I felt a desire to belong to some organised body.'[84] No one was as negative as Aine O'Rahilly, who seemed to come to an early realisation that dealing with future injury and death was a large part of the reason for the existence of the new organisation: 'My recollection of those classes is one of profound melancholy. The gloom of them was much worse than the tragedy of the Rising. I did not like the lectures about how to stop bleeding.'[85]

Mary Colum, as one of the first organisers, was anxious to establish the role of women as allies of the Volunteers, not subordinates. She emphasised that from the start the organisation:

> ... had in its body some of the gallant fighters of the Land League days – women who worked hard in that great conquering movement and saw in the new Volunteer force the salvation of Ireland. They were an inspiration to the younger women, who brought their youth and strong faith and eagerness into the new fight.[86]

While she referred to women being able to 'practice the use of the rifle', the actual role to be played by women and their ability to have a voice in the movement remained an unresolved issue. The constitution of Cumann na mBan declared its aims:

> To advance the cause of Irish liberty
> To organise Irishwomen in furtherance of the object
> To assist in arming and equipping a body of Irishmen for the defence of Ireland
> To form a fund for these purposes to be called 'The Defence of Ireland Fund'[87]

What was left unstated was the future status of Irish women – would 'Irish liberty' include women's right to citizenship in a new Ireland? Suffragist militant Hanna Sheehy Skeffington had posed some awkward questions at an early meeting of Cumann na mBan regarding 'a scheme by which rifles would be procured for the men for some undefined and undefinable end'.[88] She also asked: 'was the Irishwomen's Council to have a place in the [Volunteer] Executive? What were the liberties that Irishwomen possessed? What did Irishwomen think of the Cat and Mouse Act and the Government that foisted this alien measure on their countrywomen?'[89] A heated exchange of correspondence ensued, with Sheehy Skeffington dismissing the new organisation as 'an "animated collecting box" for men, [which] cannot have the sympathy of any self-respecting woman'.[90]

The following year, Francis Sheehy Skeffington wrote an 'Open Letter' to his old friend Thomas MacDonagh (reputed to have had the idea for Cumann na mBan), director of training for the Volunteers, asking why women had been left out of the latter: 'Consider carefully why; and when you have found out and clearly expressed the reason why women cannot be asked to enrol in this movement, you will be close to the reactionary element in the movement itself.'[91] Five months later, Constance Markievicz was to be found delivering a lecture to the Irish Women's Franchise League, admitting that 'These Ladies' Auxiliaries demoralise women, set them up in separate camps, and deprive them of all initiative and independence.'[92] Unwittingly, some of the experiences of the women would support this assessment. For example, Eilis ni Riain, a very diligent member, described a 'big parade' of Volunteers in Dublin on St Patrick's Day 1916, before going on to say, 'Cumann na mBan did not take part in this parade. They were collecting money among the crowd.' They also collected money outside Masses each Sunday; her position in Upper Gardiner Street coincided with the battalion area of the Volunteers linked to her branch of Cumann na mBan.[93]

Inghinidhe na hÉireann became a branch of Cumann na mBan, but not all members of Inghinidhe joined the new organisation. The new Inghinidhe branch was far from being a continuation of the old organisation.[94] Significant numbers of women – and the most prominent of its members – found the egalitarianism of Connolly's Irish Citizen Army (ICA) more congenial. Ann Matthews quotes from the papers of Sighle Humphreys, providing evidence that the Inghinidhe women decided to remain independent but closely associated with the ICA. In effect, as some did join Cumann na mBan, the organisation effectively split, although there is no evidence of a vote being taken.[95] In Helena Molony's experience, Connolly, as a 'staunch feminist', was 'more than anxious to welcome women into the ranks on equal terms with men, and to promote them to such rank and position as they were suited for'.[96] She had been taught to shoot by Constance Markievicz in 1910, shortly after the Fianna began, and it was the Fianna, she believed, who taught the Volunteers to shoot.[97] Markievicz's expertise was recognised by Connolly, who appointed her as one of several female officers in the ICA. During the Rising, Margaret Skinnider, a member of the ICA, argued successfully for her right to take an active military role. She was shot and badly wounded while commanding five men on a mission 'to destroy houses in Harcourt Street to cut off enemy approaches'.[98] Those who formed the Free State were less enlightened than the insurgents of 1916. When Skinnider applied for a pension in 1925 she was informed by the legal adviser to the army pensions office that he had 'no doubt' her application 'cannot be considered under the act' because the law was 'applicable to soldiers as generally understood in the masculine sense', and the definition of 'wound' in the Act 'only contemplates the masculine gender'.[99]

Jennie Wyse Power became president of Cumann na mBan after the organisation split in November 1914 over support for John Redmond and the British war effort. New members joined the organisation, which was growing increasingly militant, and branches were formed throughout the country. In Dublin, six first-aid squads were organised and allocated to the Dublin battalion of the Volunteers.[100]

Was the role of women in the nationalist movement any more than that of auxiliary to men? A conservative conception of women's role was not confined to men. Irish society was predominantly rural and inherently conservative. Although the Gaelic League was hailed for its acceptance of women as members, this was not necessarily a radical stance. As Hanna Sheehy Skeffington pointed out, because the emphasis was on teaching the language to the young, 'it is primarily in her capacity as mother' that the movement recognised women's importance.[101] Mary Butler, in a pamphlet for the Gaelic League, *Women and the Home Language*, contrasted the 'gentle low-voiced women' inculcating nationalism at the hearth with the 'shrieking viragoes or aggressive amazons' who seek a public platform.[102] Given the conservative nature of much nationalist discourse, did women believe they had the power to win equality of status within the movement?

Constance Markievicz, in her 1915 lecture to the Irish Women's Franchise League referred to earlier, gave a lecture that was a very clear summary of the past history of activist women, the problems they faced and how women themselves had the power to challenge orthodoxy and to make changes. Once again, the Ladies' Land League proved to be a crucial reference point as it had:

> ... promised better things. When the men leaders were all imprisoned it ran the movement and started to do the militant things that the men only threatened and talked of, but when the men came out they proceeded to discard the women – as usual – and disbanded the Ladies' Land League.

She regretted that women now attached to national movements were there 'chiefly to collect funds for the men to spend', and she urged women not to trust to their feminine charm and capacity for getting on the soft side of men, but to 'take up your responsibilities and be prepared to go your own way ... depending for safety on your own courage, your own truth and your own common sense, and not on the problematic chivalry of the men you may meet on the way'. With a characteristic flourish, she declared that women should 'dress suitably in short skirts and strong boots, leave their jewels and gold wands in the bank and buy a revolver'.[103] Some women did take the advice to 'buy a revolver' – but only ICA members like Margaret Skinnider. Markievicz had, says Steele, a 'commitment to establishing a precedent for the armed New Woman'.[104] In this she can be contrasted with Maud Gonne, who at the time was living in exile in France, cut off by the fighting of the First World War, and who was, with her daughter Iseult, nursing the wounded in Paris-Plage. Times had changed within the political movement in Ireland. Gonne, with her flowing gowns and particular form of theatricality, had sparked life into the cultural nationalist movement, but had never been a 'new woman'. Constance Markievicz and her Citizen Army uniform now symbolised the new woman activist.

At a time when the militant suffrage movement was at its peak, why was the demand for female equality not accepted by the ranks of advanced nationalists? The Volunteers resisted attempts to incorporate women into their movement and also refused to state where the organisation stood regarding women's suffrage. It is unfair to Cumann na mBan members to characterise them as concentrating on learning to bind wounds that would be made by others, but those who were in the organisation before the watershed of the Easter Rising seem to have accepted their auxiliary status (however reluctantly) and did not include within their constitution any objective relating specifically to women's right to equality. Only after the Proclamation, with its promise of a future Ireland based upon universal suffrage, were the principles of equal citizenship and equality of opportunity publicly accepted. The Proclamation 'legitimated women's role in the new state and gave formal recognition to their place in the nationalist movement'.[105] In addition, women, by taking their part in the dangers of armed warfare, demonstrated their capability and commitment to the cause. After that watershed Cumann na mBan felt free to include a new aim in its constitution: 'to follow the policy of the Republican Proclamation by seeing that women take up their proper position in the life of the nation'. From now on, any funds to be collected were to be for 'the arming and equipping of the men and women of Ireland'.[106]

A new, egalitarian future might have been expected, but it is clear that the leadership of the various women's organisations realised very quickly that there were obstacles in their way and they would have to work collectively if that future was ever to come about. The leaders of the Rising, almost all of whom had supported the suffrage cause, were executed by the British, and were followed by new leaders, some of whom had considerably more conservative views. Women from a wide variety of organisations came together as the 'League of Women Delegates', forming a pressure group to argue for equal representation and for women's demands to be included within the policies of Sinn Féin, now the political wing of nationalism.[107] War and civil war were to follow. After independence, women found themselves excluded from nation building because their former colleagues resurrected fears of disorderly women in order to create an independent state based on masculine authority and feminine domesticity. A gender-based juxtaposition of tradition versus modernity, first seen in the years of the Ladies' Land League, continued to be played out in the following decades of struggle, despite the many efforts made by women to claim a voice in the affairs of the nation.

8

Knowing Their Place?
Girls' Perceptions of School in
Nineteenth-Century Ireland

BRENDAN WALSH

Introduction

Very little is known about the lives of female pupils or their teachers in nineteenth-century Irish secondary schools. This task is complicated by the fact that, at the time, most teachers in girls' schools belonged to religious orders and have left little record of their personal, rather than collective, activity. Secondary schools were mostly boarding institutions and access was limited to those who could afford the fees. What constituted secondary school for girls is complicated by the fact that very often convent national schools would educate girls until the age of 14 or 16, at which stage their formal schooling was deemed complete. Hence, defining 'girls' secondary education' is difficult because the difference between national and secondary is not always clear.[1] For example, in the 1870s, the Ursuline convent in Sligo operated three schools: the boarding school (pensionnat) for fifty girls, a day school (demi-pensionnat) for approximately the same number of girls belonging to 'respectable' families in the area and a free school for poor children.[2] Orders were primarily concerned with their boarding schools. Girls were not allowed to mix with peers in the day school, and they lived an insular and pietistic life. It was not uncommon for orders to insist that girls residing in the same town attend their school as boarders. Certainly such insularity facilitated vocations. But it was not uncommon at the time for boys' schools such as Blackrock College, Dublin, St Kieran's College, Kilkenny or St Mary's College, Dundalk to cater for both lay and ecclesiastical students.[3]

As a rule, then, secondary education refers to education beyond that provided at national school level (therefore a secondary school curriculum) and, in nineteenth-century Ireland, was generally the preserve of the well-to-do. The distinction is important because, as a rule, the Irish female orders catered for the poor and, initially, operated mostly primary schools. Hence, secondary education for girls became the preserve of European orders.[4]

But we know almost nothing about their lives in school or about the women who taught them, lay or religious. Most of what we know about teachers must be inferred from what pupils have written or school journals record. The daily lives of their pupils are also only partially visible. We know, generally, what subjects were offered in schools and that they largely conformed to nineteenth-century expectations of femininity, but we know little about what these pupils were actually *like*, what they read or talked about, what interested them or how they managed the often very enclosed world of boarding school. This chapter, then, seeks to locate those lost voices and to present at least a partial picture of the female teacher and pupil in nineteenth-century Ireland. It is an attempt not only to discover what place girls felt they occupied, or should occupy, in the educational landscape but also to 'know' the physical places (schools) they occupied.

Why Explore Pupil Lives?

Feminist studies have produced remarkable insights into the education of girls.[5] But these studies have largely been concerned with the struggle for parity of treatment in terms of State examinations (the Intermediate examination established in 1878), access to higher education and access to educational opportunities generally.[6] In many ways, this struggle mirrors that of women's campaign for higher education in England, and at Cambridge in particular.[7] However, an examination of the ordinary lives of these women and girls can add to this more policy-focused research, thereby enriching both fields. The restrictions, expectations and aspirations of women in the nineteenth century cannot be detached from the notion of gender. Wider understandings of their social, private and professional roles were overwhelmingly determined and defined by this one aspect.[8] But, important as the story of women's struggle for access to higher education is, it can only be enriched by the discovery of ordinary lives, lived away from the limelight; those ordinary women who were not school founders or feminist campaigners. In many respects they had fewer advantages then their pioneering peers and because their voices were not heard in (or did not contribute to) wider debates, they are lost to mainstream history, residing in old school journals, pupil diaries or school prospectuses. Their lives have been 'of little interest or account' and it is the duty of the historian to rescue them, like all lost voices, from oblivion.[9] Another reason why these women have existed in the half-light is lack of evidence.[10] They have not left auto-biographies or been the subject of biography; they do not appear in the minutes of meetings or in the national press. Dina Copelman has called them 'shadowy figures',[11] women who are written about 'from without' and whose voices are seldom heard, too often written about as object rather than subject.[12]

Feminist and labour historians have done much to recover the voices of women and the marginalised, but the voice of the ordinary teacher and schoolgirl remains muted. In Ireland, the social history of schooling is almost unknown and if we are to recover the voices that filled classrooms we need firsthand accounts.[13] We have to be cautious of accepting what Phil Gardner (referring to the United Kingdom) describes as 'versions of history which simply catalogue the intentions of legislative activity and institutional innovation and then smuggle in the idea that these magically translated themselves … into the real world of the classroom'.[14] Rather, it is the classroom that 'ought to stand at the center of any study of educational endeavor'.[15] Too often, schooling exists on the margins of historical study, despite the fact that it was one of the first arenas in which women forged professional identities in the modern era. Female school founders and champions of equality in the nineteenth century were uncommon, strong-willed, rarefied examples of courage, but also, sometimes, of privilege. Usually educated, middle-class and articulate, they have left an abundant body of evidence in the form of letters, journals and essays. Hence, histo-rians have, understandably, been drawn to these women due to their influence and the availability of evidence; Margaret Ó hÓgartaigh's observation that 'the "revolution" in female education' in nineteenth-century Ireland was 'confined to the middle-classes [because] most second-level schools were fee-paying' reflects the social stratification of the country at a time when class rather than gender was the defining social characteristic.[16]

The 'ordinary' female teacher has not been so fortunate, and her omission leaves a gap in the narrative. Ironically, she and her pupils are the victims of the success of more formidable and noteworthy women. The danger for history is that an incomplete and merely celebratory picture emerges. Writing of American history, Marjorie Theobald notes 'it is rare to read … of the lady-teacher who taught by default, beat her students, spoke against votes for women, or married in order to escape'.[17] Again, Geraldine Clifford reminds readers that female teachers constituted 'a large part of the forgotten women of feminist history in the United States – the readied soil to catch the seeds of feminism'.[18] Nancy Hoffman points out that, in studying the lives of female teachers, the issue of gender may occlude that of teaching. The 'femaleness' of a women teacher, Hoffman argues, is the most significant factor, but only, she contends, where female teachers made it so. For most nineteenth-century teachers this idea played little or no part in their self-definition. It is Theobald who most stridently interrogates the problem and best articulates our position when she writes:

> … the grand narrative of teaching will no longer do. A monolithic feminism, such as that organized around the suffrage campaigns, can no longer frame our assumptions about the teaching profession or pre-empt the questions which we ask … the questions we ask teachers and the stories we tell about them can no longer sit unexamined beside a grand narrative of emancipation … what happened to women as teachers … may well be the antithesis of the pleasurable melodrama of emancipation experienced by nineteenth century women in the western nations.[19]

'As feminist historians', she continues, 'we have been enchanted by the marriage bars … we have thrived upon the politics of exclusion, not pausing to ask whether the generality of women wanted to stay in teaching for a lifetime. The mad-lady teacher in the attic is waiting to be heard.'[20]

While, justifiably, feminist historians argue that they cannot be separated, for the sake of clarity we might awkwardly define our task as an effort to discuss women as *teachers*, rather than teachers as *women*. Theobald's provocative question as to whether female teachers wanted to stay in teaching for a lifetime points to a very real dilemma for the historian: why did women become teachers, what was their private motivation and what was it like to be an ordinary teacher or schoolgirl in the nineteenth century? Hoffman's study of American teachers is absorbing in this respect. Despite any number of regulations governing the behaviour of women in nineteenth-century America, and the widespread notion that women were more suited to the 'motherly' art of teaching, Hoffman found that 'writing by teachers does not reveal a corresponding preoccupation; neither their love of children nor their attitude toward marriage dominates their comments', which, rather, 'indicated that they entered teaching because they needed work', while in the 'second half of the century … it allowed a woman to travel, to live independently or in the company of other women, and to attain economic security and a modest social status'.[21] Some women wanted to secure independence and avoid married life while others wished to 'foster social, political, or spiritual change'.[22] A writer in *The National Teacher* (1872) claimed that, for American women, the classroom was a 'seminary for social power' and, given the restrictions placed upon them at the period, the most rewarding and useful career open to women.[23] Gardner notes that in the United Kingdom many men and women became elementary teachers due to poverty or the inability to do other purposeful work.[24] Again, more women than men were employed as they were paid less and, as it was often combined with other work such as taking in washing, it often suited women better than men.[25]

The situation was different in Ireland, as Religious dominated the secondary schooling of girls in the nineteenth century, but, as we shall see below, lay women often worked alongside them. Women entered teaching for a multitude of reasons, most of which we cannot know. This is why firsthand accounts are invaluable. They tell us what methods were used, rather than recommended; how children were punished or rewarded; how teachers implemented (or did not) curricular changes or directives from management; how they viewed their colleagues, employers and pupils. Undermining the cherished notion of the female teacher as a 'motherly figure' which pervaded nineteenth-century discourse, the correspondence of American teachers in the mid-nineteenth century reveals that they pinched, slapped, struck, shook and 'whipped' pupils. In 1836, Adeline Reed, a Vermont elementary teacher, wrote that she 'sometimes punished a child by "putting a string around his neck attached to a nail behind him"'.[26]

When we look behind the grand narrative of women and education, therefore, we begin to encounter the ordinary – the vast cohort of women and girls who may or may not have been aware of their place in larger debates about gender and equality. These lives were 'messy', ordinary and busy. They centred on the ordinary challenges of each day, on examinations, homework, relations with pupils and management. By locating them we enter into the classroom of the nineteenth century, not as detailed in inspectors' reports or as imagined by official declamations or even by the school prospectus, but by those who taught and were taught in them. And, as in America and the United Kingdom, where the study of the lives of teachers is considerably advanced, the lives of ordinary 'lady teachers' and their pupils in Ireland can be retrieved in all their ambiguity and untidiness.

The Evolution of Girls' Secondary Schooling in Nineteenth-Century Ireland

The secondary, or Intermediate, school system dates from 1878, when the Intermediate Education (Ireland) Act provided for State funding of Intermediate schools through a system of payment by results. Prior to this date, and for many decades after independence, these schools were operated by religious orders which, particularly after Catholic Emancipation (1829), had started to establish and operate primary and secondary schools throughout Ireland. Catholic pressure had helped bring about the Intermediate system and allowed schools to access public funds. As monies were secured through open, competitive, public examination, many of these schools – some of which had developed a strong scientific base, like St Kieran's, Kilkenny – were forced to change their *modus operandi*. Little is known about this era of change and, again, the grand narrative has assumed a relatively untroubled transition when, in fact, many school managers were undecided and suspicious of the new competitive, individualistic culture. As early as 1881, for example, the principal of Blackrock College, Dublin complained that the Intermediate examination should 'not test the coaching in particular books', while past pupils instituted a separate system of prize giving for non-examination activities such as debating.[27] Girls were included in the Intermediate Education Act of 1878, but only after lobbying and negotiation, while the debate concerning their ability to compete with boys and the desirability of their taking examinations rumbled on for the first two decades of the system's operation. The contemporaneous comments of Dr Nulty, Bishop of Meath, who described the examination as unsuitable for the 'respectable middle-class female youth of Ireland, who will be the wives and mothers of farmers … merchants, manufactures and professional men of the coming generation', represented those of society generally. Such views were by no means restricted to Ireland. Joan Burstyn, in her impressive study of girls' education in Victorian Britain, notes of the period: '[c]leverness in women was measured by social success. Women achieved influence over men indirectly, by listening to them, by agreeing with them or, occasionally, offering an opinion of their own.'[28] That they should enter into public examinations and compete with boys seemed contrary to the established social order, possibly injurious to their health, antagonistic to the divine order and marital harmony and a threat to male dominance in and of the labour market.

Girls' Secondary Schools Prior to 1878

There is little doubt that, on the whole, Catholic girls' secondary schools prior to 1878 were not expected to prepare girls for work outside that of homemaking. They were essentially Victorian in attitude and culture; the girls were charged fees and usually came from middle-class families, and the schools were mostly boarding institutions.[29] Provision grew rapidly after 1829. By 1840, in Dublin alone there were seven female religious orders, representing fifteen convents, each with a school attached. By 1865 this had risen to eleven orders and forty-three convents and by 1890 there were seventeen orders with eighty-seven convents, although not all of these had schools attached. The rapid and typical expansion is exemplified by the spread of Dominican girls' boarding schools. The order founded Siena School in Drogheda, County Louth in 1725 and by 1900 had established ten such schools and eleven day schools.[30] By 1899 the following female orders had founded convent schools in Ireland: the Sisters of St Louis, the Congregation of the Faithful Companions of Jesus, the Sisters of

the Sacred Heart of Mary and the Sisters of St Joseph of Cluny. These
European orders existed alongside the indigenous Irish Congregations
of the Sisters of Mercy and Presentation and the Brigidine Sisters.
The Ursulines established a small boarding school in Thurles,
County Tipperary in 1796, charging twenty guineas per annum
(about 25 euro), although, as with many schools in nineteenth-century
Ireland, fees often remained unpaid. Between 1803 and 1816, for
example, the school tried to secure payment for three pupils (sisters)
to the amount of £133 4s 1d.[31] By the 1820s, in Thurles alone, there
were twenty-two schools for Catholics (including private fee-paying
schools), excluding those of the Christian Brothers, Presentation and
Ursulines, which catered for nearly 600 pupils. The remaining schools
catered for about 660 pupils. By the end of the nineteenth century
there were sixty-two convent boarding schools for girls in Ireland,
although only six of these were operated by Irish orders: the Sisters
of Mercy school in Ennis, County Clare, the Holy Faith school in
Glasnevin, Dublin and four Brigidine schools at Tullow, Mountrath,
Abbeyleix and Goresbridge. In the second half of the nineteenth
century a number of high (secondary) schools had been established for
girls, including the Ladies' Collegiate Institute, Belfast (1859), Strand
House School, Londonderry (1860) and Alexandra College, Dublin
(1866). The co-educational Wesley College in Dublin was founded in
1845. These schools played an important part in promoting secondary
and higher education for girls; indeed, Alexandra College acted as a spur
to Catholic secondary schools as it became prominent in the campaign
for women's access to higher education in the late nineteenth century.[32]
Its role in campaigning for the inclusion of girls in the Intermediate
Education (Ireland) Act of 1878 also prompted often unenthusiastic
Catholic high schools to enter pupils into the examinations; in effect,
the culture of competition between Protestant and Catholic schools
was given raw data in the form of Intermediate examination results and
encouraged and celebrated by the public press.[33]

Prior to the advent of the Intermediate system, schools, reflecting
social norms, tended to concentrate on 'accomplishments'. Young girls
were instructed in the domestic arts and 'feminine' disciplines such as
music, dancing and drawing.[34] We should, in passing, note that while
it is correct to characterise these as binding girls to contemporaneous
expectations of femininity we should also recall that girls had to
survive within the limitations imposed upon them. Young women

were paraded during the Dublin 'season' at the Lord Lieutenant's Ball
in Dublin Castle into the early years of the twentieth century and, for
many, marriage was the only way of avoiding becoming, in the words
of Emma Woodhouse, 'a ridiculous, disagreeable old maid'. However,
the course of studies offered was much influenced by the order.
French orders, for example, tended to emphasise the study of French
and literature.[35] Irish orders tended toward practical disciplines but not
to the exclusion of 'accomplishments'. The course of 'English, French,
Italian, History, Geography, Use of the Globes, Needlework, Writing,
Arithmetic with Music, Singing, Dancing, Drawing (offered as Extras)'
at the Brigidine Convent Boarding School in Tullow, County Carlow
is not untypical.[36] In the mid-nineteenth-century the Sacred Heart
School, Armagh offered 'English, French, Italian, History, Use of the
Globes, Writing, Arithmetic and Needlework'. The 1859 *Prospectus* of
the Dominican School in Sion Hill, County Dublin declares that the
school offers 'English, French, Italian, History, Geography, Use of the
Globes, Arithmetic, Epistolary Correspondence, Natural Philosophy,
Botany, Needlework, Music, Drawing, Dancing' while the 'other
accomplishments necessary to complete the education of a young lady,
receive attention proportionate to their importance in a polished and
fashionable education'.[37] In 1871 the Ursuline School in County Cork
offered 'English, Writing, Arithmetic, German, French, Italian, History,
Astronomy, Use of the Globes, Botany, Conchology, Mythology,
Sciences, Architecture and the elements of Geometry, Flower and
Landscape Painting and every description of useful and ornamental
work.' Extras included 'Music, Singing, Dancing, Dueling.' By 1873,
however, the Protestant Alexandra College was offering 'Mathematics,
Arithmetic, Algebra, Trigonometry, Natural Philosophy, Hebrew,
Greek, Latin, German, Geology and Biology'.[38]

Yet the type of education offered in girls' secondary schools at this
period is not easily categorised. For example, the first *Prospectus* of the
Dominican School in Cabra, founded in 1835, is unambiguous about
what the Sisters believe is the proper course for girls. The nuns:

> will not in any manner sanction the imprudence of parents, who
> attaching undue importance to what is called a fashionable education,
> waste time and money in having their children taught, to the exclusion
> of useful and necessary knowledge, accomplishments for which they
> have neither taste, capacity, nor use.[39]

Appealing as this might sound to modern sensibilities, the girls were, nonetheless, to leave Cabra in possession of 'the solid information that qualifies [them] for the due management of the domestic circle'.[40] The schools provided what was deemed necessary for the times. Most middle-class girls in the early decades of the nineteenth century did not envisage a 'career' beyond marriage and therefore were expected to be able run a household. A letter to *The Irish Times* of 1878 reflects social expectations:

> Home is the sphere of a woman; modesty is her supreme virtue; softness and sweetness are her true accomplishments; innocence is her best experience; economy is her highest ability; and constancy and self-sacrificing love her only legitimate heroism.[41]

Hence, while the number of secondary schools for girls continued to expand in the nineteenth century, it was never envisaged that these schools would prepare girls for competitive examinations with boys, for gainful employment or to work alongside men. This only began to change towards the end of the century and, even then, middle-class girls were not expected to venture into employment beyond traditional occupations such as teaching or, perhaps, nursing. It is not surprising that, as opportunities began to widen due to shifts in social understanding, greater engagement with the competitive examination system and access to higher education, criticisms of the convent education provided in earlier decades began to be voiced. Two articles in *Frazer's Magazine* in 1874 claimed that while convent education had much to offer, the curriculum was generally restrictive and of little relevance in the 'real world'.[42]

Hence, certainly prior to 1878, secondary schooling for girls was largely offered by Catholic orders in boarding schools providing a limited course of studies. However, the curriculum was not *then* considered restrictive. As we have seen above, typically, the courses offered were as varied as could be provided and reflected parental expectations. As we shall see below, many parents were opposed to their daughters entering into competitive examinations after 1878 and, while schools welcomed the access to funds which the Intermediate system introduced, they had to alter their *modus operandi* and culture to adjust to the new regime.

The Intermediate (Ireland) Act 1878

The Intermediate Act was the means by which the secondary school community in Ireland could secure public funding, allowing the government in Westminster to sidestep direct funding of denominational institutions. A system of examinations was instituted whereby subjects were awarded different marks on a sliding scale and schools could claim funding in accordance with their pupils' success in the annual 'contestation': an 'intellectual tilt and tournament' in which the schools competed.[43] The same principle had been applied to the National School system in 1870, although it was abandoned in 1889 when all parties agreed that competitive examinations encouraged rote-learning and poor teaching and were pedagogically counter-productive and inappropriate in the light of a growing understanding of childhood development and the nature of learning. A feature of schooling in the nineteenth century that has not been previously considered is how these predominantly Religious-run secondary schools were obliged to re-examine their *modus operandi* and values upon joining the Intermediate system in 1878. Religious understood education as an extension of their spiritual and social apostolate and, while examinations and hard work generally characterised their schools, the introduction of a competitive system altered the inner dynamic of these institutions in ways that are not yet understood. The unease was articulated as early as 1881, as noted above, when the principal of Blackrock College complained of '... coaching in particular books'.[44]

Certainly the Catholic hierarchy opposed the inclusion of girls in the Intermediate Bill, Cardinal Cullen writing to Chief Secretary Hicks-Beach that 'females ... go in a different direction and require other sorts of training and teaching'.[45] Cullen was doing little more than reflecting the social mores of his time. Indeed, as late as 1900 the prioress of the Sion Hill community informed Archbishop McCabe that '... the great majority of the parents express strong objections to the system and many stipulate that their girl shall not go in for the examination.'[46] However, the six Sisters from Sion Hill who left to occupy the new convent in Eccles Street, Dublin between 1882 and 1883 successfully entered girls for the Intermediate examinations from 1884.[47] Yet the Dominicans at Kingstown informed McCabe in 1883 that 'none of our Boarders ever went in for the Intermediate'.[48] They were not untypical and, nationally, the coming of public, competitive, terminal examinations shone a light into the workings of secondary schools. Not only were the examinations considered inappropriate for girls but perhaps even dangerous. Reflecting the nineteenth-century default position that anything emancipatory was probably dangerous to women's health, the Irish *Ecclesiastical Record* noted in 1883 that:

> the physical strain and nervous excitement [caused by the examination] is oftentimes decidedly and permanently injurious to the more susceptible temperament of females. If high culture can only be secured at the sacrifice of female delicacy, and the rewards of the Intermediate can only be purchased by permanent injury to health, we think the nuns are quite right in preferring maidenly modesty and healthy development of their pupils to the honours of the Intermediate Board.[49]

Such a position was neither particular to Ireland nor the nineteenth century. Concerns regarding the fitness of girls to compete in the Intermediate system were expressed throughout its existence, although the Intermediate Education (Ireland) Commission (Palles Report) of 1899 found that interested parties held often quite divergent views on the matter. Margaret Byers, principal of Victoria College, Belfast, for example, emphatically informed the Commission that 'the examinations have revolutionised girls' education. The results fees had 'enable[d] head mistresses to increase the school staff ... accommodation and general efficiency and to offer salaries that secured high-class teachers'.[50] Pupils of Victoria College 'have been in the foremost ranks at Newnham and Girton, Edinburgh and Glasgow'.[51] Byers submitted that 'her teachers are most conscientious, and repudiate teaching for results', while 'their mode of teaching is not interfered with by the system which is the most suitable to Ireland'.[52] Contrary to what might be expected, Isabella Mulvany, headmistress of Alexandra College, submitted that 'A very small proportion of children of the school go in for examination, largely on account of the objections of the parents.'[53] Alice Oldham, honorary secretary of the Central Association of Irish Schoolmistresses, submitted that 'In the Dublin schools there appears to be an increasing dislike among the most cultured parents to send their girls in for the Intermediate, owing to the high pressure, and to the fear that the girls will injure their health by over-study.' Oldham had 'personal experience of some bad cases of breakdown'.[54] The issue of health was as contentious as the system. Mr John Thompson, honorary secretary of the Dublin and Central Irish Branch of the Teachers' Guild of Great Britain and Ireland, claimed that:

> medical men have exaggerated the ill-effects on the health of the pupils of the present system. Whatever breakdowns have taken place are not inherently the fault of the system, and are often due to the over-anxiety of parents for the success of their children.[55]

Thompson's claim has a strikingly modern resonance, although the Commission's final summation that, while medical evidence is persuasive, they were not 'in a position to compare the number of students whose constitutions are injured by over-work with the number of those students who are ruined by idleness and its consequences' resounds with Victorian high-mindedness.[56]

However, we seldom hear the voice of female pupils in these debates and it is to those voices that we will now turn. It is interesting to note, for example, that seven years after the Palles Report, the magazine of Loreto College, St Stephen's Green, Dublin carried an article entitled 'Recent Reminiscences: (School girls [sic] on the Education Question)'. The anonymous author writes:

> We – girls who are undergoing the process of being educated – are so constantly talked about that it is no wonder we sometimes talk together about ourselves … we are not oppositionists to being set on the road to knowledge … we have been helped over the difficulties so far, and the greater part of the way was bright and pleasant. Certainly, neither literature, Latin, nor even mathematics have exercised a depressing or deadening influence on us … Exams after exams have left us just as awake to snatches of enjoyment as if we had nothing to occupy us seriously and busily during the greater part of the day.[57]

She continues:

> there are some trite observations [that fill] newspaper articles, and ordinary educational discussions of which we are deadly tired … One is, that our course of studies for public exams is mere cramming (This reproach chiefly falls on the Intermediate). Quite true it is, that

beginning with very empty heads, a great deal has to be got in in a given space of time … but we cannot say that the matter proposed is useless knowledge …[58]

When the first 'contestation' was held in 1879 girls represented 736 out of 3,954 candidates (11 per cent). Of these, 482 (65 per cent) secured a pass, reflecting the average pass rate during the lifetime of the Intermediate examination. The change in culture required for Catholic secondary schools to 'perform' in this new, competitive environment is reflected in their results. After a decade of examinations, only 207 girls from Catholic schools had passed the Intermediate, prompting the *Freeman's Journal* to claim in 1886 that there was 'scarcely a Catholic school left in Ireland capable of educating female pupils up to the not very exacting standard' of the Intermediate.[59] Indeed, it seemed possible that the 'ecclesiastical authorities' might, at some future date, have to consider prohibiting 'certain Catholic schools' from entering pupils, 'so that, in the race for prizes and honours with Protestant boys and girls they may not be handicapped by the ignorance of their teachers'.[60] To modern sensibilities, however, the more serious aspect of this apparent failure was that, at a time when the demand for education for middle-class girls was increasing in line with the expansion of an increasingly wealthy commercial Catholic class in the latter half of the nineteenth century, schools were failing to provide girls with the knowledge and skills necessary for employment. The era when young women were expected to rely upon their male relatives for their upkeep was passing as the century drew to its close and the new social dynamic meant that girls were increasingly entering the workplace as governesses and teachers. But these positions required a modern education. This was reflected in the changing tone in the prospectuses of some girls' schools. When the Dominican order opened their school in Eccles Street, Dublin in 1882, for example, the emphasis upon accomplishments had been replaced with the provision of a course of studies 'similar to that of the higher educational establishments', one which gave 'a thorough and special training for important duties of governesses, together with provision for training for industrial and civil posts open to females'.[61] The evident evolution in religious women's conceptualisation of their pupils' wider role may be gauged when we contrast the Dominicans' statement with that of the *Irish Ecclesiastical Record* twenty-five years *later* when it stated that:

> On Catholic principals … it is not explicitly defined that woman has the right to a living wage, or the duty of supporting herself at all. She is supposed to be shielded by her male relatives from most of the hardships and disabilities of citizenship … there is no reason why she should have any direct part in the policy of the State.[62]

It is not surprising then that the first Dominican pupils entered for the Intermediate were from this school, and by the end of the century almost all female religious orders entered their pupils for the examination.[63]

History From Beneath – The Nineteenth-Century Schoolgirl

As outlined at the beginning of this essay, historians have become increasingly interested in what (or who) lies behind the grand narrative and having traced, albeit briefly, the development of secondary schooling for girls in Ireland in the nineteenth century we turn now to that history of the ordinary. The *Loreto Magazine* essays touched upon above indicate that discussions took place among pupils concerning the most contentious issues of the day. But what of the daily, humdrum experience of girls and their teachers? In order to find out more, we must turn to two main sources: what girls wrote about school as pupils and what they later wrote as adults. In using these, we have to guard against the immaturity of the former and the sentimentalising tendency of the latter. Yet both are invaluable in recovering the past as it was actually lived.

Writing in 1921, Margaret Moore (*née* Nagle) recalled that life at the Dominican Roscrea School in the late 1850s entailed much needlework. This was common in girls' schools of the period; indeed, after 1878, the time allocated to it became a contentious issue as, increasingly, teachers and principals believed the time would be better spent on examination subjects. Moore recalled that 'warm weather stitching was unpleasant and many samples of [her] blood from badly pricked fingers stained the hard unbleached lining of the little pink dress over which [she] toiled'.[64] Again, and like most boarding pupils, Margaret recalled dressing on cold mornings in draughty dormitories, but, in an observation that permeates the recollections of all those educated by Religious, she mused:

> We did not consider how many devoted souls were already up and around working for our comfort ... No one remembered the toil incurred, the lighting of the fires, the heating of such a quantity of water and the carrying of it from the kitchen in the depths of winter ... up to five dormitories.

Adult life 'brought better understanding of the care, fatigue and sense of responsibility which caused the deaths of Choir nuns to surpass in number those of the Assistant sisters'.[65] It is interesting to note, given our earlier observation that Religious-run schools were forced to re-examine their values and *modus operandi* in 1878, that Margaret recalls a Madame Kieran who was a 'past mistress in the art of making learning, as distinct from studying, a pleasant pastime'. Madame Kieran 'taught little from school books' and Margaret 'never' forgot what she learned from her.[66] Yet girls and teachers worked hard. Almost two decades before the Intermediate, convent schools usually operated 'house' examinations and Margaret recalled that pupils busily prepared for these and 'enthusiasts besought their friends to wake them early and tucked books beneath their pillows to read at dawn'.[67] An aspect of school life which would later come under scrutiny from the Gaelic League was the anglocentric syllabus.[68] We will see below how the evolution of cultural nationalism can be traced in school publications, but in the 1860s Margaret's experience of geography lessons was typical – 'we travelled through England, told of each City [*sic*] and town' – while in English history she learned 'the story of Richard the First and the Minstrel Blondel in dealing with the Crusades'.[69] Irish history and geography are not mentioned. Recollections of unbecoming school uniforms are not uncommon in girls' recollections. The uniform worn in Roscrea in 1857 to 1858 was, according to Margaret, 'very ugly', consisting of 'brown cashmere dresses, tight fitting black jackets ... while straw bonnets [were] trimmed with cardinal red ribbon'.[70]

What is particularly striking in such memoirs is the great affection girls have for their school. Female boarding institutions, for all their rules and restrictions, became 'home' to pupils and lifelong friendships were formed. Margaret recalled that she 'slept little' the night before

she left Roscrea: 'the early train was to bear me away from all I loved
in the world ... I could hardly speak when the hurried farewells were
said and I descended the stairs for the last time. The Convent [*sic*] door
closed behind me and I faced the world alone.'[71] Often the experience
of school is portrayed as idyllic; it is a place somehow more formative
than the present. For all Roscrea's 'spartan simplicity', the girls 'were
happier and more contented than are the children today'.[72] It was a
place of 'health and happiness', of 'pure air, exercise in delightful
surroundings', where 'wholesome food' and 'quiet sleep in airy dormitories' were 'all that were required to enable us to enshrine a sane
mentality in a healthy body'.[73]

    One of the most useful sources for recollections of school life at
the turn of the century is the history of Rochelle School in Cork.
This school is particularly interesting because of its age, its history and
its origin as an all-girls school. Rochelle was founded in 1829 as a
'seminary for training young governesses'; its patroness, Hannah More,
had two older sisters who had founded a school in Bristol.[74] Their
father was a schoolmaster and the girls were 'highly educated' for the
time, although Hannah's lessons in mathematics were stopped because
'she was becoming too good at them and this was unfeminine'.[75]
The school was established at the instigation of Charlotte Abbot,
daughter of the Cork-based brewer Samuel Abbot. One of the first
teachers at this school was a Mr Lefebvre who previously ran a 'fashionable' school in Cork. In 1830 Lefebvre's wife opened a boarding
school for 'young ladies' near Glanmire, a town about five miles from
Cork City. The Lefebvre schools have left no trace, but Mrs Lefebvre's
was a boarding school and was, therefore, probably a secondary-type
school. The school was founded to cater primarily for the Protestant
community and its teachers were all laywomen. This school for
governesses, in the 1840s, offered: 'French, Italian, English, History,
Geography, Writing, Arithmetic, Geometry, Music, Drawing, plain
and fancy Needlework, Scripture and Church Catechism.'[76] One of
its later benefactors was Dr Salmon, provost of Trinity College Dublin,
who so vehemently opposed the opening of that university to women
in 1904.[77]

    Recollections of Rochelle tend to focus upon school life rather
than teachers. Miss Whately became headmistress in 1879 and was
remembered as 'sail[ing] into the classroom' making the girls open
windows on 'cold winter mornings'.[78] An unnamed French teacher

with little English was teased by the girls, who gave her 'unorthodox translations' and taught her 'unusual phrases'.[79] In 1887 Miss Whately recorded that the school had six resident English teachers:

> We used to have two foreign teachers but we prefer to have English teachers trained abroad ... All our English pupils get honours without exception in the Intermediate examinations ... We have another lady – a most valuable English teacher – and we have an English lady who has matriculated in the University of London ... One of these has been trained in the Training College of St. Andrews.[80]

When Miss Whately's successor, Miss King, died in 1892 she was succeeded by Jane Marshall, who was 'much addicted to ferocious hats' and educated at 'Mrs. Byers College' (Victoria College in Belfast). Marshall continued the connection with England, having obtained a Cambridge Higher Local Certificate and taught in Bath, Gravesend and Brighton.[81] We know that under Marshall (in 1897) the English and science teacher, Miss Maxwell, resigned and was replaced by a Miss Frances Molyneux, on the considerable salary of £50 per annum, and that in September of that year Miss Bertie Cox was admitted as a pupil teacher for one year, her fees being reduced by £10 to £20 per year.[82]

These are fragments, but they demonstrate that science was taught, that it was taught by a woman and that the school, at least on one occasion, admitted its pupils as trainee teachers. Indeed, Miss Whately had been a founder member of the Association of Irish Schoolmistresses (1882), and in 1886 the Cork Branch called for a Registry of Teachers. The proposal gained little momentum, but coupled with the pupil-teacher appointment it suggests that Rochelle was proactive in pushing for training and registration. This is further evidenced by the employment, in 1891, of a 'specially qualified instructress in the Art and Practice of Teaching', although this is not surprising as since 1884 the girls had been entering for the Royal University of Ireland (RUI) examinations, and the school had drifted from its original *raison d'être* of providing governesses for the middle classes. By 1903 five of its teachers had BA degrees and Miss J. Eveleith, Mus. Doc. Oxon. taught music. By 1909 Marshall's staff of twelve women had qualifications including the London Matriculation, Froebel, BA and LLD. In 1929 Marshall's successor, Miss Bewley, was replaced by Miss Watson, remembered as 'a most stimulating teacher, with a disconcerting gift for discerning the subtle idler', while another past pupil recalled that when Watson taught Scripture in Sixth Form for the first time one felt that 'one was learning an interesting subject and dealt with really important ... thoughts and ideas. She had an open, questing mind: she drew us out and made us think. I don't suppose a teacher could be paid a higher tribute than that.'[83]

Ruth Foley, who attended the school from 1930 to 1934, remembers Watson as a 'calm, strict' and 'aloof figure'.[84] Betty Knox, who also attended at this period, remembered that 'we all loved Mr. Sheehy', the drawing master, and 'Miss Johnson', who taught geography and was 'a very warm hearted and generous teacher and friend'.[85] Miss Bewley was remembered by Lily Fitzpatrick, who enrolled in 1918, as 'the coldest person I have ever met, with eyes like steel and no sign of affection for anyone'.[86] Others are remembered warmly: 'Miss Edwards ... whom we all loved ... Miss Smith (Domestic Science) ... nick-named ... "Big Smut" but we were all fond of her ... we had two male teachers ... dear old Billy Sheehy our drawing master' and Dr Eveleigh, who taught music and 'whom I loathed'.[87]

Girls who attended Rochelle have left valuable information about school life in the nineteenth century. Frances Moran, who enrolled in 1875, recalled that servants made up her bed and she herself took 'many meals at the "Disgrace Table"' for unrecorded misdemeanours. Lily Jellet, who attended in the mid-1870s, remembered her schooldays as 'harsh and severe', although 'she enjoyed her lessons and the good teaching'.[88] Pupils rose at 7 a.m., studied from 7.30 to 8.30 and ate breakfast at 8.45, consisting of bread and butter and tea, followed by prayers and classes until 11.30. Lunch was 'a slice of dry bread', after which classes resumed until dinner: 'there was one course: meat, potatoes and vegetables ... the meat was often uneatable and the cooking abominable'.[89] After dinner the girls walked 'two by two' along the road near the school; their evening meal was tea and dry bread, followed by study until 7.30 p.m. and bed at 8.30. She also recalls that the procession of young trainee-governesses to church on Sunday was 'of great interest' to the medical students at the South Infirmary, who would 'assemble en masse' to observe the parade.[90] The girls would also drop notes from the music-room window during lessons, to be collected by boys from the local grammar school, and a visiting teacher who worked in various schools in the locality allowed his hat to be used 'as a post office by boys and girls, who slipped notes inside it'.[91] Despite the harshness of the regime, or perhaps because of it, Jellet won a first-class prize in the Intermediate examinations of 1878.

Frances Maybury, who enrolled in 1885, was 'very unhappy' at the school. Pupils rose at 6 a.m., the food was 'dreadful' and, according to the school historian, she was 'particularly horrified by sheep's head served complete with eyes and eyelashes staring at her from the dish'.[92] As in other early nineteenth-century schools, classes were often taught in one large room. Harriette Hore attended Rochelle while Marshall was headmistress and recalled that 'Miss Acheson ... sometimes in desperation put up a baize screen to separate her class from the others'.[93] Margaret Fitzgerald, who attended from 1892 to 1896, remembered five or six classes being held simultaneously in one large room.[94] Mabel Lethbridge was a pupil there in 1914 and in her novel *Fortune Grass* has her narrator describe how:'the school food was dreadful ... the dormitories were unheated and I would like awake at nights numb with cold'.[95] Lunch was secured by 'brute force', the girls having to jostle to ensure they got a portion of the 'small slices of bread and margarine'.[96] Lethbridge's fictional schoolgirl was 'teased endlessly for [her] flat chest ... ever after [she] clothed and unclothed [her]self beneath [her] nightdress'.[97]

Teachers' recollections are, unsurprisingly, different. Mrs White, who taught under Bewley for five 'pleasant years', recalled them as 'passed in pleasant surroundings ... pleasant hours passed on lawns and tennis courts, in music rooms and on the playing field'. 'Of course,' she adds, 'we worked hard.'[98]

Schools reinforced the influence of wider social norms, regardless of the era. Rochelle – a Protestant lay foundation for girls – operated in an almost identical way to the Dominican Convent in Cabra, Dublin, a typical foundation of the period. Founded in 1819, its Rules of 1914 reflect the same expectations and concerns. Girls were forbidden to purchase 'novels or periodicals at Railway stations' or to 'introduce such into the school', expected to write home 'once a week ... acquire a ladylike easy manner, and a refined pleasing accent', while 'useless and unnecessary correspondence with friends' was not permitted.[99] In a regulation immersed in the gendered expectations of the period, they were warned to avoid using 'vulgarisms, slang or certain phrases, which, used by their brothers, would be harmless and inoffensive, but when spoken by young ladies would betray a great want of self-respect and refinement'.[100] Pupils were also forbidden to 'give orders' to 'Lay Sisters or maids'.[101] Others remember small luxuries. Stanley Lyon, for example, entered St Mary's College, Dundalk in 1893 and remembered the installation of 'the modern type of bath with hot and cold water', making the winter morning ablutions less severe. His 1961 observation that the 'present generation' would scarcely believe the 'Spartan conditions', which made it 'hard going for small boys', reflects almost exactly Margaret Moore's 1921 comment concerning the rudimentary environment of nineteenth-century boarding schools. But it is noteworthy that almost half a century separates their experiences.

Experimental schools, such as those established by A.S. Neill or Patrick Pearse, may operate as agents of transformation but more generally schools reflect and encapsulate wider social change (or stagnation).[102] Girls' schools, in particular, tend to capture changing notions of femininity through items such as photographs, prospectuses and regulations. Debates concerning femininity became more dominant in school literature from the mid-1960s, as pupils of both sexes began to chafe against restrictions placed upon dress, hairstyle and behaviour. Indeed, it is remarkable how persistently concepts such as 'being ladylike' permeated the culture of girls' schools. The first (1850) prospectus of Loreto School, Bray, for example, stated that one of the aims of the school was to 'aid young ladies in the acquirement of suitable accomplishments'.[103] Fifty-seven years later, pupils were still graded (in in-house examinations) on 'Ladylike Deportment' and, while the school boasted of the bathing amenities at Bray, a Josephine Murphy was 'devastated' to learn in the early 1920s that pupils of the school were also expected to wear their swimsuit in the bath tub.[104] Loreto was not alone in this stipulation, and it appears that pupils commonly dipped their costumed in the tub and then bathed in the customary manner.[105]

The Ursulines at Sligo, in 1850, offered a wide course of studies, including 'all those attainments which are necessary, useful and ornamental in society'.[106] At the same time, the nuns of the Sacred Heart wished to encourage in their pupils the 'ability to think for oneself' and the acquisition of 'a breadth of view, strength of judgment and fineness

of perception'.[107] This independence of thought is reflected in the fact
that the nuns did not enter pupils for the Intermediate examination
until 1931. But the Sisters of St Louis (Monaghan), also a French order,
entered girls in the early 1880s, held *soirées* once a month and were the
first female order to embrace the Gaelic Revival and offer Irish (Celtic)
in their schools. In short, there was no single type of female education
in the nineteenth century. Girls had different experiences depending
upon their school and its ethos. There are, of course, commonalities, but
we need to guard against overlooking everyday events that reveal quite
different ways of operating in diverse institutions.

Katherine Tynan, author of *Twenty-Five Years*, was enrolled at the
Dominican Siena Convent in Drogheda from 1872 to 1874. Even at
this period, she felt the school to be out of touch, the prohibition
of newspapers and magazines being unnecessarily restrictive. For the
teaching nuns, 'the progress of the world had stopped ... some ten or
twenty or thirty or forty years before'.[108] Like others, Tynan praised
her teachers for bringing 'whatever of ladyhood [*sic*]' was 'in a girl to
perfection', but believed that the nuns knew little of the needs of Irish
women of the time – describing the 'House-mother' who 'cannot
cook, cannot sew, cannot wash, cannot clean'.[109] These observations
foreshadowed an acerbic attack upon convent education written by
P.H. O'Donnell in 1902. His *The Ruin of Education in Ireland* was an
immoderate polemic against the standard of education at the turn of
the century, but it contained elements of truth, particularly regarding
the inability of lay teachers to gain work in the largely Religious-
dominated system and the lack of accountability of schools generally.
His most stinging criticisms, however, were reserved for the 'Female
Orders', whose 'inculcation of pietistic ignorance ... disqualifies
multitudes of Irish girls for the duties of home and the holiest hopes
of womanhood', making their schools a 'fount of unpractical living
and uncultured thinking ... a perpetual agency for idleness, shift-
lessness ... and emigration'.[110] While O'Donnell's remarks appear
to damn convent education, they are, in fact, significant for what
they reveal. Convent education is judged a failure because Irish girls
are not being prepared, in 'unpractical schools', for 'the duties of
home'. As we shall see below when we encounter essays written by
pupils from Loreto on the Green, Dublin some ten years previously,
they, and Irish girls more widely, were not inclined to be, primarily,
prepared for 'the duties of the home'.

We have already noted that senior girls at Loreto on the Green held strong opinions regarding their involvement in the Intermediate system. The girls were evidently reflecting upon the issue but, as their essays demonstrate, their deliberations were informed by notions of what we would now term 'feminism'. It is difficult to gauge to what extent this was the result of school culture. Certainly the girls would have been influenced by their peers and parents. The school was situated in the heart of the city so they had access, albeit probably quite limited, to libraries, newspapers, magazines and the general culture of news that tends to be generated in urban centres. Reading material is important and historians have all but ignored what pupils in this period did and did not have access to. For example, a note in the *Loreto Magazine* of 1895 asks pupils to submit reviews of books they are reading and suggests titles including *Lorna Doone*, *Cranford*, *Three Men in a Boat*, *The Moonstone* and *The Adventures of Sherlock Holmes*. Magazines include *The Century*, *The Strand*, *The Windsor*, *Atlanta*, *The Idler*, *Harper's* and *Cassell's Saturday Journal*. Generally, these are standard fare. However, the American *Century Magazine* existed as *Scribner's Monthly* between 1870 and 1881. Infused with a Christian ethos and generally popular in tone, it was nonetheless an unlikely precursor to the reading fare of girls in an Irish Catholic school at the turn of the century. In November 1870, for example, *Scribner's* published an article entitled 'Papa and the Dogma', concerning the relationship between European political powers and the Vatican.[111] These powers, it noted,

> have no respect for His Holiness. They are powers born of Protestantism. Education and freedom from priestly domination have made them great ... The Pope has failed to make his subjects happy, failed to make them prosperous, failed to secure their affection, failed to educate them ... failed to enlighten the masses under his influence ... failed to make them moral and religious, failed to secure their unity against the aggressions of Protestant power, failed to do anything for human progress, failed utterly as a temporal ruler ...[112]

We are not suggesting that such material was available to Loreto girls in 1870, or indeed any other year, but we cannot know for certain. What we do know is that the piece just quoted appeared in the precursor of a periodical recommended by the girls in their school magazine two decades later. Again, given the girls' views on the role of women and equal pay (see below), it is worth noting that the same periodical, like so many others in the 1870s, argued that, while we may 'feel intuitively' that women and men should be paid the same for equal work, that work is not equal when it is physical: 'The owner of the mastiff that turns a churn cannot expect to receive for his work the same as the man who furnishes a horse to perform the same service. The horse is a hundred times more valuable than the dog as a motive power.'[113] While accepting that in the creative arts parity of pay should be *de rigueur*, the piece concludes that 'so long as man alone has the power to deal with the rough forces of nature, and to practice the arts of production and commerce, so long will his time be adjudged of greater value than woman's'.[114] After 1881, when *Scribner's* became *The Century*, it became increasingly secular in outlook, promoting science (publishing an essay by Thomas Edison on roentgen rays in 1896), publishing essays by atheists, including Bertrand Russell in 1923, and supporting women's suffrage in 1926.

The dual thinking of the *Scribner's* piece regarding pay and opportunity for women was replayed in the essays in the *Loreto Magazine* some twenty-five years later, and these reflect the wider debate in Ireland at the end of the nineteenth century. What is interesting is that they take place in the Loreto school magazine, from which we can only conclude that they were either encouraged or at the least sanctioned by the Loreto Sisters. They are worth quoting at length. An essay in the 1895 Midsummer edition by 'Y.Y.', entitled 'The New Woman', notes (incorrectly) that in the past women were allowed access to education and cites 'Miss Austen' and 'George Eliot' and 'Mrs. Browning' as examples. But, the author continues:

[women] have always exercised a second-rate intellectual capacity ... Let us confess it – women have had their chance as well as men, and they have fallen into their proper position. They are physically weaker and mentally more superficial. They cannot join in men's sports, nor rise high in men's professions. The can be, and should be, educated, mentally and physically, so as to develop all their powers. They can be brilliant musicians, but not great composers; helpful nurses, but not famous surgeons, pleasing writers, but not inspired poets. And they have undoubtedly the right to earn their bread in whatever way they are able, and be paid for it as well as men, provided always that their work

is as good. Those who clamour so loudly to be equal to men should remember that, by the very act, they renounce their claim to woman's privileges. Let them have votes for Parliament, and enter it if they like ... but then let them be content to stand in the tramcar, and push their way at the railway station ...[115]

This piece is followed immediately by 'Another View of "Woman's Progress"' by 'M.E.', in which the writer states:

> If we look at the lives of our sisters at the beginning of the century [we see that] the prejudices, the so-called safeguards of a most narrow-minded age, fettered and bound them down [but] now take a rapid glance at the bands of noble women and girl-professionals of to-day. Laurel-crowned pioneers of our cause, they have sounded the trumpet of freedom from unjust trammels, and are daily adding recruits to their ranks in their chosen careers of science, medicine, law, art, and literature. In their train follow the home workers ... They, too, are coming forward, in no small measure, to take part in the grand struggle, and to help their professional sisters by their intelligent sympathy. They also do good work by interesting themselves in schools, visiting the sick the old, and the destitute ... There are churches to be decorated, bazaars and concerts for charities to be worked up, and impulse given to literary circles ...[116]

This second piece reflects the contemporaneous notion that, regardless of education, middle-class women were expected to engage in philanthropic and cultural activities. Indeed, early feminists were anxious not to omit these for fear of claims by their opponents that they were 'unsexing' women. But the language employed in this piece is intriguing: 'our sisters'; 'the so-called safeguards' of a 'most narrow-minded age'; 'fettered and bound'; 'our cause'; 'the trumpet of freedom'; 'the ranks'; 'the grand struggle'; 'professional sisters'. It is rhetorically militant and military, designed to inspire and reassure, and by including 'home workers' (note the term 'workers' rather than 'makers', 'wives', etc.) the writer establishes an all-inclusive cohort of womanhood. But this is not an early feminist tract; it is an article in the magazine of Loreto on the Green, Dublin, written and produced by schoolgirls.

But, despite the evident influence of early feminist thought, the tension of the dual role underlies other essays. This is perhaps best illustrated by Marion Mulhall's 1897 contribution, in which the schoolgirl sets out to demonstrate that the 'New Woman' is in fact nothing of the sort: 'Woman has, from the earliest ages, aspired to a higher position than that accorded her by man. Her position in those primitive times was certainly not that given to her by the great Creator, *but one which arose out of the existing forms of Society* [*sic*, my emphasis].' We cannot know if the writer was aware of the insight implied by her last sentence where, in effect, she employs the theory of social reproduction to denounce the role assigned to women in late nineteenth-century Ireland. Man, being physically stronger, has assumed a dominant role ever since the evolution of the earliest communities, when physical strength was necessary for the survival of the group. However – highlighting the advantages of an education in the classics – she also refers to Strabo's observations regarding Celtic women accompanying their husbands into battle and how those of the German tribes had fought the legions of Marius. Accepting that 'girls should be taught to earn their bread in an honourable and 'suitable' occupation, and, above all, that they should be 'well trained in domestic economy', Mulhall proceeds to critique the curriculum of Irish schools:

> The present age is one of rapid progress, and it is almost a necessity for girls to know two or three modern languages … The art of education is, or should be, progressive, and many distinguished authorities, both in England and America, think the system of education in these countries is too exclusively literary …[117]

Mulhall is writing in summer 1897. February of that year saw the publication of the first report of the Commission on Manual and Practical Instruction (Belmore Commission). The Commission was established in response to growing concern regarding the lack of practical and manual subjects offered in Irish national schools. The final report of the commission was published in June 1898 and included the following recommendation:

> We may at once express our strong conviction that Manual and Practical Instruction ought to be introduced, as far as possible, into all schools where it does not at present exist, and that, in those schools where it does exist, it ought to be largely developed and extended.

We are satisfied that such a change will not involve any detriment to the literary education of the pupils, while it will contribute largely to develop their faculties, to quicken their intelligence, and to fit them better for their work in life.[118]

Writing four or five months later, Mulhall noted that a literary/classical education was increasingly being scrutinised by the authorities as to its general usefulness, and concluded:

The requirements of our own time point to the urgency of making technical, practical and manual instruction a principal feature of education. Industrial teaching does not mean a lessening of intellectual vigour, and there is no reason why the discipline of head and hand should not flourish together, side by side ...[119]

Certainly, the reports of the Belmore Commission were being discussed in the public press some months before Mulhall's essay but her piece illustrates her, and presumably her peers', familiarity with debates concerning educational policy, and also that they had taken positions on various sides of the discussion. Hence we find in the summer of 1898 – the same period that witnessed the publication of the final report of the Belmore Commission Report – an article by W.Z. Ella Hannon in the magazine, ostensibly about the role of poetry in education. However, the essay addresses the fundamental issue of the purpose of education in terms of the perennial distinction between liberal and vocational forms. Addressing the rhetorical question as to why one should study poetry, surely a private pleasure, Hannon muses that if, as some hold, education is to be entirely utilitarian, to do with mastering skills that might be called into use 'at some future period', the advocates of this view would, surely, then 'set aside all branches of knowledge, the end of which is not plainly visible'.[120] But this, she argues, is to misunderstand the purpose of education, which is 'the forming and perfecting of intellect'.[121]

These essays are not untypical of other school publications at the time, but they are particularly articulate and demonstrate the level of interest in topical affairs and discussion taking place in this school at a particular moment in history. Behind them lies a body of silent teachers, mostly Religious. Did they facilitate debate on these topics? Did they lead the girls to editorials or press articles of note to spark their interest, and was the general culture of the school one of intellectual curiosity and engagement? There is much evidence from later decades to suggest that they did.[122]

Another striking demonstration of the intellectual vitality of this school, captured at a transitional moment in Irish history, appeared in 1900 when the school magazine marked the visit of Queen Victoria (aged 81) to Loreto on the Green.[123] Enthused by the increasingly popular Irish cultural and linguistic revival, the review of the royal visit appears alongside other pieces about the Irish language and history. The school magazine, like others such as the *Clongownian* and *Belvederian*, which so poignantly captured the tensions aroused by the Easter Rising and the involvement of past pupils in the Great War, perfectly reflects wider social and political events.[124] Hence the 1901 Christmas edition includes a drama entitled *Oisin*, an article about the Irish language and another about Thomas Davis signed by 'A Grand-Daughter of a "Young Irelander", Loreto College, Stephen's Green'. In the summer edition, 'Hugh Kennedy B.A., Auditor of the Literary and Historical Society, University College, St. Stephen's Green' praises the 'Sisters of Loreto' who 'had determined to give their pupils facilities in the study of the Irish language'.[125]

In the Christmas edition of 1902, the influence of the Revival permeates all. The articles include 'A Summer School in Kerry' (a course in Irish run in Glenbeigh). The article, by past pupil Clare O'Sullivan, captures the mood:

> England knew, as did Rome in the days of old, that the surest way to kill the spirit of a nation was to deprive it of its own language … But the spirit of the nation was hard to kill. The natives of the Glen are intensely Irish in every way … Gaelic is the language of their home life; they are Irish in their amusements, in their mode of thought … A holiday in a place like this is an unfailing Irish antidote to counteract the effects of the Anglicisation of centuries …
>
> And we have sore need to stand together in this, the latest struggle in Ireland's chequered career. It is a bloodless fight, this for the restoration of our language, but none the less fierce and desperate for that. It has been waged for years, in silence and in solitude, against crushing persecution, against the most scathing ridicule and contempt … Perhaps this resurrection of our old tongue is the first fruit of that seed of generous blood shed apparently so vainly for Ireland …[126]

This issue also carries one of the first essays in the Irish language. The date of this edition (1902) coincides with that of O'Donnell's *The Ruin of Education in Ireland*, in which he described the teaching Religious as 'clerical smatterers'.[127]

While there is no doubt that, to modern sensibilities, schools were conservative and restrictive, reflecting the values and customs of their time, the evidence of the *Loreto Magazine* suggests (and there is no reason to suspect that it differed to any great degree from similar school publications, given women's involvement in the Gaelic League and entry to the National University of Ireland in 1913) that its mixture of feminism, inculcation of independent thought and cultural politics implies that, more widely, school cultures existed that were far removed from the archetypical late-Victorian model we have presumed.

Conclusion

Much remains unknown about the life of women in nineteenth-century schools. This essay has focused primarily on the experiences of female pupils, but we have much to learn about those who taught them. Educational studies have, as we suggested at the beginning of this essay, tended to focus upon the leading lights of education for girls, those who led high-profile campaigns, gave evidence before parliamentary enquiries, founded prestigious schools or records of their work. What we know less about are the ordinary teachers and their pupils. In particular, we know very little about those from modest backgrounds. Many of these attended the convent 'pay' schools operated by the Mercy and Presentation Sisters. These, usually urban schools, catered for girls whose parents could not meet the cost of boarding school but in most other respects were similar. Professor James Kavanagh explained before the Powis Commission that the schools were 'middle class schools ... above the primary while being below the regular convent boarding school'.[128] Pay schools reflected a crucial characteristic of nineteenth-century life that transcended gender and, on occasion, religion. They were, Kavanagh explained, 'an acknowledgement of the social distinctions that existed in society'.[129] Pay schools were inexpensive but never attracted large numbers. Because convent national schools retained pupils until they were as old as 16, they grew increasingly popular with the expanding Catholic middle class and formed, along with convent boarding schools, the two pillars of girls' education in nineteenth- and twentieth-century Ireland. The creation of the Intermediate system forced secondary-type schools to change their curriculum to suit the payment-by-results model. The extent to which this change reflected or facilitated the continued expansion of the Catholic mercantile middle class remains uncertain but, as the nineteenth century drew to a close, Catholic (and Protestant) parents recognised that by securing the Intermediate examinations their daughters could, at last, acquire a modicum of financial independence. This was significant for two reasons. Firstly, the swelling ranks of middle-class women entering the workplace in this period could now do so in possession of a formal, certified qualification. Secondly, it quickly facilitated the changing middle-class perception of schooling by equating education with opportunity in terms of labour. The disappearance of 'accomplishments' can hardly be a cause for regret, but the close identification of education with the possibilities of the marketplace was contested, at least by Ella Hannon, who tried to persuade her peers at Loreto on the Green that education was 'the forming and perfecting of intellect', rather than simply the 'mastering [of] stuff'.[130]

It is Ella's voice that has been missing in the grand narrative of education. One wonders where her incisive schoolgirl's mind led her in later life. Perhaps she and similarly clever schoolgirls were the precursors, for example, of Kathleen M. Lowndes, a past pupil of Dominican Convent in Muckross, who, when named as the first female president of the Veterinary Medical Association of Ireland, told the media that 'she accepted the office because she was a staunch feminist and regarded it as a challenge',[131] or of retired teacher Margo [pseudonym], who described the Dominican nuns who taught her in the 1950s as 'feminists with a big F',[132] or of the girls attending Sacred Heart School in Roscrea in the 1940s, who were praised by a (male) Department of Education inspector as 'able to give their own views on every question and to support these views [and] not ready to accept his if he disagreed with what they considered right',[133] or of Sister Fionnuala's [pseudonym] teachers who, also in the 1940s, created a school culture where 'it was ... in your consciousness that women should be leaders',[134] or of Sister Patrick who, at Muckross College, gave the girls 'books which were banned at the time, but

which she knew were good literature'.[135] What Ella Hannon and
her peers' essays demonstrate is that they engaged intelligently
and enthusiastically with the beguiling times in which they lived,
and they cannot have been alone in this. The period witnessed
the beginnings of a feminist consciousness in Ireland, the gradual
opening of university education to women, and the intellectual
exhilaration of the Revival, with its attendant opportunities for
women to share platforms with men in public debate or mix as
equals at Irish language classes and summer Gaeltacht retreats. These
essays reveal young Irish women interrogating old assumptions in
a new world. In 'talk[ing] together about ourselves' they enter into
acts of self-definition, couched as debates about their place within a
school system that is beginning to offer significant opportunities but
is increasingly at odds with definitions of liberal education which
some of them hold as fundamental intellectual positions. Again,
these girls' self-scrutiny as women migrates into, or includes, new
debates about the self and nationhood, and self-definition in terms
of opposition – in 'counteract[ing] the effects of the Anglicisation
of centuries'.[136] In these essays new thoughts for a new country are
articulated in new languages as pupils intellectually and socially
redefine themselves and the 'place' they inhabit: 'professional sisters'
interrogating a 'narrow-minded age' or 'need[ing] to stand together
in … the latest struggle in Ireland's chequered career' – the 'fight for
the restoration of [its] language'. These essays reveal young women
interrogating their *place*, both internally and externally; they are
iridescent with the earnestness of youth, certainly, but they demonstrate the importance of school culture in facilitating (or subduing)
the early steps towards intellectual independence and the donning of
adult personality.

Schools influence their pupils, often in remarkable ways.[137] Peter
Parker's study of the British public school ethos and the Great War
is a sobering testament to this relationship in dark times.[138] Anne
V. O'Connor noted in 1986 that 'by 1900 Catholic girls in Ireland were
educationally poised to enter the new century on more equal terms
with boys than could reasonably have seemed possible 20 years earlier'.[139]
Some of these girls were shaped by and later shaped schools, and in doing
so they shaped the early decades of Irish independence, but in what
ways? We have attempted here to give voice to a very small number of
them and, in doing so, have suggested that their lives are a 'place' we still

do not know. It is time, in Jane Martin's words, to seek 'a theoretically informed "people's history" of education that learns from life histories' and that democratises 'the act of historical production' by 'tak[ing] into account the people who inhabit classrooms and the forms, dimensions and the meaning of their experience, to ensure ... the story ... [is] not forgotten'.[140]

Appendix

SUSAN M. PARKES

List of Irish Students who attended Cambridge Women's Colleges College 1875–1904 with year of entry and school

Newnham College

1875	Mary Hutton	–
	Alice M. Townshend	University Coll. Bristol
	Mary H. Townshend	University of Bristol
1878	Elizabeth Finlay	St Leonard's-on-Sea
	Alice Mary Lloyd	private school
1879	Agnes Perry	Bedford College, London
	Lucy Ann Earl	D'Israeli School, Rathvilly
1880	Frances Ralph Gray	Plymouth High School
1881	Lizzie Davison	Queen's University, Belfast
	Anne W. Richardson	private school
1882	Henrietta White	Alexandra College
1885	Edith Badham	–
	Constance M. Crommelin	Alexandra College
1888	Elizabeth Graham	Victoria College, Belfast
	Blanche Vernon	private tuition
	Mary Pakenham Walsh	French School, Bray

1889	Ilsa Bury	private school
1890	Elizabeth Lyster	Alexandra College
	Yolande G. Raymond	Clergy Daughters' School, Bristol
	Edith Stoney	private tuition
1891	Rosa Patterson	Victoria College, Belfast
	Alice Shackelton	Alexandra College
	Mary Stokes	Howell's School, Llandaff
1892	Margaret Gardner	Downpatrick
1895	Maria H. Meade	St Margaret's Hall
1897	Margaret A. MacAlister	Roedean School
	Hertha H.C. Sollas	Alexandra College
1899	Helen Letitia Dodd	McCutcheon's School, Dublin
1901	Geraldine A. Townshend	private tuition
1904	Annie Cecilia Aimers	Alexandra College
1905	Edith Stewart Dodd	Alexandra College

Newnham Staff

1880	Mary Jane Martin	private tuition
1882	Jane Lee	Alexandra College
1903	Igerna B. J. Sollas	Alexandra College

Irish Students who attended Girton College

1869–70	Isabella Townsend	private tuition
1882	Amy Barrington	private tuition
	Charlotte Young	private tuition
1883	Anna Hogben	day school, L'derry
	Catherine Jebb	Alexandra College
1884	Hilda Pomeroy	Cheltenham Ladies' College
	Mary Raymond	Clergy Daughters' School, Bristol
	Georgina Young	Alexandra College
1885	Mary Kennedy	Ladies' Collegiate School L'derry
1886	Alice Everett	Methodist College
	Annie Russell	Victoria College, Belfast
1887	Clara Carnegie	Alexandra College
	Mary McAfee	Methodist College
1888	Sara Annesley	private school and in Germany
	Wilhelmina Joyce	private school L'derry

	Evelyn Macdonald	Queen's School, Chester
	Annie Warnock	L'derry High School
1889	Mary Dick	L'derry High School
	Jane Pollock	Victoria College
1891	Margaret Cunningham	Victoria College, L'derry
1893	Etelka Beamish	at home
1894	Elizabeth Leebody	private school, Magee College
1896	Katherine McCutcheon	Methodist College
1897	Edith Bailey	private school, L'derry
1899	Edith Thompson	High School, Chiswick
1900	Leota Bennet	private school, Belfast
	Violet Bolton	Victoria High School, L'derry
	Sara Smiley	Methodist College
1901	Mary Acheson	Alexandra School, Portadown
	Elizabeth McCallum	Victoria College, Belfast
1902	Annie Cunningham	Alexandra College
1903	Charlotte Warner	Victoria High School, L'derry
1904	Hanna Dunne	private school, Waterford
	Margaret Willis	Brookvale Collegiate School, Belfast
1905	Marjorie Long	Victoria College, Belfast
	Anne Shillington	Methodist College
1906	Margaret Brown	Victoria School, L'derry

Mistresses of Girton

1885–1903 Elizabeth Welsh	home and private school
1925–51 Edith Major	Methodist College

Girton Staff

1888	Margaret Meyer	North London Collegiate
1899	Mildred Barwell	Baker Street High School
1911	Marian Beard	Alexandra College

Notes

Introduction

1 Germaine Greer, *The Female Eunuch* (London: Fourth Estate, 1970; this ed. 2012), 332-3.

2 Maryann Valiulis and Mary O'Dowd (eds), *Women and Irish History* (Dublin: Wolfhound Press, 1997), 9.

3 Sheila Rowbotham, *Hidden from History: 300 Years of Women's Oppression and the Fight Against It* (London: Pluto Press, 1975); Renate Bridenthal and Claudia Koonz, *Becoming Visible: Women in European History* (London: Houghton Mifflin, 1977).

4 Valiulis and O'Dowd (eds), *Women and Irish History*, 9.

5 *Ibid.*

6 In Judith Harford, *The Opening of University Education to Women in Ireland* (Dublin: Irish Academic Press, 2008), 30.

7 See Susan M. Parkes (ed.), *A Danger to the Men? A History of Women in Trinity College Dublin, 1904–2004* (Dublin: Lilliput Press, 2004) *passim.*

8 While largely only relevant to middle-class women it is nonetheless worth recording that in Britain, in the 1880s, both the Dress Reform Movement and the Rational Dress Society strove to inform society about the health implications of fashionable, restrictive clothing for women. In this period manufacturers routinely advertised corsets that would ensure a small waist even in the third trimester of pregnancy. The less restrictive garments

chosen by advocates of 'rational dress' often adorn the female figures in the paintings of the Pre-Raphaelite Brotherhood. On the regulation of the female body see note 14 below.

9   See Lucinda Hawksley, *March Women March: Voices of the Women's Movement from the First Feminist to Votes for Women* (Andre Deutsch Books, London, 2013)

10 Joan N. Burstyn, *Victorian Education and the Ideal of Womanhood* (New Brunswick, NJ: Rutgers University Press, 1984), 30.

11 Cited in *ibid.*, 33.

12 Cited in *ibid.*, 38.

13 *The Irish Times*, 4 May 1878.

14 On the regulation of schoolgirls see Brendan Walsh and Majella McSharry, 'Fostering Complicit Femininity: Epoch, Education and the Young Female Body', in Peter Kelly and Annelies Kamp (ed.), *A Critical Youth Studies for the 21st Century* (Leiden: Brill, 2014).

15 See, for example, Anne V. O'Connor and Susan Parkes, *Gladly Learn and Gladly Teach: Alexandra School, 1866–1966* (Dublin: Blackwater Press, 1984); Anne V. O'Connor, 'The revolution in girls' secondary education in Ireland 1860–1910', in Caitriona Clear (ed.), *Nuns in Nineteenth-Century Ireland* (Dublin: Gill and Macmillan, 1987); Deirdre Raftery and Susan Parkes, *Female Education in Ireland 1700–1900* (Dublin: Irish Academic Press, 2007); Harford, *The Opening of University Education to Women in Ireland*.

16 *Intermediate Education (Ireland) Commission. Appendix to the Final Report of the Commissioners. Part II. Miscellaneous Documents* (Dublin: Stationery Office, 1899). [C.-9513]. Section E. – Digest of Minutes of Evidence, 274.

17 *Ibid.*, 246.

18 *Intermediate Education (Ireland) Commission. Appendix to the Final Report of the Commissioners. Part II. Miscellaneous Documents* (Dublin: Stationery Office, 1899). [C.-9513]. Section E. – Digest of Minutes of Evidence, 283.

19 Ged Martin, *Hughes Hall Cambridge 1885–2010* (London: Third Millennium, 2010), 55-56.

20 See Margaret McCurtain and Mary O'Dowd (eds), *Women in Early Modern Ireland* (Dublin: Wolfhound Press, 1991). See also Deirdre Raftery, *Women and Learning in English Writing, 1600–1900* (Dublin: Four Courts Press, 1997).

21 Oxoniensis, 'The Education of Women', *Christian Observer* 64 (London, 1865), 547.

22 'Miss Becker on the Mental Characteristics of the Sexes', *The Lancet* (London, 1868), 320.

23 Remarks by R.S. Charnock in Emma Wallington's 'The Physical
    and Intellectual Capacities of Woman Equal to Men', *Anthropologia*
    (London Anthropological Society, 1874), 563.

1. 'Starry Eyed'

1   Sean Duke, *How Irish Scientists Changed the World* (Dublin: Londubh,
    2013).

2   Mark McCartney and Andrew Whittaker (eds), *Physicists of Ireland:
    Passion and Precision* (Bristol and Philadelphia: Institute of Physics
    Publishing, 2003).

3   Ken Houston (ed.), *Creators of Mathematics: The Irish Connection*
    (Dublin: University College Dublin Press, 2000).

4   Deasmumhan Ó Raghallaigh, *Three Centuries of Irish Chemists*
    (Cork: Cork University Press, 1941).

5   Charles Mollan, *Its Part of What We Are: Some Irish Contributors to
    the Development of the Chemical and Physical Sciences*, 2 vols (Dublin:
    Royal Dublin Society, 2007). The women included are Catherine
    Boyle (*c.*1588–1630), Agnes Mary Clerke (1842–1907), Mary Ward
    (1827–69), Margaret Lindsay Huggins (1848–1915) and Kathleen
    Lonsdale (1903–71).

6   Charles Mollan, William Davis and Brendan Finucane (eds), *Irish
    Innovators in Science and Technology*, (Dublin: Royal Irish Academy, 2002);
    Charles Mollan, William Davis and Brendan Finucane (eds), *Some
    People and Places in Irish Science and Technology* (Dublin: Royal Irish
    Academy, 1985); Charles Mollan, William Davis and Brendan Finucane
    (eds), *More People and Places in Irish Science and Technology* (Dublin: Royal
    Irish Academy, 1990). The women included are Mary Ball (1812–98),
    Agnes Mary Clerke (1842–1907), Phyllis Clinch (1901–84), Margaret
    Lindsay Huggins (1848–1915), Ellen Hutchins (1755–1815), Matilda
    Knowles (1864–1933), Kathleen Lonsdale (1903–71), Annie Massy
    (1867–1931), Mary Parsons, Countess of Rosse (1813–85), Dorothy
    Stopford Price (1890–1954) and Mary Ward (1827–69).

7   Mollan, Davis and Finucane (eds), *Irish Innovators in Science and
    Technology*, iii.

8   Susan McKenna-Lawlor, *Whatever Shines Should Be Observed
    [quicquid nited notandum]* (Dublin: Samton, 1998).

9   Mary Mulvihill (ed.), *Stars, Shells and Bluebells: Women Scientists and
    Pioneers* (Dublin: WITS, 1997).

10 Mary Mulvihill (ed.), *Lab Coats and Lace: The Lives and Legacies of
    Inspiring Irish Women Scientists and Pioneers* (Dublin: WITS, 2009).

11 www.siliconrepublic/innovation, accessed 1 October 2013.
    The chosen winner was Dorothy Stopford Price.

12   McKenna-Lawlor, *Whatever Shines Should Be Observed*, 11.

13   For example, Mary Ward wrote as the 'Hon. Mrs. W.'.

14   Helena C.G. Chesney, 'The young lady of the lichens' in Mulvihill (ed.), *Stars, Shells and Bluebells*, 28-39.

15   Intermediate Education (Ireland) Act 1878.

16   See, for example, Mary Cullen (ed.), *Girls Don't Do Honours: Irish Women in Education in the 19th and 20th Centuries* (Dublin: Women's Education Bureau, 1987); Susan Parkes, 'Intermediate education for girls', in Deirdre Raftery and Susan M. Parkes (eds), *Female Education in Ireland 1700–1900* (Dublin: Irish Academic Press, 2007), 69-104; Susan M. Parkes and Judith Harford, 'Women and higher education in Ireland', in Raftery and Parkes (eds), *Female Education in Ireland 1700–1900*, 105-43; Anne V. O'Connor, 'Influences affecting girls' secondary education in Ireland, 1860–1910', in *Archivium Hibernicum*, 41 (1986), 83-98; Judith Harford, *The Opening of University Education to Women in Ireland* (Dublin: Irish Academic Press, 2008); Eileen Breathnach, 'Women and higher education in Ireland', in *The Crane Bag*, 4 (1) (1980), 47-54.

17   *Report of the President of Queen's College, Belfast, for the session 1882–3*, p. 5, H.C. 1883 [C 3758], xxvi, 317-42. The Queen's College in Cork first admitted women in 1885 and the Queen's College in Galway in 1888. Trinity College Dublin admitted women in 1904 and from 1908, with the passing of the Universities' Act, women were admitted to all degrees in Ireland's universities, including the new National University of Ireland.

18   Denis Crowley, 'Chemistry', in James Meenan and Desmond Clarke (eds), *RDS: The Royal Dublin Society, 1731–1981* (Dublin, 1981) 169.

19   *Report of the local Committee to the Subscribers to the Local Fund, with the List of committees, statement of Accounts, and list of Subscribers [to the British Association Dublin meeting 185]7* (Dublin: 1858) 20.

20   *Report from the Commission on the Science and Art Department in Ireland, Vol. I. 1868–9*, p 400, H.C. 1868–9 [4103], xxiv. The *Freeman's Journal* of 2 April 1870 reported that Trinity College Dublin established examinations for women (twenty-eight candidates presented themselves) and 'the successful candidates will receive notifications of their success addressed to their residences'.

21   *Thirteenth Annual Report of the Dublin Mechanics' Institution, Lower Abbey Street; presented by the retiring Board of Directors, January 13, 1851* (Dublin: Mechanics' Institution, 1851), 8.

22   John Sproule (ed.), *The Irish Industrial Exhibition of 1853: A detailed catalogue of its contents, with critical dissertations, statistical information,*

and accounts of manufacturing processes in the different departments
(Dublin: McGlashan, 1854).

23 A.T.Q. Stewart, *Belfast Royal Academy: The First Century, 1785–1885*
(Antrim: BRA, 1985); quoted by Helena C.G. Chesney,
'Enlightenment and education', in J.W. Foster and H.C.G. Chesney
(eds), *Nature in Ireland: A Scientific and Cultural History* (Dublin:
Lilliput, 1997), 380.

24 *Reports from the Select Committees on Foundation Schools and Education
in Ireland; together with the Minutes of Evidence, Appendix and Index*
[Wyse] Part I: 1835, Part II: 1836, p. 327, H.C. 1835 (630). Evidence
of D.B. Bullen, 13 August 1835.

25 Kathleen Lonsdale, 'Women in science: reminiscences and
reflections', in *Impact of Science on Society*, 20:1 (1969), 46.

26 See Clara Cullen, 'The Museum of Irish Industry and the Irish
people', in Michael S. O'Neill, Clara Cullen, Colman Dennehy
(eds*)*, *History Matters* (Dublin: University College Dublin School
of History and Archives, 2004), 23-32; Clara Cullen, 'Women,
the Museum of Irish Industry, and the pursuit of scientific learning
in nineteenth century Dublin', in Ciara Meehan and Emma Lyons
(eds), *History Matters II* (Dublin: University College Dublin School
of History and Archives, 2006), 9-19; Clara Cullen, '"Laurels for
fair as well as manly brows": women at Dublin's Museum of Irish
Industry, 1854–1867', in Mulvihill (ed.), *Lab Coats and Lace*, 1-13;
Clara Cullen, 'The Museum of Irish Industry, Robert Kane and
education for all in the Dublin of the 1850s and 1860s', in *History
of Education* 38 (2009), 99-113; Clara Cullen, 'Women and the
pursuit of scientific knowledge in mid-Victorian Dublin', in Donna
Spalding Andréolle and Véronique Molinari (eds), *Women and
Science, 17th Century to Present: Pioneers, Activists and Protagonists*
(Newcastle-upon-Tyne: Cambridge Scholars, 2011), 89-98;
Patrick Keating, 'Sir Robert Kane and industrial education at the
Museum of Irish Industry and Queen's College, Cork' (MEd thesis,
University College, Dublin, 1979).

27 The building at 51-52 St Stephen's Green which housed the
museum is still in existence. It is now an office of the Department
of Justice and Equality. For a history of the building see Simon
Lincoln, *Mansions, Museums and Commissioners: An Architectural
History of the Office of Public Works on St. Stephen's Green* (Dublin:
Office of Public Works, 2002).

28 Museum of Irish Industry, *General Descriptive Guide to the Museum of
Irish Industry, Dublin* (Dublin: [Thom], 1857), 3.

29 *Ibid.*, 3.

30 *Report from the Select Committee on Scientific Instruction; together with the Proceedings of the Committee, Minutes of Evidence and Appendix ... 1868*, 152, 1867–8, H.C. (432), xv, 1.

31 *Report upon the Royal Dublin Society, the Museum of Irish Industry, and on the System of Scientific Instruction in Ireland ... 1862*, 94, H.C. 1863 [3180], xvii, Pt. I, 1.

32 According to family records, his father John Kean (d. 1832), who came from Westmeath, settled in Dublin, married Eleanor Troy, the niece of the Catholic Archbishop of Dublin, and was a United Irishman who had been forced in 1798 to flee to France. John Kean changed his name to John Kane when he returned to Ireland in 1803.

33 Robert John Kane, *The Industrial Resources of Ireland*, 2nd ed. (Dublin: Hodges and Smith, 1845), ix.

34 *The Irish Times*, 21 October 1859.

35 *Freeman's Journal*, 29 May 1856.

36 *Freeman's Journal*, 7 October 1856.

37 Government School of Science applied to the Arts, Museum of Irish Industry, *Programme of Educational Arrangements for the Session of 1856–1857* (Dublin: Thom, 1856).

38 *Third Report of the Department of Science and Art*, 191, H.C. 1856 [2123] xxiv. 1.

39 Department of Science and Art, *Annual reports*, 1–13 (London: HMSO, 1854–67).

40 *Freeman's Journal*, 29 May 1856.

41 *Ibid.*

42 *Saunder's News-letter*, 26 May 1856; *Freeman's Journal*, 29 May 1856.

43 *Fourth Report of the Department of Science and Art ... [1856]*, 99, H.C. 1857 Session 2 [2240], xx, 1; *Sixth Report of the Science and Art Department ... [1858]*, 73-4, H.C. 1859, Session 1 [2502], xxi, Pt. 2, 433; *Thom's ... 1857* (Dublin: Thom, 1857), 1305; *Saunder's*, 26 May 1856; *Freeman's Journal*, 29 May 1856; *Evening Post*, 27 November 1856, 11 May 1858; *Daily Express*, 14 June 1858.

44 *Freeman's Journal*, 15 June 1858.

45 *Thom's Irish Directory and Official Almanac ... 1857* (Dublin: Thom, 1857), 1018; *Thom's ... 1861* (Dublin: Thom, 1861), 1335; *Thom's ... 1867* (Dublin: Thom, 1867), 470, 1356.

46 *Freeman's Journal*, 21 October 1859.

47 *Daily Express*, 22 December 1858. Both Hester and Harriet Harman, then at the School of Art in Cork, were medal winners at the national exhibitions in 1854. In 1856 all three Harmans, Harriet E., Henrietta E. and Hester Anne, won awards at the School of Art in Dublin; in 1860 Harriet and Hester were on the prize winner lists

of the National Art Competition; and in 1861 and 1862, Harriet
E. Harman was awarded prizes in the national competition.

48 University College Dublin Archives (UCDA), Museum of Irish
    Industry monthly consolidated cash accounts, 1853–59 (UCDA MII/5).

49 1901 England Census, http://ancestry.co.uk, accessed 3 February 2014.

50 *Report upon the Royal Dublin Society, the Museum of Irish Industry,
    and on the System of Scientific Instruction in Ireland ... 1862*, 97, H.C.,
    1863 [3180], xvii Pt. I, 1.

51 *Thom's ... 1864* (Dublin: Thom, 1864), 1633; *Thom's ... 1866* (Dublin:
    Thom, 1866), 1787; *Thom's ... 1872* (Dublin: Thom, 1872), 1828.

52 Anne V. O'Connor and Susan M. Parkes, *Gladly Learn and Gladly
    Teach: Alexandra College and School, 1866–1966* (Dublin: Blackwater
    Press, 1984), 4.

53 *Eleventh Report of the Department of Science and Art*, 210, H.C. 1864
    [3335] xix, Pt. I. 1; *Twelfth Report of the Department of Science and Art*,
    260-1, H.C. 1865 [3476] xvi, 301.

54 Katherine to Alexander Leeper, 6 March 1886; quoted by John
    Poynter, *Doubts and Uncertainties: A Life of Alexander Leeper*
    (Melbourne: Melbourne University Press, 1997), 145.

55 Katherine to Alexander Leeper, 12 July 1921; quoted by Poynter,
    Doubts and Uncertainties, 399.

56 *Report from the Commission on the Science and Art Department in
    Ireland*, Vol.2, Minutes of evidence, appendix and index, 374,
    H.C. 1868–69 [4103-1], xxiv, 43.

57 *Freeman's Journal*, 21 October 1859.

58 *The Irish Times*, 4 October 1861.

59 *Report upon the Royal Dublin Society, the Museum of Irish Industry,
    and on the System of Scientific Instruction in Ireland*, 97, H.C., 1863
    [3180], xvii. Pt. I. 1.

60 *Sixth Report of the Science and Art Department ... [1858]*, 73, H.C. 1859,
    Session 1 [2502], xxi, Pt. 2, 433; *Tenth Report of the Science and Art
    Department ... [1862]*, 216-17, H.C. 1863 [3143], xvi, 21; *Daily Express*,
    11 June 1858; *The Irish Times*, 12 April 1861; *Evening Packet*, 14 April 1862.

61 Lydia Ernestine Becker, 'On the study of science by women',
    in *Contemporary Review*, x (1869), 396.

62 UCDA, Royal College of Science for Ireland (RCScI). Minutes of
    meeting of council, 28 November 1867 (UCDA, RCSI/1).

63 *Ibid.*, 28 November and 7 December 1867 (UCDA, RCSI/1).

64 Becker, 'On the study of science by women', 395.

65 'Return from Alexandra College', *Royal Commission on ... primary
    education (Ireland): Vol. VIII, miscellaneous papers and returns ...*, 241-3,
    H.C. 1870 [C.6 –VII], xxviii Pt.V, 917.

66 See Brian Kelham, 'The Royal College of Science for Ireland
    (1867–1926)', in *Studies* 56 (1967), 297-309; George Sigerson, 'The Royal
    College of Science for Ireland', in *Modern Ireland: Its Vital Questions, Secret
    Societies and Government; by an Ulsterman* (London: Longmans, 1868),
    197-206; W.F. Barrett, *An Historical Sketch of the Royal College of Science from
    its Foundation to the year 1900* (Dublin: Falconer, 1907).

67 *Report of the Select Committee on Scientific Institutions (Dublin) …
    together with the proceedings of the Committee, minutes of evidence,
    appendix, and index*, H.C. 1864 (495), xiii, 1.

68 Barrett, *An Historical Sketch of the Royal College of Science*, 7-8.

69 Clara Cullen, '"A pure school of science": the Royal College of
    Science for Ireland and scientific education in Victorian Ireland',
    in Juliana Adelman and Éadaoin Agnew (eds), *Science and Technology in
    Nineteenth-Century Ireland* (Dublin: Four Courts Press, 2011), 136-49.

70 *The College of Science for Ireland: its origin and development, with notes on similar
    institutions in other countries and a bibliography of the work published by staff and
    students (1900–1923)* (Dublin: College of Science Association, 1923).

71 *Report of the Commission on the Science and Art Department in Ireland …*,
    2 vols. H.C. 1868–69 [4103], xxiv, 1, H.C. 1868–69 [4103-1], xxiv, 43,
    Vol. 1, xxxiii.

72 *Fifteenth Report of the Department of Science and Art*, 293, H.C. 1867–68
    [4049], xxvii.

73 UCDA, RCScI Council Minute Book, 7 December 1867
    (UCDA, RCSI/1).

74 UCDA, RCScI Register of Occasional and non-Associate Students
    1867/8–1905/6 (RCSI/65).

75 *Sixteenth Report of the Department of Science and Art*, 431, H.C. 1869
    [4136] xxiii.

76 Barrett, *An Historical Sketch of the Royal College of Science*, 9.

77 UCDA, RCScI Register of Associate Students, 1867/8–1904/5
    (RCSI/63).

78 UCDA, RCScI Register of Occasional and non-Associate Students
    1867/8–1905/6 (RCSI/65).

79 O'Connor and Parkes, *Gladly Learn and Gladly Teach*, 50.

80 UCDA, RCScI Register of Occasional and non-Associate Students
    1867/8–1905/6 (RCSI/65).

81 UCDA, RCScI Register of Occasional and non-Associate Students
    1867/8–1905/6 (RCSI/65); Irene Finn, 'Women in the medical
    profession in Ireland, 1876–1919', in Bernadette Whelan (ed.), *Women
    and Paid Work in Ireland, 1500–1830* (Dublin: Four Courts Press, 2000),
    102-19; Laura Kelly, *Irish Women in Medicine, c. 1880s-1920s: Origins,
    Education and Careers* (Manchester: Manchester University Press, 2013).

82 For further information on the RCScI at Merrion Street see Clara Cullen and Orla Feely (eds), *The Building of the State: Science and Engineering with Government on Merrion Street* (Dublin: University College Dublin, 2011) and at www.ucd.ie/merrionstreet.

2. 'The Fun of Being Intellectual'

1 J[ane] L[evett], 'An impression of undergraduate days', 2, Maude Clarke Papers, Somerville College, Oxford, hereafter CP, Obituary and Letters of Appreciation file. Thanks to Somerville College, University of Oxford for permission to quote the Clarke Papers. Levett credits Maude Clarke, hereafter MVC, with teaching her 'the fun of being intellectual'.

2 V.H. Galbraith, hereafter VHG, quoted in Norman Cantor, *Inventing the Middle Ages: The Lives, Works, and Ideas of the Great Medievalists of the Twentieth Century* (New York: William Morrow, 1991), 385.

3 Helen Waddell, hereafter HW, letter to George Pritchard Taylor, hereafter GPT, [November 1915], Helen Waddell Papers at Kilmacrew House, County Down, Northern Ireland, hereafter WP, box 17. Square brackets indicate dates derived from internal evidence. Thanks to Louise Anson for permission to quote from these papers and from HW's unpublished writings held elsewhere.

4 M.T. Clanchy, *Abelard: A Medieval Life* (1997; Oxford: Blackwell, 1999), 328.

5 L[evett], 'An impression of undergraduate days', 2-3, CP, Obituary file.

6 HW to GPT, 21 July 1918, WP, box 16.

7 HW and MVC, *Discipline*, WP, box 5; HW to GPT, 24 September 1918. Jennifer FitzGerald is preparing an edition of *Discipline* for publication.

8 Thanks to Lorraine Daston for pointing this out.

9 O. Douglas, *The Day of Small Things* (London: Hodder & Stoughton, 1930), 188.

10 George Birmingham, *The Hymn Tune Mystery* (1930; Indianapolis: Bobbs-Merrill Company, 1931), 21.

11 MVC and VHG, 'The Deposition of Richard II', *Bulletin of the John Rylands Library, Manchester* 14, no. 1 (Jan. 1930), 125-81, repr. in L.S. Sutherland, hereafter LSS, and M. McKisack (eds), *Fourteenth Century Studies*, hereafter FS (Oxford: Clarendon Press, 1937), 53-98; Gillian Olivier, *The Broomscod Collar* (London: William Heinemann, 1930). I have revised my previous association of *The Broomscod Collar* with MVC's research on the Wilton Diptych; see Jennifer FitzGerald, *Helen Waddell and Maude Clarke: Irishwomen, Friends and Scholars*, hereafter *HW and MC* (Oxford: Peter Lang, 2012), 132.

12 St Hilda's College Centenary Register, 1924; St Hilda's College,
    Oxford, manuscript register of students. Olivier remained in Oxford
    for the academic year 1928/29, taking the Oxford Training Course
    for Teachers, during which she may have discussed new material on
    Richard II with Maude, including the National Gallery's acquisition
    of the Wilton Diptych. Thanks to St Hilda's College for providing
    this information; evidence of MVC's discussing her research appears
    in KMEM's letters, *passim*.

13 K.M.E. Murray, hereafter KMEM, to Kate Maitland Murray,
    hereafter KMM, 15 November 1931, Murray Papers, Accession 9601,
    West Sussex Public Records Office, Chichester, Sussex, hereafter
    MP, box 17. Thanks to West Sussex Public Records Office and to
    John Murray for permission to quote from these papers.

14 Olivier, *The Broomscod Collar*, 44, 119; MVC, 'Forfeitures and Treason in
    1388', *Transactions of the Royal Historical Society*, hereafter *TRHS*, 4th ser.,
    14 (1931), 65–94, repr. in *FS*, 117. Olivier calls her novel 'an imaginative
    biography', claiming to base it 'on a careful study of Richard the Second
    as he appears in contemporary chronicles and records, and in the pages
    of the chief modern authorities on his reign' (Prefatory Note).

15 Samantha Ellis, 'Richard of Bordeaux, London 1933', *Guardian*,
    9 April 2003; Gordon Daviot, *Richard of Bordeaux: A Play in Two Acts*
    (Boston: Little, Brown, 1933).

16 John Gielgud, 'Foreword', in Gordon Daviot, *Plays, 2 vols* (London: Peter
    Davies, 1953), 1, ix; Niloufer Harben, *Twentieth-Century English History
    Plays* (Basingstoke: Macmillan, 1988), 92; MVC's student, Betty Murray,
    reported Oxford gossip that 'the plot and even some of the words' were
    'bagged … from a novel written by one of Clarke's pupils' (KMEM to
    KMM, 17 March 1934), confirmed by Helen Cam twenty-five years
    later: *Historical Novels* (London: Historical Association, 1961), 16.

17 Vera Brittain, *The Dark Tide* (London: Grant Richards, 1923).
    For similarities between MVC and the character, and for MVC's
    reaction to this novel, see *HW and MC*, 95–8.

18 L[evett], 'An impression of undergraduate days', 2–3, CP, Obituary file.

19 HW to Margaret Martin, hereafter MM, [summer 1912], WP, box 11.

20 There was 'intermittent strife' between HW and Smith 'on the
    matter of feminism in the University and other minor feuds', HW
    to GPT, [July/August 1915], WP, box 17.

21 G. Gregory Smith, 'The Middle Scots Anthologies', in A.W. Ward
    and A.R. Waller (eds), *Cambridge History of English Literature*, vol. 2:
    The End of the Middle Ages (Cambridge: Cambridge University
    Press, 1908), 319; William E. Mead, 'The Prologue of the Wife of
    Bath's Tale', *PMLA*, new ser., 9, no, 3 (1901), 397.

22 Myrtle Mann Gillet, 'Woman in German Literature before and after the Reformation', *Journal of English and Germanic Philology* 17, no. 3 (July 1918), 349.

23 HW, Helen Waddell Papers, hereafter QUL, Special Collections and Archive, Queen's University Belfast, MS 18/1/c, 41. Thanks to Queen's University Library for permission to quote from these papers. I have italicised 'Roman' for clarity.

24 HW to MM (spring/summer 1913), WP, box 11; James Legge, *The Chinese Classics: with a Translation, Critical and Exegetical Notes, Prolegomena, and Copious Indexes*, vol. 4, parts 1 and 2 (Hong Kong: At the Author's, 1871).

25 HW refers to Walter de la Mare's review in a letter but the review itself has not been traced, HW to Lynda Grier, 18 June 1923, Lady Margaret Hall Helen Waddell Papers; AE [George Russell], review of HW, *Lyrics from the Chinese, Irish Homestead,* 27 December 1913, 1078. Thanks to Lady Margaret Hall, University of Oxford for permission to quote from the Waddell Papers.

26 See David Burleigh, 'Chinese Originals: Helen Waddell and Arthur Waley' in Jennifer FitzGerald (ed.), *Helen Waddell Reassessed: New Readings,* hereafter *HWR* (Oxford: Peter Lang, 2013), 258–66; Harriet Monroe and Alice Corbin Henderson, 'Introduction', Harriet Monroe (ed.), *The New Poetry: An Anthology* (New York: Macmillan, 1917), xi; and Eunice Tietjens, 'On Translating Chinese Poetry II', *Poetry* 20, no. 8 (September 1922), 328–9. See also Helen Carr, 'Wandering Poets and the Spirit of Romance in Helen Waddell and Ezra Pound' in *HWR*, 246–50.

27 Samuel Waddell to HW, 29 July 1912, WP, box 5. Sam was HW's point of contact with the Celtic Revival, with Gaelic Leaguers such as Robert Lynd, with journalist Jimmy Good and artist Paul Henry; Sam's brother-in-law, Joseph Campbell, was another Irish Imagist. For HW's essays and reviews, see Jennifer FitzGerald (ed.), 'Helen Waddell Bibliography', in *HWR*, 301–5.

28 HW to GPT, [5 November 1916], WP, box 16.

29 Review of HW, *The Wandering Scholars*, hereafter *WS* (London: Constable, 1927), *The Times*, 29 April 1927.

30 HW to GPT, 23 March 1919, WP, box 17.

31 HW to GPT, 21 June 1916, WP, box 16; *HW and MC*, 91–3.

32 'Woman in the Drama before Shakespeare' is published in *HW and MC*, 187–230; see also *HW and MC*, 56–9; Ina Schabert, 'A Double-voiced Discourse: Shakespeare Studies by Women in the Early 20th Century', in Miriam Kauko, Sylvia Mieszkowski and Alexandra Tischel (eds), *Gendered Academia: Wissenschaft und Geschlecterdifferenz 1890–1945* (Munich: Wallstein, 2005), 255–77.

33 HW, lectures and fragments, 'The Mime in the Middle Ages', WP, box 6.

34 HW, draft letter to G.G. Coulton, [spring 1931], WP, box 2. See
    Jennifer FitzGerald, 'Women, Love and Mime: The Evolution of
    The Wandering Scholars' in *HWR*, 81–103.

35 HW, *The Desert Fathers: Translations from the Latin* (London:
    Constable, 1936), viii.

36 HW to MM, [12 May 1925], WP, box 11.

37 In 1930 the University Grants Committee explicitly stated that
    a 'university teaching post should first of all offer to a man the
    prospect of marrying and maintaining himself and his family',
    quoted in Fernanda Perrone, 'Women Academics in England,
    1879–1930', *History of Universities* 12 (1993), 358.

38 HW to MM, [February? 1926], WP, box 11.

39 Gianna Pomata, 'Amateurs by Choice: Women and the Pursuit of
    Independent Scholarship in Twentieth-Century Historical Writing',
    Centaurus 55, no. 22 (May 2013), 196–219.

40 HW, 'Pelagia of Antioch', *Nineteenth Century and After* 107, no. 638
    (April 1930), 556.

41 Review of *WS*, *The Times*, 29 April 1927.

42 Review of *WS*, *British Weekly*, 26 May 1927.

43 *Observer*, 1 May 1927; *The Times*, 31 December 1927.

44 F.M. Powicke, hereafter FMP, review of *WS*, *Scottish Historical
    Review* 24, no. 96 (July 1927), 300.

45 See Jennifer FitzGerald, 'Reading (into) *The Wandering Scholars*:
    The (Inter)textual Text', in *HWR*, 173–95.

46 See reviews of HW, *Mediaeval Latin Lyrics*, hereafter *MLL* (London:
    Constable, 1929): J.H.F. Peile, *Church Quarterly Review* (April 1930),
    167; E.F. J[acob], *English Historical Review*, hereafter *EHR*, 46, no. 181
    (January 1931), 152; Gerard Murphy, review of *MLL*, *Irish Statesman*
    13, no. 20 (January 1930), 395.

47 Reviews of *MLL*: J[acob], 152; D.S. Mirsky, *London Mercury* 16, no. 94
    (August 1927), 416; *Life and Letters* 5, no. 8 (August 1930), 131.

48 Review of *MLL* and Stephen Gaselee, *Book of Medieval Latin Verse*,
    Times Literary Supplement, 26 December 1929, 1095; see HW's
    response, *Times Literary Supplement*, 9 January 1930, 28; Murphy,
    review of *MLL*, 398.

49 John Scattergood, Introduction, *MLL* (Dublin: Four Courts Press,
    2008), xxxiv.

50 Susan Bassnett, 'Transplanting the Seed: Poetry and Translation' in
    Susan Bassnett and André Lefevere, *Constructing Cultures: Essays on
    Literary Translation* (Clevedon: Multilingual Matters, 1998), 74.

51 Peile, review of *MLL*, 170.

52 HW, Preface, *MLL*, xl; xli.

53 HW to William Rothenstein, 22 October [1933], in William Rothenstein, *Since Fifty: Men and Memories, 1922–1939: Recollections* (London: Faber, 1939), 119.

54 See Constant J. Mews, 'Helen Waddell and Heloise: The Continuity of a Learned Tradition', in *HWR*, 21-37.

55 HW, 'Medieval Sojurn', Wings 7, no. 10 (October 1933), 9. The French sentence, which translates as 'She always speak Abelard', is perhaps a mistake for 'Elle parle toujours d'Abelard' – 'she always speaks of Abelard'. However, Stephen Kelly points out that the line as written also 'perhaps inadvertently re-asserts Waddell's strong identification with the philosopher'. Stephen Kelly, 'The Ghost of a Voice: Waddell's Peter Abelard between Benjamin and Collingwood', in *HWR*, 113-14, n19.

56 T.B. Rudmose-Brown, review of HW, *Peter Abelard* (London: Constable, 1933), *Dublin Magazine*, new ser. 9, no. 1 (January-March 1935), 71.

57 HW, *Dublin Magazine*, new ser. 9, no. 2 (April-June 1934), 79.

58 Elizabeth Maslen, 'Women's Novels Between the Wars' in Patrick Parrinder and Andrzej Gasiorek (eds), *The Oxford History of the Novel in English, vol. 4: The Reinvention of the British and Irish Novel 1880–1940* (Oxford: Oxford University Press, 2011), 420.

59 Because medieval ideology considered that the physicality of sex, including 'conjugal voluptuousness', fatally compromised the intellect as well as the soul, Abelard's reputation for chastity had to be maintained for his academic career to advance. Clanchy, *Abelard*, 46.

60 Kelly, 'The Ghost of a Voice', 110; 108.

61 See Mews, 'Helen Waddell and Heloise', 12-16 and Norman Vance, 'Beyond Rome and Geneva', in *HWR*, 219-22; see also Jennifer FitzGerald, '"Love's Martyr or Truth's Martyr": Helen Waddell's *Peter Abelard*', *Colby Quarterly* 36, no. 2 (June 2000), 176-87.

62 HW to Basil Blackett, [1932?], WP, box 2.

63 HW, *Peter Abelard: A Novel* (London: Constable, 1933), 303-4; Mews, 'Helen Waddell and Heloise', *HWR*, 33-4.

64 HW, *Beasts and Saints: Translations* (London: Constable, 1934), xi.

65 HW, *Desert* Fathers, 29; viii.

66 HW to the Association of Writers for Intellectual Liberty, 14 March 1940, For Intellectual Liberty Papers, Cambridge University Library MS. Add. 9369, A6/24. Thanks to the Syndics of Cambridge University Library for permission to quote this letter.

67 HW to E.K. Rand, 4 May 1944, Autograph Letters, Autograph File, Houghton Library, Harvard University.

68 HW, *Lament for Damonis*, tr. from the *Epitaphium Damonis* of John Milton (privately printed, 1943).

69 HW, *More Latin Lyrics: From Virgil to Milton*, ed. Felicitas Corrigan (London: Constable, 1976).

70 HW, *Poetry in the Dark Ages: The Eighth W.P. Ker Memorial Lecture* (Glasgow: Jackson, 1948).

71 Although it too could have been jeopardised by family duty: MVC's mother was institutionalised in 1913 after many years of mental instability, delaying but not preventing MVC's studies at Oxford; see *HW and MC*, 40.

72 HW to George Saintsbury, [21 March 1919], QUL uncatalogued.

73 HW to GPT, 9 November 1919, WP, box 17; KMEM to KMM, 10 March 1934, MP, box 17.

74 HW to MM, [March 1926]; [7 May 1926], WP, box 11.

75 *SCR*, 382; 97-8; 380-1. Mary Macaulay's husband, Frederick Oglivie, was vice-chancellor of Queen's University Belfast from 1934 to 1938. Evangeline Evans, lecturer in modern history at Somerville from 1947 to 1965, was also MVC's student. *SCR*, 107.

76 Harriet Spiegel, 'Mary Dominica Legge (1905–1986)', in Jane Chance (ed.), *Women Medievalists and the Academy* (Madison, WI: University of Wisconsin Press, 2005), 616; 613.

77 Anne Whiteman, 'Lucy Stuart Sutherland, 1903–1980', *Proceedings of the British Academy* 69 (1983), 612-13.

78 *SCR*, 394; 150; 395.

79 KMEM to KMM, 9 March 1929; 16 February 1929, MP, box 18.

80 KMEM to KMM 24 May 1931, MP, box 17. Murray's spelling is very unreliable; the word 'reconstruction' is a guess.

81 KMEM to KMM, 24 May 1931; MVC, 'Purpose of the General Paper', CP, box 1; KMEM to KMM, 12 May 1929, MP, box 18.

82 KMEM to Alice Burnet, 22 March 1931, MP, box 44; KMEM to KMM, 27 October 1929, MP, box 18.

83 FMP, rev. of *FS, Manchester Guardian*, 10 August 1937; Vera Brittain, *Testament of Friendship: the Story of Winifred Holtby* (1940; London: Virago, 1980), 85; KMEM to Alice Burnet, 28 November 1935, MP, box 44.

84 KMEM to Alice Burnet, 28 November 1935, MP, box 44; KMEM to KMM, 8 May 1932, MP, box 17.

85 Kathleen Fitzpatrick, *Solid Bluestone Foundations and Other Memories of a Melbourne Girlhood, 1908–1928* (1983; Melbourne: University of Melbourne Press, 2003), 218.

86 *HW and MC*, 99; 111.

87 MVC to Somerville College Council, 14 March 1919, CP, Testimonials file; *Register of the Priory of the Blessed Virgin at Tristernagh, Transcribed and Edited from the Manuscript at the Cathedral Library, Armagh*, ed. MVC (Dublin: Stationery Office, 1941).

88 William Stubbs, *Constitutional History of England*, 3 vols (Oxford: Clarendon Press, 1874–8), 1, 544; Geoffrey Templeman, 'The History of Parliament in the Light of New Research', *University of Birmingham Historical Journal*, 1, no. 3 (1948), 202-31.

89 MVC, *The Medieval City State: An Essay on Tyranny and Federation in the Later Middle Ages* (London: Methuen, 1926).

90 Helen M. Cam, review of *MRC*, *EHR* 51, no. 204 (October 1936), 701.

91 MVC and VHG, 'Deposition of Richard II', *FS*, 79. *FS* omits the text of 'The Chronicle of Dieulacres Abbey'.

92 *The Times*, 29 January 1930.

93 MVC, 'The Wilton Diptych', *Burlington Magazine* 58 (June 1931), 283-94, repr. in *FS*, 272; J.J.N. Palmer, *England, France and Christendom, 1377–99* (London: Routledge & Kegan Paul, 1972), 243; MVC, 'Wilton Diptych', *FS*, 284-92.

94 John Harvey, 'The Wilton Diptych: A Re-examination', *Archaeologia*, 2nd ser., 98 (1961), 1-29. In 1997 every contributor to a definitive work on the Wilton Diptych referred to the impact of MVC's work and of John Harvey's. Dillan Gordon, 'The Wilton Diptych: An Introduction', in Dillan Gordon, Lisa Monnas and Caroline Elam (eds), *The Regal Image of Richard II and the Wilton Diptych* (London: Harvey Miller, 1997), 20.

95 MVC, 'William of Windsor in Ireland, 1369–1376', *Proceedings of the Royal Irish Academy*, 41C (August 1932), 55-130, repr. in *FS*, 146-241.

96 MVC, 'The Origin of Impeachment', in FMP (ed.), *Oxford Essays in Medieval History presented to Herbert Edward Salter* (Oxford: Clarendon Press, 1934), repr. in *FS*, 265.

97 MVC, 'Committee of Estates and Deposition of Edward II', in J.G. Edwards, VHG and E.F. Jacob (eds), *Historical Essays in Honour of James Tait* (Manchester, for subscribers, 1933), 27-45.

98 KMEM to KMM, 30 October 1932, MP, box 17.

99 MVC to LSS, [28 July 1934], Sutherland Papers, Bodleian Libraries, University of Oxford, box 3. Thanks to Bodleian Libraries, University of Oxford and to the principal of Lady Margaret Hall, Oxford for permission to quote from these papers.

100 MVC, *Medieval Representation and Consent: A Study of the Early Parliaments in England and Ireland, with special reference to the Modus Tenendi Parliamentum,* hereafter *MRC* (London: Longmans, 1936), 109.

101 *MRC*, 261-2; 296-8; 317.

102 Reviews of *MRC*: G[alliard] L[apsley], *Cambridge Review* (5 February 1937), 237; George L. Haskins, *American History Review* 42, no. 4 (July 1937), 733; *Times Literary Supplement*, 2 January 1937, 6. The criticism of Richardson and Sayles focused in particular on the texts of the *Modus*: see *HW* and *MC*, 173.

103 VHG, 'The Modus Tenendi Parliamentum', *Journal of the Warburg
     and Cortauld Institutes* 16, no. 1/2 (1953), 85, n1 and Gailliard Lapsley,
     'The Interpretation of the Statute of York, Part I', *EHR* 56, no. 221
     (January 1941), 24; Edmund Curtis, *History of Medieval Ireland*,
     rev. edn (London: Methuen, 1938), 292 and A.J. Otway-Ruthven,
     A History of Medieval Ireland, 2nd edn (New York: St Martin's Press,
     1980), 355-6 – this despite H.G. Richardson's refutation: 'Historical
     Revision, VII: The Preston Exemplification of the Modus Tenendi
     Parliamentum', *Irish Historical Studies* 3 (1942), 187-92.

104 It is cited regularly from the 1930s to the 1990s. In 1980 it was still
     considered 'the fullest and most complete' analysis of the treatise.
     Nicholas Pronay and John Taylor, Introduction, *Parliamentary Texts
     of the Later Middle Ages* (Oxford: Clarendon Press, 1980), 2. A 2010
     article plays with its title: Peter Crooks, 'Representation and Dissent:
     "Parliamentarism" and the Structure of Politics in Colonial Ireland,
     c. 1370–1420', *EHR* 125, no. 512 (February 2010), 1-34.

105 MVC, 'England C14', 1; 27; 32, CP, box 1.

106 Woodward, 'Memoir', xiv; MVC, Chaucer Notebook; 'England
     C14', 33, CP, box 1.

107 May McKisack, Preface, *Oxford History of England,* vol. 5:
     The Fourteenth Century: 1307–1399 (Oxford: Clarendon Press, 1959).

108 Herbert Fisher to Helen Darbishire, 18 November 1935, CP,
     Obituary file.

109 'Miss M.V. Clarke', *The Times,* 18 November 1935; reviews of *MRC*:
     Times Literary Supplement, 2 January 1937; H.J. Laski, *New Statesman,*
     5 October 1936; *Church of Ireland Gazette,* 8 May 1936.

110 FMP, Presidential Address to Royal Historical Society,
     11 February 1937, repr. in FMP, *Modern Historians and the Study of
     History: Essays and Papers* (London: Oldhams, 1955), 207.

111 HW to GPT, [*c.* 13 October 1918], WP, box 16; E.M. Jamison,
     'In Memoriam Maude Violet Clarke', *The Brown Book: The Lady
     Margaret Hall Chronicle* (December 1935), 84.

112 *HW and MC*, 136, n69; FMP, review of *FS*; MVC, 'Stages of
     Mental Development Necessary for Historical Study (or better)
     The Equipment of a Historian' and 'Historiography', repr. in *HW
     and MC*, 237-40 and 240-5.

113 HW to GPT, [*c.* 13 October 1918], WP, box 16.

114 Recognised as such by her friend and student, May McKisack:
     'Obituary: Maude Violet Clarke', *Oxford Magazine* 54
     (21 November 1935), 186.

115 MVC, 'Stages of Mental Development', in *HW and MC*, 236.

116 'The historian ... re-enacts the past in his mind', R.G. Collingwood,

'Outlines of a Philosophy of History' (1928), in Jan Van de Dussen (ed.), *The Idea of History*, rev. edn with Lectures 1926–1928 (Oxford: Oxford University Press, 1994), 444. For the 1936 lecture, 'History as Re-enactment of Past Experience', see 282-302.

117 MVC's brother Stewart (Chang), an Oxford archaeologist of classical Greece, is likely to have known Collingwood, an Oxford archaeologist of Roman Britain who conducted excavations almost every summer. With J.N.L. Myres, Collingwood wrote the first volume of the *Oxford History of England*, to which MVC was also asked to contribute.

118 Virginia Woolf, *To the Lighthouse* (1927; Harmondsworth: Penguin, 1974), 215.

119 MVC, 'Historiography', in *HW and MC*, 242.

120 R.G. Collingwood, 'Oswald Spengler and the Theory of Historical Cycles', *Antiquity* 1, no. 3 (1927), 315. MVC refers to 'Collingwood's formula of dominant and recessive' discussed in this article in 'England C14', 3-6, CP, box 1.

121 MVC, 'Methods of Thinking', in *HW and MC*, 232; Benedetto Croce, *History: Its Theory and Practice* (New York: Harcourt, Brace and Co., 1921), 19.

122 MVC, 'Methods of Thinking', in *HW and MC*, 231.

123 Excerpts are published in *HW and MC*, 231-3; 233-40.

124 MVC, 'Stages of Mental Development' and 'Historiography', in *HW and MC*, 235; 244.

125 HW, 'Miss N.V. Clark' [*sic*], *The Times*, 25 November 1935; Josiah C. Russell, review of *MRC*, *Speculum* 12, no. 1 (January 1937), 118.

126 MVC, *MRC*, 6; MVC to LSS, 4 August 1931, Sutherland Papers, box 3. This characteristic was detected by readers: T.F. Plucknett, review of *MRC*, *Journal of Comparative Legislation and International Law*, 3rd ser., 19, no. 1 (1937), 148; Palmer, *England, France and Christendom*, 243.

127 VHG, 'Maude Violet Clarke', *DNB* (1949), 183; review of *WS*, *Daily News*, 28 April 1927.

128 MVC to Helen Darbishire, 23 June 1935, CP, Memorial Fund file; HW to Rubie Warner Somerset, [2] November 1935, in private hands.

129 HW to GPT, 19 August 1919; [June-July 1916], WP, box 17.

130 HW to GPT, 17 August 1919, WP, box 17.

131 HW to Monica Brooksbank, 12 April 1937, WP, box 2; HW to MM, 15 September [1942], WP, box 13.

132 HW to MM, 15 September 1942, WP, box 13. On 28 August 1942 *The Times* published HW's letter of protest against the government of Northern Ireland who had refused six young IRA men the right to appeal against their death sentences.

133 David Fitzpatrick, *'Solitary and Wild': Frederick MacNeice and the Salvation of Ireland* (Dublin: Lilliput Press, 2012), 108 and 135; for Revd Clarke's Covenant signature see http://applications.proni.gov.uk/UlsterCovenant/image.aspx?image=M0006710002.

134 E.R. Dodds, *Missing Persons: An Autobiography* (Oxford: Clarendon Press, 1977), 34; HW to GPT, 16 June 1918, WP, box 16.

135 HW, 'Biographical Note', WP, box 2; HW to MM, [*c.* 1932], WP, box 11.

136 HW to GPT, 4 February 1917, WP, box 16.

137 HW, 'Biographical Note', WP, box 2; HW to GPT, 22 November [1917], WP, box 16. See Nini Rodgers, 'Helen Waddell and the Victorian Family', in *HWR*, 277-98.

138 HW, 'Address at a Memorial Festival for Elgar and Holst', June 1934, WP, box 2.

139 HW, Foreword, W. Haughton Crowe, *New Education for Old* (Belfast: William Mullan & Son, 1944), 9. HW is buried close to this roofless Church of Ireland church (replaced by a new building at some distance in 1886), which is across the road from the Magherally Presbyterian Church where HW's brother-in-law, J.D. Martin, was minister from 1883 to 1946.

140 HW, 'Biographical Note', WP, box 2.

141 HW to Harold Rubinstein, 24 February 1941, WP, box 2.

142 HW to MM, undated, WP, box 11.

143 P.G. Walsh, in 'Waddell, Helen Jane (1889–1965)', in H.C.G. Matthew and Brian Harrison (eds), *Oxford Dictionary of National Biography* (Oxford: Oxford University Press, 2004); online edn, ed. Lawrence Goldman, May 2009, www.oxforddnb.com/view/article/36670, accessed 13 January 2014, states that HW was a member of the Royal Irish Academy, which, however, has no record of her election. Email from Petra Schnabel, Deputy Librarian, Royal Irish Academy, 8 January 2014. It is likely that Walsh meant to refer to the Irish Academy of Letters, of which HW became an associate member in 1932. Kathleen White, president of the Irish Literary Society of London, affirms HW's vice-presidency: Kathleen White, 'The Dream of Helen Waddell', *Belfast Telegraph*, 13 March 1965.

144 Amanda Tucker, 'Reviving Helen Waddell's Lost Decade: Ireland and the Transnational Imaginary', in *HWR*, 127-45; Norman Vance, 'Helen Waddell, Presbyterian Medievalist' (Belfast: Presbyterian Historical Society of Ireland, 1996), repr. in *HWR*, 147-71. HW's teacher, Gregory Smith, and her mentor, George Saintsbury, were among the pioneers of comparative literary studies: Saintsbury edited the series Periods of European Literature (of which he wrote three volumes and Smith one), the aim of which was 'to exhibit

European literature from the comparative point of view'. George
Saintsbury, *The Later Nineteenth Century* (Edinburgh: Blackwoods,
1907), vii. See also G. Gregory Smith, 'The Foible of Comparative
Literature', *Blackwoods Edinburgh Magazine* 169 (January 1901), 38-48
and 'Some Notes on the Comparative Study of Literature', *Modern
Language Review* 1, no. 1 (October 1905), 1-8. A review of HW's
WS dubbed it 'comparative literature with a vengeance, in the very
best manner of George Saintsbury, W.P. Ker, and Gregory Smith'.
Percy S. Allen, review of *WS*, *Speculum* 3, no. 1 (January 1928), 110.

145 HW, *Poetry in the Dark Ages*, 7.

146 HW, *WS* 47-8. These glosses were published in Whitley Stokes and
John Strachan (eds), *Thesaurus Palaeohibernicus: A Collection of Old
Irish Glosses, Scholia, Prose and Verse*, 2 vols (Cambridge: Cambridge
University Press, 1903), 2, 49–224.

147 Mews, 'Helen Waddell and Heloise', in *HWR*, 21-2; Douglas Hyde
[An Craoibhín Aoibinn], 'O King of the Friday', *Abhráin Diadha
Chúige Connacht: The Religious Songs of Connacht*, intr. Dominic Daly,
2 vols (London: Fisher & Unwin, and Dublin: Gill, 1906; Shannon:
Irish University Press, 1972), 2, 7-8.

148 Mews, 'Helen Waddell and Heloise', in *HWR*, 34; E.A. Lowe (ed.),
The Bobbio Missal. A Gallican Mass-book (MS Paris lat. 13246), Henry
Bradshaw Society lviii, lxi (London: Henry Bradshaw Society,
1920–24, repr. as one vol., 1991), 62, no. 200.

149 *WS*, 28; 34.

150 Charles Lock, 'Scholar of the Dark: Helen Waddell and the Middle
Ages', in *HWR*, 42-3. This reading overlooks evidence of the
'quarrel between letters and religion' in the monastic records
described by Robin Flower, *The Irish Tradition* (1947; Oxford:
Clarendon Press, 1978), 44-50.

151 The editor might have felt that the first review on 28 June 1927
was too humorous to befit the acclaim emerging from scholarly
quarters, publishing a more serious review on 13 August 1927.

152 E.B. FitzMaurice and A.G. Little (eds), *Materials for the History of the
Franciscan Province of Ireland, 1230–1450*, British Society for Franciscan
Studies 9 (Manchester: Manchester University Press, 1920), xxii–
xxiv; MVC, 'Irish Parliaments in the Reign of Edward II', *TRHS*,
4th ser., 9 (1926), 29-60, repr. in *FS*, 11 n1.

153 H.I. Bell, 'Robin Ernest William Flower', *Proceedings of the British
Academy* 32 (1946), 362; 360; HW to MM, [31 May 1930], WP, box 11.

154 HW, Preface to *WS*, v. Flower printed his translation privately in
a brochure, *Trirech inna n-En*, sent out as a Christmas card in 1926;
it was published in his *Poems and Translations* (London: Constable,

1931), 129–30; no doubt HW had a hand in securing the volume for
Constable's. It is possible that HW had heard the poem as early as 1910;
Okey Belfour, who lectured her in Old English at Queen's University
Belfast, had a cat named Pangur Bán and read the translation out to his
colleague, Rubie Warner. Warner identified Flower's as the translation
she had heard 'in Okey Belfour's home in 1910 in Belfast' but it is
likely that the version Belfour read was Whitley Stokes's. Charles Lock,
Ladies, Prisoners, Professors: English Studies at Queen's during the Great War
(Belfast: Queen's University Gender Initiative, 2010), 7; Whitley Stokes
(ed.), *Thesaurus Palaeohibernicus*, 2, 293–4. Flower was still a beginner
in Irish when he was granted leave in 1910 to attend lectures on Old
and Middle Irish language and literature in Dublin. Bell, 'Robin Ernest
William Flower', 362.

155 HW, epigraph, *WS*, omitted from some editions; Kuno Meyer (ed.),
     The Vision of Mac Conglinne, A Middle Irish Wonder-Tale (London:
     David Nutt, 1892), 8–9.

156 Flower, *The Irish Tradition*, 76–7.

157 For Florence McLoughlin: *Victoria College Magazine* 49 (July 1903):
     95; *SCR*, 375–6; J.N.L. Myres, 'May McKisack', in F.R.H. du
     Boulay and Caroline M. Barron (eds), *The Reign of Richard II:
     Essays in Honour of May McKisack* (London: University of London,
     The Athlone Press, 1971), xiii. Mary Coate held the position
     temporarily from 1918 to 1919. *SCR*, 376.

158 Goddard Henry Orpen, *Ireland under the Normans,* vols 1 and 2:
     1169–1216 (Oxford: Clarendon Press, 1911), vols 3 and 4: *1216–1333*
     (Oxford: Clarendon Press, 1920); Edmund Curtis, Foreword, *A
     History of Medieval Ireland from 1110 to 1513* (Dublin: Maunsel, 1923),
     quoted in Preface, *A History of Medieval Ireland from 1086 to 1513*, rev.
     edn (London: Methuen, 1938), vi.

159 It is very likely that Dodds would have at least talked to another
     medieval historian about MVC, for whom he had felt 'a romantic
     but distant admiration'. Dodds, *Missing Persons,* 61; 46.

160 MVC, 'Irish Parliaments', in *FS*, 5.

161 MVC, review of Newport B. White (ed.), *Ormond Deeds: The Red
     Book of Ormond*; Edmund Curtis (ed.), *Calendar of Ormond Deeds*,
     Irish Manuscripts Commission (Dublin: Stationery Office, 1932),
     EHR 49, no. 194 (Apr. 1934), 331; 330.

162 MVC, 'Irish Parliaments', *FS*, 16.

163 MVC, *MRC*, 36.

164 MVC, reviews of: *Ormond Deeds* (see note 161); Agnes Conway,
     Henry VII's Relations with Scotland and Ireland, 1485–98, with a chapter
     on the Acts of Poynings' Parliament, 1494–5 by Edmund Curtis

(Cambridge: Cambridge University Press, 1932), *EHR* 48, no. 191
(July 1933), 473-5; M.J. Hynes, *The Mission of Rinuccini, 1645–1649*
(Dublin: Browne & Nolan, 1932) *EHR* 49, no. 194 (Apr. 1934), 329-32;
R.F. D'Arcy, *Life of John, first Baron Darcy of Knayth, 1280–1347* (London:
Eyre & Spottiswoode, 1933) and Donough Bryan, *Gerald Fitzgerald,
the Great Earl of Kildare, 1456–1513* (Dublin: Talbot Press, 1933), *EHR*
50, no. 197 (January 1935), 166-7 and 169; Edmund Curtis (ed.),
Calendar of Ormond Deeds 1172–1359, vol. 1, ed, and Newport B. White
(ed.), *Ormond Deeds: The Red Book of Ormond*, Irish Manuscripts
Commission (Dublin: Stationery Office, 1932), *Bulletin of the Institute
of Historical Research* 13, no. 38 (Nov. 1935), 95-7; Edmund Curtis (ed.),
Calendar of Ormond Deeds, 2, 1350–1413 (Dublin: Stationery Office,
1934), and W.L. Renwick (ed.), *Spenser's View of the Present State of
Ireland*, vol. 4 of *The Complete Works of Edmund Spenser* (London:
Partridge, 1934), *EHR* 51, no. 203 (July 1936), 518-20 and 548.

165 'List of Irish Parliamenta in Edward II's Reign', appendix
to 'Irish Parliaments', in *FS* 30-35; 'Parliament and Council
Proceedings - Chancery', appendix to 'William of Windsor in
Ireland', in *FS*, 182-241; 'The Latin Text of the English *Modus*;
The Latin Text of the Irish *Modus*', *MRC*, 373-92.

166 Peter Crooks, 'Factions, Feuds and Noble Power in the Lordship of
Ireland, *c.* 1356–1496', *Irish Historical Studies* 35, no. 140 (November
2007), 433; 432-3.

167 Helen Cam, 'Stubbs Seventy Years After', *Cambridge Historical
Journal* 9, no. 2 (1948), 145-7; Helen Cam to Helen Darbishire,
19 November 1935, CP, Obituary file and note 201 below.

168 Peter Crooks, 'The Lecky Professors', in Peter Crooks (ed.),
*Government, War and Society in Medieval Ireland: Essays by Edmund
Curtis, A. J. Otway-Ruthven and James Lydon* (Dublin: Four Courts
Press, 2008), 48-50.

169 Curtis, *History of Medieval Ireland*, rev. edn, 248-9, 252, 292;
Otway-Ruthven, *A History of Medieval Ireland*, 170 n101, 298 n47,
299 n50, 303 n59, 304 n60, 307 n66, 356 n34; James Lydon, 'The Irish
Church and Taxation in the Fourteenth Century', *Irish Ecclesiastical
Record* 103 (1965), 158-9 and 'William of Windsor and the Irish
Parliament', 1965, in Crooks (ed.), *Government, War and Society*, 90-5.

170 Crooks, 'Lecky Professors', 41, quoting H.G. Richardson, 'English
Institutions in Medieval Ireland', *Irish Historical Studies* 1, no. 4
(September 1939), 383, a point he had made a year earlier, in his
review of *MRC*, *History* 22 (June 1937), 67.

171 MVC, review of Conway, *Henry VII's Relations with Scotland and
Ireland*, 474.

172 Crooks, 'Lecky Professors', 41.

173 Woodward, 'Memoir', *FS*, x; MVC, 'O'Clery i.e Clarke', CP, box 1.

174 Michael O'Clery, Cucogry O'Clery, Ferfeasa Mulconry, Conary O'Clery, *Annala Rioghachta Éireann* [*Annals of the Kingdom of Ireland*], ed. John O'Donovan, 7 vols (Dublin: Hodges and Smith, 1851), cited in *MRC*, 101 n3.

175 MVC to LSS, 19 September 1932 and 28 July 1934, Sutherland Papers, box 3 and Woodward, 'Memoir', xii. MVC also helped her brother, Revd H.J.St.J. Clarke, with his research for *Thirty Centuries in South-East Antrim* (Belfast: Quota Press, 1938).

176 R.R. Davies, 'In Praise of British History', in *The British Isles 1100–1500: Comparison, Contrasts and Connections* (Edinburgh: J. Donald, 1988), 23. Thanks to Marie Therese Flanagan for drawing my attention to this parallel.

177 Robin Frame, Introduction, *The Political Development of the British Isles, 1100–1330* (Oxford: Oxford University Press, 1990), 3-4.

178 R.R. Davies, 'A Farewell Speech', in Huw Pryce and John Watts (eds), *Power and Identity in the Middle Ages: Essays in Memory of Rees Davies* (Oxford: Oxford University Press, 2007), 262; Robin Frame, Preface, *The Political Development of the British Isles* (Oxford: Oxford University Press, 1990), vii. MVC's Welsh colleague, J.G. Edwards, would also count as an all-Britain historian. J.F.A. Mason, 'Edwards, Sir (John) Goronwy (1891–1976),' in Matthew and Harrison (eds), *Oxford Dictionary of National Biography*; online ed., ed. Goldman, www.oxforddnb.com/view/article/31064, accessed 13 January 2014.

179 Christopher Hobhouse, *Oxford as it was and as it is To-day* (1939; London: B. T. Batsford, 1948), 101-3.

180 Carol Dyhouse, *No Distinction of Sex? Women in British Universities, 1870–1939* (London: UCL Press, 1995), 147.

181 KMEM TO KMM, 15 February 1931, MP, box 17; Cam to Darbishire, 19 November 1935, CP, Obituary file.

182 HW to MM, [March 1925], WP, box 11.

183 FMP, review of *FS*; Brittain, *Testament of Friendship*, 85; HW to GPT, 11 March 1917, WP, box 16.

184 HW to MM, [*c*. October 1921], WP, box 11.

185 KMEM to KMM 27 October 1927, MP, box 18; HW, *The Times*, 25 November 1935.

186 HW to MM, [March 1925], box 11; Evelyn M. Jamison, 'In Memoriam Maude Violet Clarke', *The Brown Book: The Lady Margaret Hall Chronicle* (December 1935), 84; Woodward, 'Memoir', xix.

187 KMEM to KMM, 26 May 1929, MP, box 18; KMEM to Alice Burnet, 2 July 1934, MP, box 45.

188 HW to Enid Starkie, [14? October 1935], Starkie Papers, Bodleian Libraries, University of Oxford, box 2. Grateful acknowledgements to the Bodleian Libraries, University of Oxford and to Alma Starkie for permission to quote from these papers.

189 MVC to Enid Starkie, 1 August 1935, Starkie Papers, box 2.

190 *HW and MC*, 180-1.

191 Thomas Pynchon, Introduction, *Slow Learner: Early Stories* (Boston: Little, Brown, 1984), 8.

192 Roy Rosenstein, 'Helen Waddell at Columbia: Maker of Medievalists', in Richard Utz and Elizabeth Emery (eds), *Cahier Calin: Makers of the Middle Ages: Essays in Honor of William Calin* (Kalamazoo, MI: Studies in Medievalism 2011), 15, http://works.bepress.com/richard_utz/86.

193 Étienne Gilson, *Heloise and Abelard*, 1948, tr. L.K. Shook (London: Hollis and Carter, 1953), xii; Ernst Curtius, 'The Medieval Bases of Western Thought', *European Literature and the Latin Middle Ages*, 1948, tr. Willard R. Trask (Princeton, NJ: Princeton University Press, 1953), 597.

194 Rosenstein, 'Helen Waddell at Columbia', 15.

195 The number of anthologies is too unwieldy to record; among scholarly uses, see C.A. Patrides (ed.), *Milton's Lycidas: The Tradition and the Poem* (New York: Holt, Rinehart and Winston, 1961), which sets HW's translation of Milton's 'Epitaphium Damonis' alongside H.W. Garrod's and 'Lycidas', and HW's version of Petronius's 'Foeda Est In Coitu Volupto' alongside those of Ben Jonson, Jack Lindsay, John Press, Judy Spink, Michael Lebeck and J.P. Sullivan: 'Foeda Est In Coitu Volupto: Versions', *Arion* 2, no. 1 (Spring 1963), 82-4.

196 Anthony Steel, who did not know Maude, 'should have liked to dedicate' his biography of Richard II to her memory. *Richard II* (Cambridge: Cambridge University Press, 1941), x.

197 VHG, 'Clarke, Maude Violet (1892–1935)', Revd K.D. Reynolds, in Matthew and Harrison (eds), *Oxford Dictionary of National Biography*; online ed., ed. Goldman, www.oxforddnb.com/view/article/31064, accessed 13 January 2014.

198 Margaret Hastings to Helen Cam, 14 March 1960, Helen Maud Cam's Personal Papers, GCPP Cam 2/7/7, Girton College, Cambridge. Thanks to the mistress and fellows of Girton College, Cambridge for permission to quote this letter. Every reasonable effort has been made to trace Margaret Hastings's copyright holders but without success.

199 *Ibid.* Cam had given Hastings feedback on the rough draft of this essay; it is clear that, according to Cam, Hastings had overlooked

MVC's contribution. The published article acknowledges MVC's
work on the reign of Richard II and 'other work so brilliantly begun
on the constitutional developments of the fourteenth century'.
Margaret Hastings, 'High History or Hack History: England in
the Later Middle Ages', rev. edn, in Elizabeth Chapin Furber (ed.),
Changing Views on British History: Essays on Historical Writing since 1939
(Cambridge, MA: Harvard University Press, 1966), 72.

200   HW to E.K. Rand, 18 November 1934, Papers of Edward Kennard
Rand, Correspondence 1934–1942, Folder W, Harvard University
Archives. Quoted courtesy of the Harvard University Archives.

201   MVC to HW, 2 October 1913, WP, box 2.

202   HW to GPT, 10 July 1917, WP, box 16. The book she borrowed was
volume 5 of Alexander B. Grosart (ed.), *The Life and Complete Prose
and Verse of Robert Greene*, 12 vols, of which fifty copies were printed
in 1881–2 for private circulation in the Huth Library collection.

3. Intellectual Lives and Literary Perspectives

1   For a consideration of Irish female writers living and publishing in
England, see Rolf Loeber and Magda Stouthamer-Loeber, 'Literary
Absentees: Irish women authors in nineteenth-century England',
in Jacqueline Belanger (ed.), *The Irish Novel in the Nineteenth
Century: Facts and Fictions* (Dublin: Four Courts, 2005): 167-86.
Many of the writers who travelled and resided in Europe can be
discussed in these contexts too.

2   There are numerous accounts of emigration and/or travel away
from Ireland during the nineteenth century. See, as a starting point,
Chapter 3 in Gerardine Meaney, Mary O' Dowd and Bernadette
Whelan, *Reading the Irishwoman: Studies in Cultural Encounters and
Exchange, 1714–1960* (Liverpool: Liverpool University Press, 2013), 88.

3   Hannah Lynch, *Jinny Blake: A Tale* (London: J. M. Dent & Company,
1897), 13 and 167 respectively.

4   Lynch, *Jinny Blake*, 16.

5   This neglect, especially of writers who chose foreign settings
and who lived abroad themselves, began with the Irish Literary
Revival, as Heather Ingman notes in her discussion of the Irish
New Woman: 'Like Sydney Owenson earlier in the century and
Charlotte Riddell mid-century, they crossed the Irish Sea in search
of publishers and London became the center for New Woman
writers, several of whom – George Egerton, Sarah Grand, Beatrice
Grimshaw – were Irish in origin. Living abroad inevitably affected
their writing, and the foreign settings of their fiction, as John
Wilson Foster and others have point out, is one reason why these

writers were ignored by the Irish Literary Revival'. Heather
Ingman, *Irish Women's Fiction: From Edgeworth to Enright* (Dublin:
Irish Academic Press, 2013), 34. See also Margaret Kelleher's
discussion of reasons for neglect, particularly for the second half of
the nineteenth century, in '"Wanted: an Irish Novelist": The Critical
Decline of the Nineteenth-Century Novel' in Belanger, *The Irish
Novel in the Nineteenth Century: Facts and Fictions*, 187-201.

6 See Ingman, *Irish Women's Fiction*, 1-17.

7 Joe Cleary, 'The Nineteenth-Century Novel: Notes and
Speculations on Literary Historiography' in Belanger, *The Irish
Novel in the Nineteenth Century: Facts and Fictions*, 221. There are
several studies, especially on late nineteenth-century writing, that
focus on different transnational contexts. See, for example, Andrea
Bobotis, 'From Egypt to Ireland: Lady Augusta Gregory and
Cross-Cultural Nationalisms in Victorian Ireland' in *Romanticism and
Victorianism on the Net* 48 (November 2007), Doi: 10.7202/017439ar,
http://id.erudit.org/iderudit/017439ar.

8 Gillian Dow, Introduction, 'Women Readers in Europe: Readers,
Writers, Salonnières, 1750–1900', *Women's Writing* 18. no. 1 (2011): 2.
http://dx.doi.org/10.1080/09699082.2011.525003, accessed
26 March 2013. See also studies such as Margaret Cohen and
Caroline Dever (eds), *The Literary Channel: The International Invention
of the Novel* (Princeton: Princeton University Press, 2002). There
is now considerable critical attention paid to transnationalism,
cosmopolitanism and late eighteenth-/early nineteenth-century
Irish women writers such as Lady Blessington, Lady Sydney
Morgan and Maria Edgeworth. For example, Julia Donovan
discusses 'Owensons's cosmopolitanism as the means by which she
exhorted Ireland to reclaim a transnational identity increasingly lost
in the colonial orbit' in *Sydney Owenson, Lady Morgan and the Politics
of Style* (Palo Alto: Academia Press, 2009), 16.

9 Marguerite Corporaal and Christina Morin, 'The Cultural Mobility
of the Irish in Europe in the Long Nineteenth Century', *Europe and
its Worlds*, Radboud University Nijmegen, 16-18 October 2013.

10 Meaney, O' Dowd and Whelan, *Reading the Irishwoman*, 3.

11 *Ibid.*, 65.

12 *Ibid.*, 41. See Gillian Dow on the need for a fuller examination
of female reading, writing and translation networks, especially
cross-culturally (Introduction, 'Women Readers in Europe',
1-14). The UK RED (Reading Experience Database) offers one
important resource for this burgeoning field: www.open.ac.uk/
Arts/reading/UK/index.php. Within Franco-Irish contexts, a recent

study on translation and cultural exchange marks the emergence of
another important area of scholarship. See Michele Milan, 'Found
in Translation: Franco-Irish Relationships in Nineteenth-Century
Ireland' (DPhil diss., Dublin City University, 2013).

13 Mary Pierse's edited publications *Irish Feminisms, 1810–1930*, 5
    vols (Oxon: Routledge, 2010) follow on most directly from the
    Field Day volumes. See also, for example, John Wilson Foster's
    The Cambridge Companion to the Irish Novel (Cambridge: Cambridge
    University Press, 2007) and his *Irish Novels 1890–1949: New Bearings
    in Culture and Fiction* (New York: Oxford University Press, 2008).
    James H. Murphy offers a more specific insight into a broad range
    of writing in his *Irish Novelists and the Victorian Age* (Oxford: Oxford
    University Press, 2011).

14 'The lack of a large market and readership for their works drove
    many Irish authors to Britain, but it was also the case that the
    flourishing book trades in British cities such as London and
    Liverpool simply offered many more employment opportunities for
    Irish authors.' Loeber and Stouthamer-Loeber, 'Literary Absentees:
    Irish women authors in nineteenth-century England', 171.

15 Murphy addresses the difficulties with this term in *Irish Novelists
    and the Victorian Age*: 'there is a problem with the use of the
    adjective Victorian when it comes to Ireland. Even though there
    was a good deal of cultural convergence between Britain and
    Ireland during the period, especially at the middle-class level, there
    was considerable political divergence, with the rise of increasingly
    assertive forms of Irish nationalism. Most scholars have baulked at
    using the phrase Victorian Ireland' (10).

16 Jill Brady Hampton, 'Ambivalent Realism: May Laffan's "Flitters,
    Tatters, and the Counsellor"', *New Hibernia Review* 12. no. 2
    (2008), 130.

17 See Foster, *The Cambridge Companion to the Irish Novel* and *Irish Novels
    1890–1949*; Murphy, *Irish Novelists and the Victorian* Age; Ingman, *Irish
    Women's Fiction*; and Tina O'Toole, *The Irish New Woman* (Basingstoke:
    Palgrave Macmillan, 2013). For the fullest and most sustained
    attention to a diversity of Lynch's work, see Faith Binckes and
    Kathryn Laing, 'Irish Autobiographical Fiction and Hannah Lynch's
    Autobiography of a Child', *English Literature in Transition* 55, no. 2 (2012):
    195-218; Binckes and Laing, 'A Vagabond's Scrutiny: Hannah Lynch
    in Europe' in Elke D'hoker, Raphaël Ingelbien and Hedwig Schwall
    (eds), *Irish Women Writers: New Critical Perspectives* (Oxford: Peter Lang,
    2011): 111-31; Binckes and Laing, 'A Forgotten Franco-Irish Literary
    Network: Hannah Lynch, Arvède Barine and Salon Culture in

Fin-de-Siècle Paris', *Etudes Irlandaises*, 36, no. 2 (2011), 159-60; Binckes and Laing, 'From "Wild Irish Girl" to "Parisianised Foreigner": Hannah Lynch and France' in Eamon Maher and Eugene O' Brien (eds), *War of the Words: Literary Rebellion in France and Ireland* (Haute Bretagne: TIR, 2010): 41-58.

18 Anna and Fanny Parnell, who established the Ladies' Land League in 1881 in response to the growing land war crisis and the imprisonment of their brother and promoter of Home Rule, Charles Stuart Parnell, were, like Lynch, educated and well-travelled. As Michael Wainwright highlights: 'Physical separation from Ireland enabled both girls to appreciate the interacting and often conflicting relays of imperial and parochial power that raked their homeland.' 'Female Suffrage in Ireland: James Joyce's Realization of Unrealized Potential', *Criticism* 51, no. 4 (Fall 2010): 655.

19 Tina O'Toole, 'Ireland: The *Terra Incognita* of the New Woman Project' in Heidi Hansson (ed.), *New Contexts: Re-Framing Nineteenth-Century Irish Women's Prose* (Cork: Cork University Press, 2008), 129.

20 Foster notes how the 'Europeanized Lynch's field of view was far wider than Irish nationalism's', in *Irish Novels 1890–1949,* 278.

21 Lynch, *Jinny Blake*, 192.

22 Lynch published several novels and short stories set in European contexts, often with Irish protagonists. See, for example, *Rosni Harvey: A Novel*, 3 vols (1892) and 'Dr Vermont's Fantasy' in *Dr Vermont's Fantasy* (1886).

23 Heidi Hansson, 'Introduction', *New Contexts*, 3.

24 Margaret Kelleher, 'Prose writing and drama in English, 1830–1890: from Catholic emancipation to the fall of Parnell' in Margaret Kelleher and Philip O' Leary (eds), *The Cambridge History of Irish Literature Vol. 1. to 1890* (Cambridge: Cambridge University Press, 2008), 450.

25 M.R., 'Sketches in Irish biography, No. 17 – Kathleen O'Meara' in the *Irish Monthly* 17, no. 196 (October 1889): 527. www.jstor.org/stable/20497958, accessed 27 March 2013. O'Meara was an important contributor of fiction to this magazine under the pen name of Grace Ramsay. Her fiction draws on both Irish and European contexts and settings. For further details about her writing, see Rolf Loeber and Magda Loeber, with Anne Mullin Burnham, *An Electronic Version of A Guide to Irish Fiction 1650–1900*, created by An Foras Feasa, NUI Maynooth. www.lgif.ie.

26 Julia Kavanagh, *English Women of Letters: Biographical Sketches.* Vol. 2 (London: Hurst and Blackett Publishers, 1863), 311-12.

27 Lynch, *Jinny Blake*, 42.

28 Lynch, *French Life in Town and Country* (New York and London: G.P. Putnam's Sons, 1901), 47.

29 Hannah Lynch, *Autobiography of a Child* (Edinburgh: William Blackwood and Sons, 1899), 211. For a detailed discussion of *Autobiography*, see Binckes and Laing, 'Irish Autobiographical fiction and Hannah Lynch's *Autobiography of a Child*', 195-218.

30 Tina O'Toole, 'Ireland: The *Terra Incognita* of the New Woman Project' in Hansson, *New Contexts*, 131.

31 Review by FYE, 'The Paris Correspondent Once More: *French Life in Town and Country* by Hannah Lynch', *Speaker* (March 1901), 663.

32 Hannah Lynch, 'Impressions of the Canary Isles: Teneriffe' in *Good Words* (January 1896), 741. For further discussion of Lynch and the trope of the vagabond, see Binckes and Laing, 'A Vagabond's Scrutiny', 111-31.

33 She recalls these semi-comic instances in several travel essays. For example, visiting the military town of Rochefort, she finds herself an uncomfortable object of fascination: 'I was beginning myself to regard a woman as a rare and strange-looking animal in this stagnant town of uniformed males'. Lynch, 'A Day in Pierre Loti's Town', *Speaker*, 10 (13 October 1894), 409

34 Hannah Lynch, *Rosni Harvey: A Novel*, Vol. 2, London: Chapman and Hall, 1892), 29.

35 *Ibid.*, 53.

36 Lynch, *Jinny Blake*, 15.

37 *Ibid.*, 220.

38 *Ibid.*, 147, 96.

39 *Ibid.*, 62.

40 *Ibid.*, 13, 98.

41 *Ibid.*, 194, 67.

42 Lynch, 'The Senora of Today', *Freeman's Journal* (24 March 1894), 6. This is one of numerous articles Lynch wrote on Spain, many commenting on the position of women.

43 Fauset notes the immense popularity, for example, of *Grace Lee* with American readers. *The Politics of Writing* (Manchester: Manchester University Press, 2009), 73.

44 See Binckes and Laing, 'A Vagabond's Scrutiny', 124 for a discussion of Lynch's contributions to the *Irish Monthly*.

45 Kathleen O'Meara's fiction 'had a considerable range, from espousing women's suffrage to exploring eastern European revolution. Much of it however, was on explicitly Catholic themes.' Murphy, *Irish Novelists and the Victorian Age*, 160. Selina Bunbury, 1802–82, is another writer whose travels through Europe have received critical attention

and could be included alongside Kavanagh and O'Meara. See for
example, essay in Hansson, *New Contexts*, 55–77.

46 Fauset, *The Politics of Writing*, 42.

47 *Ibid.*, 2.

48 Mrs Charles Martin, 'The Late Julia Kavanagh' in the *Irish Monthly*,
Vol. 6, (1878): 96. www.jstor.org/stable/20502138, accessed
27 March 2013.

49 Cited in Fauset, *The Politics of Writing*, 17.

50 See, for example, Marguerite Power, Countess of Blessington,
The Idler in Italy, 2 vols (London: Colburn, 1839) and Sydney
Owenson (Lady Morgan), *Italy*, 2 vols (London: H. Colburn
and Co., 1824).

51 Julia Kavanagh, *A Summer and Winter in the Two Sicilies*, Vol. 1
(London: Hurst and Blackett Publishers, 1858), 16.

52 *Ibid.*, 103.

53 Giorgia Alù, *Beyond the Traveller's Gaze: Expatriate Ladies Writing in
Sicily 1848–1910* (Bern: Peter Lang, 2008), 45.

54 Kavanagh, *A Summer and Winter in the Two Sicilies*, Vol. 1, 111.
The comparison of jealous husbands with Turks is a common one
in travel writing at this time. For further discussions of Orientalism,
gender and travel, see, for example: Sarah Mills, *Discourses of Difference:
An Analysis of Women's Travel Writing and Colonialism* (London and
New York: Routledge, 1991) or Mary Louise Pratt, *Imperial Eyes: Travel
Writing and Transculturation* (London and New York: Routledge, 1992).

55 Kavanagh, *A Summer and Winter in the Two Sicilies*, Vol. 1, 102–3.

56 Writing governess fiction and/or experiencing the life of a
governess is another link between many of the Irish female writers
under discussion, from Edgeworth and Morgan to Hannah Lynch.
It is a promising area for further examination in relation to the
intellectual and writing lives of these Irish writers.

57 Such thematic connections between travel, travelogues and fiction
can be traced back to Sydney Morgan, Maria Edgeworth and Lady
Blessington too. See Susanne Schmid, *British Literary Salons of the
Late Eighteenth and Early Nineteenth Centuries* (New York: Palgrave
Macmillan, 2013), for her discussion of Lady Blessington.

58 Julia Kavanagh, *Grace Lee*, Vol. 1 (London: Smith, Elder & Co, 1885), 23.

59 'Grace Lee is one of Kavanagh's more independent and resilient
heroines who, like most of her main protagonists, is not
conventionally beautiful, but has qualities of strength, endurance
and kindness in her nature. The genesis of the resilient and
independent heroine lies in earlier writers and, of course, is not
unique to Kavanagh (or Brontë). Arguably the qualities invested in

Grace Lee and Jane Eyre are characteristic of mid–century domestic fiction' (Fauset, *The Politics of Writing*, 73).

60 Fauset argues that the novel not only draws on the romance conventions of domestic fiction, it is also 'experimental', venturing 'further into the realms of fantasy and surrealism' (72-4).

61 Kavanagh, *Grace Lee*, Vol. 1, 21.

62 Fauset suggests that Kavanagh may have drawn on both 'Madame de Stael's enigmatic heroine, Corinne, in Grace's desire for liberty', as well as 'the Catholic scholar Lamartine's account of Lady Esther Stanhope, who he met in his travels in the orient' (*The Politics of Writing*, 79).

63 Kavanagh, *A Summer and Winter in the Two Sicilies*, Vol. 2, 34.

64 Kate O'Brien inherits and explores this trope in her fiction in the twentieth century.

65 Kavanagh, *Grace Lee*, Vol. 1, 24.

66 Fauset, *The Politics of Writing*, 79.

67 Kavanagh, *Grace Lee*, Vol. 1, 34.

68 *Ibid.*, 47.

69 Murphy, *Irish Novelists and the Victorian Age*, 107.

70 Julia Kavanagh, *Natalie: A Tale*, 1850 (New York: D. Appleton & Company, 1881), 18.

71 *Ibid.*, 32.

72 Murphy, *Irish Novelists and the Victorian Age*, 107. Commentary on the condition of Ireland refracted through the French setting could be extended. For example, M. de Sainville, with whom Natalie falls in love, is a feudal ruler in his home and on his estate. His apparently motiveless dismissal of a faithful gardener is criticised by Natalie and his aunt, who describes it as an act of 'despotism and caprice' (Kavanagh, *Natalie*, 73).

73 The domestic novel was also known as 'sentimental fiction' or 'women's fiction'. See Nancy Armstrong, *Desire and Domestic Fiction: A Political History of the Novel* (Oxford: Oxford University Press, 1989).

74 Fauset, *The Politics of Writing*, 50. The influence of Charlotte Brontë and the literary exchange between Brontë and Kavanagh is a particularly interesting one. Brontë may be read as another literary foremother for many Irish female writers, including Lynch, whose *Autobiography of a Child* can be read as a partial reworking of the novel. See Binckes and Laing, 'Irish Autobiographical fiction and Hannah Lynch's *Autobiography of a Child*', 208.

75 Kavanagh, *Natalie*, 135.

76 *Ibid.*, 387.

77 *Ibid.*, 423.

78 Implicit analogies between Ireland and France evident in the novel
    are made much more explicit in Kavanagh's discussion of Maria
    Edgeworth in *English Women of Letters: Biographical Sketches*. In the
    two countries, '[t]he same oppression, the same poverty, sprang from
    very similar causes' (Vol. 2, 168).

79 Binckes and Laing, 'From "Wild Irish Girl" to "Parisianised
    Foreigner": Hannah Lynch and France', 44.

80 *Ibid.*, 47.

81 Lady Blessington, also publishing during the earlier part of the
    century, offers another potentially fruitful intersection to explore.
    She was best known for her 'silver fork novels' and scandalous
    lifestyle, but she also 'inaugurated a new genre', the governess novel.
    In addition, her writing about Ireland and English society was shaped
    by European travel and she published several popular travel books.

82 Jinny is the daughter of a popular Irish tragedian, Herbert Blake;
    her mother has died young. Lynch herself may have felt a certain
    connection with Owenson, born of Catholic and non-Catholic
    parents as well as enduring the life of a governess. In the novel,
    the fictional Herbert Blake is more successful than Owenson's
    father, who went bankrupt. Lynch's near contemporary, L.T. Meade,
    also makes clear allusions to Owenson and the 'wild Irish girl'
    in many of her novels for girls. See Beth Rogers, 'Irishness,
    Professional Authorship and the "Wild Irish Girls" of L.T. Meade'
    English Literature in Transition, 1880–1920, 56, no. 2 (2013), 146–66,
    http://muse.jhu.edu/journals/elt/summary/v056/56.2.rodgers.html.

83 Ingman describes Owenson foreshadowing the New Woman in
    another novel too, *Florence Macarthy*: 'destabilising her society's
    notions of the proper – that is domestic sphere for women' (*Irish
    Women's Fiction*, 13).

84 Roy Foster in *Words Alone: Yeats and His Inheritances* comments
    on the continental dimensions of Owenson's work, noting how
    'The upper-class Irish Catholics in *The O'Briens and the O'Flahertys*
    slip constantly into French and Italian – an indication of their
    enforcedly peripatetic lives as well as their cultural education'.
    Likewise in Edgeworth, there is evidence of 'the Continentalism
    of elite Catholic Irish manners in *Ormond* and elsewhere'
    (Oxford: Oxford University Press, 2011, 38).

85 Edith Somerville and Martyn Ross, *Irish Memories* (New York:
    Longmans, Green & Co., 1918), 53. The impact of Edgeworth's
    writing on Somerville and Ross has been discussed by numerous
    commentators, including Julie Ann Stevens, *The Irish Scene in
    Somerville and Ross* (Dublin: Irish Academic Press, 2007) and

Maureen O'Connor, *The Female and the Species: The Animal in Irish Women's Writing* (Oxford: Peter Lang, 2010). Lady Gregory is also cited as an admirer of Edgeworth, although a more ambivalent one. See Claire Connolly, *A Cultural History of the Irish Novel, 1790–1829* (Cambridge: Cambridge University Press, 2012), 21.

86 Heidi Hansson, *Emily Lawless 1845–1913: Writing the Interspace* (Cork: Cork University Press, 2007), III.

87 Lawless's biography has also been described as 'a major feminist or proto-feminist work', establishing Edgeworth as a literary foremother. James M. Cahalan, 'Forging a Tradition: Emily Lawless and the Irish Literary Canon', *Colby Quarterly*, vol. 27, no.1 (1991): 35.

88 Kavanagh, *English Women of Letters: Biographical Sketches*. Vol.1 (1863), n.p.

89 Fausset, *The Politics of Writing*, 37. For a detailed discussion of Kavanagh's biographical sketches and their significance, see Joanne Wilkes, *Women Reviewing Women in Nineteenth-Century Britain: The Critical Reception of Jane Austen, Charlotte Bronte and George Eliot* (Surrey: Ashgate, 2010) and Rohan Maitzen, '"This Feminine Preserve": Historical Biographies by Victorian Women', *Victorian Studies* 38 no. 3 (Spring 1995): 371-93.

90 There is a considerable range of material that engages with the impact of travel and reading continental fiction on Morgan and Edgeworth. See, for example, Meaney, O' Dowd and Whelan (eds), *Reading the Irishwoman*, 65-73 and Isabelle Bour, 'What Maria Learned: Maria Edgeworth and Continental Fiction' in *Women's Writing*, 18, no. 1 (February 2011), 34-49.

91 Julia Kavanagh, *English Women of Letters: Biographical Sketches* vol. 2, 311.

92 *Ibid.*, 103, 149.

93 *Ibid.*, 308.

94 *Ibid.*, 332.

95 Meaney, O' Dowd and Whelan (eds), *Reading the Irishwoman*, 73.

96 Kavanagh, *English Women of Letters: Biographical Sketches*. Vol. 2, 353.

97 Stevens, *The Irish Scene in Somerville and Ross*, 8.

98 Foster, *Words Alone*, xiv.

4. General Practice?

1 *The Lancet*, 24 January 1931.

2 *Ibid.*

3 *British Medical Journal*, 12 June 1937.

4 *Irish Press*, 12 July 1934.

5 *British Medical Journal*, 21 July 1934.

6 *Ibid.*, 8 March 1941.

7   *Ibid.*, 11 October 1930.

8   Dr Brendan Kelly, University College Dublin, is currently completing a major biography of Dr Ada English, which will be published by Irish Academic Press; I am grateful to Dr. Kelly for sharing his great knowledge of Dr English with me.

9   For a full examination of Lynn's political career, see Chapter Two, 'Rebellious Womanhood' of my *Kathleen Lynn, Irishwoman, Patriot, Doctor* (Dublin and Portland, 2006 and 2011).

10 Lynn's diary, 6 May 1916, courtesy of the Royal College of Physicians in Ireland, RCPI. My thanks to Margaret Connolly who transcribed the 600,000 words in Lynn's diary; the record was kept from 1916 to 1955.

11 For Lord Mayor Lawrence O'Neill, see the biography by Tom Morrisse; the exact quotation from Lynn comes from Lynn's First Witness Statement to the Bureau of Military History, now available on the National Archives of Ireland website.

12 Lynn's diary, 21 April 1925, RCPI.

13 Interview with William Wynne, December 1996.

14 Dr Dorothy Price, in Liam Price (ed.), *An Account of Twenty Years' Fight against Tuberculosis in Ireland* (Oxford: Oxford University Press, 1957), 5. Dr Anne Mac Lellan, Connolly Memorial Hospital, is currently completing a biography of Dr Price which will be published by Irish Academic Press and I have learned much from her.

15 *British Medical Journal*, 22 August 1931.

16 *Ibid.*, 8 September 1906.

17 *Ibid.*

18 *The Irish Times*, 10 February 1938.

19 *St. Stephen's*, November 1904.

20 *Alexandra College Magazine,* June 1924, 33. For further information on the Sunshine Home, see Laura Kelly's article in Anne Mac Lellan and Alice Mauger (eds), *Growing Pains: Childhood Illness in Ireland 1750–1950* (Dublin: Irish Academic Press, 2013), 141-58. I am grateful to the editors for giving me a copy of this excellent book.

21 *The Irish Times,* 27 August 1946.

22 *Ibid.*

5. Intellectual Women

1   John A. Murphy, *The College: A History of Queen's/University College, Cork* (Cork: Cork University Press, 1995); Brian Walker and Alf McCreary, *Degrees of Excellence: The Story of Queen's Belfast, 1845–1995* (Belfast: Institute of Irish Studies, 1994); Tadhg Foley, *From Queen's College to National University: Essays on the Academic History*

of QCG/UCG/NUI, Galway (Dublin: Four Courts, 1999); Donal McCartney, *A National Idea: The History of University College, Dublin* (Dublin: Gill & Macmillan, 1990); John Luce, *The First Four Hundred Years: Trinity College Dublin, 1592–1992* (Dublin: 1992).

2   Alison Jordan, *Mrs. Margaret Byers, A Pioneer of Women's Education and Founder of Victoria College, Belfast* (Belfast: Institute of Irish Studies, 1994).

3   Anne V. O'Connor and Susan M. Parkes, *Gladly Learn and Gladly Teach: A History of Alexandra College and School, 1866–1966* (Dublin: Blackwater Press, 1984).

4   Mary Cullen and Maria Luddy (eds), *Women, Power and Consciousness in Nineteenth Century Ireland* (Dublin: Attic Press, 1995); Deirdre Raftery and Susan M. Parkes, *Female Education in Ireland, 1700–1900: Minerva or Madonna* (Dublin: Irish Academic Press, 1997); Janice Holmes and Diane Urquhart (eds), *Coming into the Light: The Work of Politics and Religion in Ulster, 1840–1940* (Belfast: Institute of Irish Studies, 1994).

5   Patricia Phillips, 'The Queen's Institute (1861–81): The First Technical College for Women in the British Isles', in Norman Macmillan (ed.), *Prometheus's Fire: The History of Scientific Technological Education in Ireland* (Carlow: Tyndale Publications, 2000), 446–63.

6   O'Connor and Parkes, *Gladly Learn and Gladly Teach*, 3-33; Anne V. O' Connor, 'Anne Jellicoe' in Cullen and Luddy (eds), *Women, Power, and Consciousness*, 125-60.

7   *Dublin University Calendar*, 1887, *Regulations for the Examinations for Women*.

8   Raftery and Parkes, *Female Education in Ireland*, 69-105.

9   Mary Cullen (ed.), *Girls Don't Do Honours: Irish Women in Education in the Nineteenth Century* (Dublin: Woman's Education Bureau, 1987); Judith Harford, *The Opening of University Education to Women in Ireland* (Dublin: Irish Academic Press, 2008).

10   Lucinda Thomson, 'The Campaign for Admission, 1870–1904' in Susan M. Parkes (ed.), *A Danger to the Men? A History of Women in Trinity College Dublin, 1904–2004* (Dublin: Lilliput Press, 2004), 19-54.

11   The Central Association of Irish Schoolmistresses was founded in 1882 to support girls' schools. Raftery and Parkes, *Female Education in Ireland*, 76-92.

12   Under the '*ad eundem gradum*' privilege, students could be examined by one of the universities and awarded the degree by another. Oxford did not award degrees to women until 1919 and Cambridge not until 1948. Susan M. Parkes, 'Trinity College, Dublin and the Steamboat Ladies, 1904–07', in M.R. Mason and D. Simonton (eds), *Women and Higher Education, Past, Present and Future* (Aberdeen: Aberdeen University Press, 1996).

13   *Calendar of the Royal University of Ireland for 1909*, 3.

14 The Tripos examination consisted of two separate parts, I and II, which were taken in two consecutive years.

15 Susan Manning, 'Women from Scotland at Newnham: the early years', in Mason and Simonton (eds), *Women and Higher Education*, 231-44.

16 Felicity Hunt and Carol Barker, *Women at Cambridge, A Brief History* (Cambridge: Cambridge University Press, 1998), 4.

17 Janet Sondheimer, *The Girls' Public Day School Trust, 1872–1972: A Centenary History* (London: GPDST, 1973). Among the early high schools were Blackheath, Croydon, Putney and South Hampstead.

18 *Girton College Register, 1869–1946* (Cambridge, Girton College, 1948); *Newnham College Register,* Vol. I, 1871–1971 (Cambridge, Newnham College, 1979).

19 Rachel Cook, daughter of Revd John Cook, professor of ecclesiastical history at St Andrew's University, married Charles Scott of the *Manchester Guardian* and was an active advocate of women's education in Manchester. Louisa Lumsden was to have a distinguished career in women's education, for which she was awarded a DBE in1925. She became the pioneering head of St Leonard's School in St Andrew's and later the first female warden of University Hall for Women Students at St Andrew's. Sarah Woodhead was a Quaker and the daughter of a Manchester grocer. She sat for the Cambridge Mathematical Tripos in 1873. She taught mathematics at Manchester High School for Girls and was later headmistress of Silverwell School, Bolton. In 1875 she married Christopher Corbett, a chartered surveyor.

20 [Anon], *Emily Townshend* (privately published, 1926; copy in Cambridge University Library), 29, quoted in Felicity Hunt, *Lessons for Life: The Schooling of Girls and Women, 1850–1950* (Oxford: Blackwell, 1987, 175-6).

21 *Girton Register,* 1.

22 *Ibid.,* 20

23 *Ibid.,* 24.

24 *Ibid.,* 26

25 *Ibid.,* 31.

26 Students are listed in the university register by the year of entry rather than graduation.

27 *Ibid.,* 32.

28 *Ibid,* 34. Women HMIs had been appointed from 1896. J.E. Dunford, *Her Majesty's Inspectors from 1944: Standard Bearers or Turbulent Priests?* (London: Woburn Press, 1998).

29 *Girton Register,* 627; Rita Tullberg McWilliam, *Women at Cambridge,* (Cambridge, CUP, 1998), 90-118.

30 *Girton Register,* 629-30.

31 The Girls' Day School Trust, formerly the Girls' Public Day School Trust (established at the Girls' Public Day School Company in 1872) is the largest group of independent schools in the United Kingdom.

32 A. Price and N. Glenday, *Reluctant Revolutionaries: A Century of Headmistresses, 1874–1974* (London: Pitman, 1974).

33 Obituary, *The Times*, 19 May 1951; Girton College Scrapbook, Girton College archives, 'Obituary', *Girton Review*, Easter Term 1951, No.146, 9–14.

34 *Girton Register*, 37, 40.

35 Mary Mulvihill (ed.), *Lab Coats and Lace: The Lives and Legacies of Inspiring Irish Women Scientists and Pioneers* (Dublin: WITS, 2009), 73–85. Everett published with her father a book on lens and glass, translated from a German book by H. Horestadt, J.D. Everett and Alice Everett (eds & trans), *Jena Glass and its Scientific and Industrial Applications* (London: Macmillan, 1902).

36 *Girton Register*, 40; Mulvihill, *Lab Coats and Lace*, 74–82.

37 Pam Hirsch and Mark McBeth, *Teacher Training at Cambridge: The Initiatives of Oscar Browning and Elizabeth Hughes* (London: Woburn Press, 2004).

38 *Girton Register*, 54

39 M. Bottrall, *Hughes Hall, 1885–1985* (Cambridge: Rutherford Publications, 1985).

40 *Girton Register*, 58.

41 Clarissa Pilkington, 'Trinity Hall', in Parkes (ed.), *A Danger to the Men?*, 237–54; Rosa Pilcher, *A History of Trinity Hall, 1908–2002* (Dublin: Hinds, 2013).

42 *Ibid.*

43 *Girton Register*, 101; Margaret J. Tuke, *A History of Bedford College for Women, 1849–1937* (Oxford: Oxford University Press, 1939); K.S.H. McCutcheon and Julia Grant, *The History of St. Leonard's School, 1877–1927* (Oxford: Oxford University Press, 1927).

44 Georgina Fitzpatrick, *St Andrew's College, 1894–1994* (Dublin: St Andrew's College, 1994), 18–28; *Girton Register*, 85.

45 Rita McWilliams Tulberg, *Women at Cambridge* (London: Gollancz, 1975), 37–55.

46 K. Rathbone (Dixon, 1880) in Ann Phillips (ed.), *A Newnham Anthology* (Cambridge: Cambridge University Press, 1979), 21.

47 *Ibid.*, 22.

48 Newnham Register, 59; W.J.R. Wallace, *Faithful to our Trust: A History of the Erasmus Smith Trust and the High School Dublin* (Dublin: Columba Press, 2004); Maurice Wilkins, *The Third Man of the*

Double Helix: The Autobiography of Maurice Wilkins (Oxford: Oxford University Press, 2003).

49 Newnham Register, 67; Michael Quane, 'D'Israeli School, Rathvilly', *Royal Society of Antiquarians of Ireland, Journal*, Ser. 7, Vol. xxviii, 11-23, 1948. The period school building is still extant.

50 C.B. Firth, *Constance Louisa Maynard: Mistress of Westfield* (London: George Allen & Unwin, 1949); Constance Maynard, *Between Terms* (London: James Nisbet, 1910); Newnham Register, 70.

51 Martha Vicinus, *Independent Women: Work and Community for Single Women, 1850–1920* (London: Virago, 1985); Elizabeth Alden Green, *Mary Lyon and Mount Holyoke: The Opening of the Gates* (New Hampshire: University Press of New England, 1979).

52 Frances Ralph Gray, *Gladly wolde He Lerne and Gladly Teche: Chaucer – A Book about Teaching and Learning* (London: Sampson Low, 1931).

53 Janet Sondheimer, *Castle Adamant in Hampstead: A History of Westfield* (London: Westfield College, 1983). Westfield merged with Queen Mary's College, London in 1989.

54 Newnham Register, 77; O'Connor and Parkes, *Gladly Learn and Gladly Teach*, 53-86.

55 Parkes (ed.), *A Danger to the Men?*, 6-70.

56 Newnham Register, 85; Roedean School in Brighton was founded by Penelope Lawrence and her two sisters in 1885 to prepare girls to enter the Cambridge women's colleges. It was to become one of the most prestigious schools in England.

57 Newnham Register, 79; Patrick Wyse Jackson, 'Grenville Arthur James Cole, 1859–1924', *Dictionary of Irish Biography* (Cambridge: Cambridge University Press, 2009).

58 G. and B. Cole, *As We Ride* (Dublin: written and published for the Royal City Hospital, 1902). I am indebted to Dr Patrick Wyse Jackson for information on Blanche Vernon Cole.

59 Margaret Ó hÓgartaigh, *Kathleen Lynn, Irishwoman, Patriot, Doctor* (Dublin: Irish Academic Press, 2006), 71. The Sunshine Home provided an open-air convalescent and holiday home for children from the inner city. It is still open.

60 Newnham Register, 143, 9; Patrick Wyse Jackson, 'William Johnson Sollas, 1849–1936', *Dictionary of Irish Biography*.

61 Jennifer Flegg, *The French School, Bray, Remembered* (Dublin: A.& A. Farmar, 2006).

62 Newnham Register, 99; William Marshall, 'Irish Clergy Abroad', in T.C. Barnard and W.G. Neely (eds), *The Clergy and the Church of Ireland, 1000–2000* (Dublin: Four Courts Press, 2006), 268.

63 Dartford College of Physical Education was founded in

1895 by the Swedish pioneer of physical education, Madame
Bergman-Osterberg.

64 *Royal Commission on University Education (Ireland)* (Robertson); *First
Report*, 1901–3, HC 1902 [C.825-6.] xxxi, 21: *Second Report*, 1902
[C. 899-900.] xxxi, 459; *Third Report*, 1902 [C. 1228-9.] xxxii. i.;
Final Report, 1903 [C1483-4.] xxxii.i.

65 T.W. Moody and J.C. Beckett, *Queen's University 1845–1945:
The History of a University*, Vol. I (London: Faber & Faber, 1949).

66 *Robertson Commission, Third Report, Minutes of Evidence*, 319;
Robertson Commission, First Report, Minutes of Evidence, 218-21;
Robertson Commission, Third Report, Minutes of Evidence, 357-9.

67 *Robertson Commission, First Report, Minutes of Evidence*, 209-15.

68 Harford, *The Opening of University Education to Women in Ireland*,
99-128.

69 *Robertson Commission, Third Report*, 64-65.

70 *Robertson Commission, Final Report*, 46-50.

71 Irish Universities Act, 1908 (8 Edw.VII.c.38).

72 O'Connor and Parkes, *Gladly Learn and Gladly Teach*; Harford,
The Opening of University Education to Women in Ireland, 127-8.

73 Parkes (ed.), *A Danger to the Men?*; Parkes, 'The Steamboat
Ladies and Trinity College' in Mason and Simonton, *Women and
Higher Education*.

74 Bryant was born in Belfast and succeeded Miss Buss as head of
North London Collegiate School. She was the first woman to be
awarded a London University DSc degree. Barlow was a well-known
author of Irish novels, her most popular being *Irish Idylls* (1892).

75 George Johnstone Stoney was secretary of the Queen's University
of Ireland from 1857 to 1879 and was an advocate of the higher
education of women.

76 *Newnham College Letter*, 1904, 37-43; *Newnham Register*, 107.

77 Parkes (ed.), *A Danger to the Men?*, 89.

78 *University of Dublin Calendar for the year 1904–5*, degrees conferred, 64-9.

79 *Newnham Register*, 111.

80 *Ibid.*, 106.

81 Pilcher, *Trinity Hall, 1908–2008*.

82 *Girton Register*, 130.

83 Felicitas Corrigan, *Helen Waddell: A Biography* (London: Gollancz,
1986); Jennifer FitzGerald, 'The Queen's Girl: Helen Waddell and
Women at Queen's University Belfast, 1908–20', in Judith Harford
and Claire Rush (eds), *Have Women Made a Difference? Women in
Irish Universities, 1850–2010* (Oxford: Peter Lang, 2009), 77-194;
Jennifer FitzGerald, *Helen Waddell and Maude Clarke: Irishwomen,*

Friends and Scholars (Oxford: Peter Lang, 2012). I am grateful to Jennifer FitzGerald for details on McCallum; *Girton Register*, 136.

84 *Girton Register*, 165.

85 *Girton Register*, 198. I am indebted to Debbie Wheeler, her granddaughter, for details.

86 *Robertson Commission on University Education Ireland, Final Report*, 49.

87 Parkes (ed.), *A Danger to the Men?*, 55–86.

88 Harford, *The Opening of University Education to Women in Ireland*, 99–128.

89 Intermediate Board Exams: in 1898 123 girls sat the senior grade; by 1915 the number had risen to 501. Raftery and Parkes, *Female Education in Ireland*, 86, 93.

90 James Albisetti, 'Unlearned Lessons from the New World? English Views of American Co-education and the Women's Colleges, c. 1865–1910', *History of Education*, vol. 29, no 5 (2000), 473–89.

91 Orla Egan (ed.), *Women Staff in Irish Colleges* (Dublin: Higher Education Equality Unit, 1995).

I wish to thank the libraries of both Girton and Newnham Colleges for facilitating my research.

6. A Woman's Reply

1 E.A.Y. [anon.], *Annals of fashionable gallantry: a collection of remarkable trials for crim. con., divorce, adultery, seduction, cruelty, and c.; The whole forming a complete history of the private life and amours of many characters in the most ellvated [sic] sphere, interspersed with many curious anecdotes of supreme bon ton* (London: printed for private circulation, 1883), 81-2. Like many collections of this kind, Irish cases were interspersed with those from the rest of the UK. See also Charles Phillips, *The speech of Mr. Philips, delivered in the Court of Common Pleas, Dublin, in the case of Guthrie v. W. P. B. D. Sterne, for Crim. Con.* (Bristol: Joseph Routh, 1815) and Charles Philips (ed.), *The Speeches of Charles Philips, Esq. delivered at the Bar, on various public occasions, in Ireland and England* (London: William Hone, 1817).

2 This association with the upper echelons of society was at least partly related to the cost of divorce. E.A.Y. [anon.], *Annals of Fashionable Gallantry*, iii.

3 *Ibid.*

4 *Ibid.*, 50.

5 *Ibid.*, iii.

6 W.E. Vaughan and A.J. Fitzpatrick (eds), *Irish Historical Statistics, 1821–1971* (Dublin: Royal Irish Academy, 1978), 241-2 and 246.

7 *Ibid.*, 87-9.

8 An invalid marriage could be annulled. See Roderick Phillips, *Untying the Knot: A Short History of Divorce* (Cambridge: Cambridge University Press, 1991), 2-6.

9 That Plowden still deemed separation the 'best accommodation for conjugal disagreement' is indicative of the difficulties of divorcing at this juncture. Separation was also known as *divorce à mensâ et thoro*. Francis Plowden, *Crim. Con. Biography: or celebrated trials in the ecclesiastical and civil courts for adultery and other crimes connected with incontinency, from the period of Henry the Eighth to the present time* (London: M. Iys, 1830), iii.

10 A parliamentary divorce could cost between £200 and £5,000 and take years to complete. See Gail L. Savage, 'The operation of the 1857 Divorce Act, 1860–1910: a research note', *Journal of Social History* 16, no. 4 (Summer, 1983), 103.

11 Anon., *Authentic report of the crim. con trial of Joynt v. Jackson, in the Exchequer Court, Dublin, commencing May 10th, 1880* (Dublin: Edward Smyth, 1880), 28.

12 This increase continued: an average of one Irish divorce act was passed per annum in the 1907–10 period, with the rate increasing steadily thereafter. Evidence of James Roberts to the Royal Commission on Divorce and Matrimonial Causes, *Minutes of Evidence* 3 (London: HMSO, 1912), 465.

13 See, for example, James Patrick Byrne, *The New Law of Divorce and Matrimonial Causes applicable to Ireland ... Popularly Explained* (Dublin: E.J. Milliken, 1859).

14 The Westropp case is further discussed in Diane Urquhart, 'Irish divorce and domestic violence, 1886–1922', *Women's History Review*, 22 no. 5 (2013): 820-37. A further twenty-four Irishwomen presented divorce bills to Westminster from 1900 to 1922. To contextualise these figures in relation to Irishmen: women brought 45 per cent of all Irish divorce bills to Westminster from 1900 to 1922 and 54 per cent of bills from 1914 to 1922 (Records of the House of Commons, Minutes of Proceedings on Irish Divorce Bills [1907–1922] (4 vols., HC/CL/CO/BF/1-4)).

15 House of Lords debates, 28 July 1859, vol. 155, cc 510-18.

16 See, for example, William G. Brooke, 'Report on the differences in the law of England and Ireland as regards the protection of women', *Report to the Council of the Statistical and Social Inquiry of Ireland* (21 January 1873) and 'Rights of married women in England and Ireland' in *The Irish Law Times and Solicitors' Journal* (31 May 1873), as well as A.W. Samuels, 'The law of divorce in Ireland', *Report of Statistical and Social Inquiry of Ireland* IV (June 1887). Although

Wicklow believed divorce opposed the sacraments, he frequently
championed Irish divorce law reform on the grounds of equality
between Ireland and the rest of the UK under the Union.

17 The Marchioness of Westmeath (Emily Anne Bennett Elizabeth
Nugent), *A narrative of the case of the Marchioness of Westmeath*
(London: James Ridgway, 1857) (British Library, 6497.c.13).

18 Lawrence Stone, *Broken Lives: Separation and Divorce in England,
1660–1857* (Oxford: Oxford University Press, 1993), 298. Lord Devlin
was promoted from Irish earl to Irish marquess by the Tory
government in 1822 and was elected an Irish life peer in the Lords
in 1831.

19 *Ibid.*, 285-6. George inherited the Westmeath title and estates
in 1814. See E.H. Chalus, 'Cecil, Mary Amelia, marchioness of
Salisbury (1750–1835)', *Oxford Dictionary of National Biography*
(Oxford: Oxford University Press, 2004); online edn, www.
oxforddnb.com/view/article/68357, accessed 24 July 2013.

20 In the Westmeaths' 1827 Court of Arches case, Nicholl believed that
this was proof of 'contrivance … deception … concealment' on
Lord Westmeath's part (cited in Westmeath, *Narrative*, 17).

21 Cited in Stone, *Broken Lives*, 303.

22 Wood also acted as a trustee for the Marchioness of Westmeath.
Wood brought a case against the Marquess of Westmeath in the
Court of King's Bench, 1820. See Anon, *Reports of some cases,
in which the Marquess and Marchioness of Westmeath have been litigant
parties* (London: np, 1825), 30-60.

23 Cited in Stone, *Broken Lives*, 307.

24 Cited in Anon, *Reports of some cases*, 60-5.

25 Restitution of conjugal rights proceedings could force a spouse to
return home and cohabit with their partner.

26 *Freeman's Journal*, 27 March 1820.

27 Cited in Stone, *Broken Lives*, 291.

28 Anon, *Reports of some cases*, 16.

29 Westmeath, *Narrative*, 6.

30 Being accessory to the adultery, connivance, collusion or
condonation were peremptory bars to a divorce whilst
recrimination, cruelty, desertion, wilful separation, wilful neglect,
misconduct and unreasonable delay were classified as discretionary
bars. The sexual double standard, however, meant that less weight
was attached to a wife's condonation of her husband's infidelity.

31 *Freeman's Journal*, 27 March 1820.

32 *Ibid.*

33 *Ibid.* See also the comments of Lord Westmeath's lawyer, Attorney

General J.S. Copley, later Lord Lyndhurst, in relation to the deeds of 1817 and 1818 in Anon, *Reports of some cases*, 19 and 22. The Lord Chancellor concurred in 1820, noting the case was 'not only important as to the parties, but to the public at large'. Anon, *Reports of some cases*, 22.

34 *Freeman's Journal*, 27 and 29 March 1820. Each would steal the other's correspondence and would pay for evidence.

35 *Ibid.*, 29 March 1820.

36 *Ibid*, 6 April 1830.

37 In 1830 Lord Westmeath also appealed in the House of Lords to have the 1818 deed removed.

38 *Freeman's Journal*, 6 April 1830.

39 Stone, *Broken Lives*, 315. See also the pro-Marchioness of Westmeath pamphlet, Anon, *Reports of some cases*.

40 Cited in Anon, *Reports of some cases*, 56.

41 Cited in *ibid.*, 30.

42 Letter from Lady Westmeath to William Leake, 21 October 1832 cited in Westmeath, *Narrative*, 189.

43 The marquess appealed the verdict. See *The most noble George Thomas John, Marquess of Westmeath, appellant, against the most mobile Emily Anne Bennett Elizabeth, Marchioness of Westmeath (his wife), respondent: an appeal from the Arches Court of Canterbury* (London: Samuel Brooke, 1828).

44 Stone, *Broken Lives*, 331-2. George appealed to the Court of Delegates in 1829, refusing to pay Emily's expenses of £1,500 and alimony. Emily sued him for contempt of court and he 'claimed immunity from arrest by virtue of his privilege as an Irish peer'. However, it was found that a writ of contempt from a Church court 'was not enforceable in law against a peer'. Lord Brougham's reaction to this was to introduce the Ecclesiastical Court Powers Bill of 1832. In 1853 some costs were still outstanding and thus Emily sued her spouse for unpaid alimony. He successfully appealed against the scale of payment. The amount was reduced by the Judicial Committee of the Privy Council to £315 per annum but he had to pay £20,000 in arrears from 1822 to 1833 and costs (*ibid.*).

45 Cited in Westmeath, *Narrative*, 13.

46 *Ibid.*, 22 and 28.

47 *Ibid.*, 17.

48 Fourteen letters dating from 1813 from Lady Westmeath to her spouse were used against her, as they made no reference to her abuse.

49 Cited in Westmeath, *Narrative*, 44-7. After another incident, Lady Westmeath feared a strike to her breast 'would end in a cancer' and

asked a servant to fashion a 'handkerchief to hide it' at the Duke of Leinster's house (*ibid*).

50 *Ibid*., 19-20.

51 See John M. Biggs, *The Concept of Matrimonial Cruelty* (London: Athlone Press, 1962) and Elizabeth Foyster, *Marital Violence: An English Family History, 1660–1857* (Cambridge: Cambridge University Press, 2005).

52 Westmeath, *Narrative*, 76.

53 Byrne, *New Law of Divorce*, 27. This approach was also taken by Irish reformer Frances Power Cobbe. See, for example, her article, 'Wife-torture in England' (1878), reprinted in Sheila Jeffreys (ed.), *The Sexuality Debates* (New York and London: Routledge and Kegan Paul, 1987), 219-53. Lord Westmeath appealed unsuccessfully against the 1827 judgement in the Court of Delegates and then in the Commission of Review.

54 The pamphlet was published by the Independent Press, Dublin (British Library, 1609/4162).

55 Westmeath, *Sketch*, 6.

56 *Ibid*., 16, 21-2, 37-29 and 91.

57 *Ibid*., 12. The latter was inferred in the 1827 Ecclesiastical Court of Arches case where 'making no allusion to those occasional acts of harshness' was deemed 'not discreditable to Lady Westmeath'. Rather 'by conciliatory conduct, she hoped to soften the violence of her husband's temper' (cited in Westmeath, *Narrative*, 15-16).

58 Westmeath, *Sketch*, 6-7.

59 *Ibid*., 9-10.

60 *Ibid*., 12-13. The fact the under civil law, such witnesses gave evidence to the ecclesiastical court in private and '*back to back*' to interrogatories was further used by Westmeath in an attempt to discredit them, asking why none had been called to give evidence in common law proceedings where they would have to be '*face to face*' with the court (*ibid*., 14-15). Claims that Emily paid witnesses to lie were not proven and she and her attorney were cleared in 1822 when George sued the witnesses for conspiracy before the Commission Court in Dublin. Three people, including George's alleged mistress, Anne Connell, were found guilty. They were fined and sentenced to eighteen months.

61 *Ibid*., 43.

62 *Ibid*., 30.

63 *Ibid*., 45.

64 *Ibid*., 46-7.

65 Cited in *ibid*., 10-11. A housekeeper, for example, defied George's authority as she was Emily's employee. Stone, *Broken Lives*, 309.

66 Westmeath, *Sketch*, 15-16.

67 Cited in *ibid.*, 21.

68 Westmeath, *Narrative*, 3 and 104.

69 *Ibid.*, 104 and 127.

70 Caroline Norton, *A Letter to the Queen on Lord Chancellor Cranworth's Marriage and Divorce Bill* (London: Longman, Brown, Green and Longmans, 1855), 4, 5, 33, 48, 67 and 79.

71 Westmeath, *Narrative*, 103-4.

72 *Ibid.*, 2.

73 Stone, *Broken Lives*, 342. Westmeath bequeathed £600 per annum jointure to this mistress and £10,000 to his three children by her, although the deaths of two of these children pre-dated his own death.

74 Westmeath, *Narrative*, 118, 124 and 139.

75 Cited in Stone, *Broken Lives*, 298-9.

76 Cited in Westmeath, *Narrative*, 8.

77 Cited in *ibid.*, 76-8.

78 Lord Salisbury cited in *ibid.*, 101. Lord Salisbury died in 1823.

79 Westmeath, *Narrative*, 129, 131 and 133. Fearing perjury, Emily also refused to try and secure a Scottish divorce in 1823–4.

80 Cited in *ibid.*, 107-8. See also Lord Westmeath, *A Reply to the 'Narrative of the case of the Marchioness of Westmeath'* (London: np, 1857), 40 (British Library, 16417.g.57). Lord Westmeath countered this claim by noting that she refused alimony in the Lords in 1821 when the suit for restitution of conjugal rights was pending, on the grounds that to accept it could invalidate the deed of 1818.

81 Emily persuaded Wellington to secure places for some of her Irish witnesses in, for example, the Ordnance Office (although one was unable to write English), and McGuire, her attorney, was appointed as government solicitor; this served to discredit Wellington (see Stone, *Broken Lives*, 326).

82 *Ibid.*, 333.

83 For example, the Irish Lord Lieutenant opposed this pension and it was questioned, but not withdrawn, in 1833 (*ibid.*, 335-6).

84 Westmeath, *Narrative*, 3.

85 *Ibid.*, 128.

86 *Ibid.*, 213.

87 Stone, *Broken Lives*, 341.

88 James Grant, for example, offers an unflattering portrait of the Tory Westmeath in the Lords in *Random Recollections of the Lords and Commons*, vol. 1 (London: Henry Colburn Publishers, 1838), 86.

89 House of Lords debates, 25 May 1857, vol. 140, cc 809-12.

90 Westmeath, *Reply*, 5-6.

91 *Ibid.*, 95–6 and see Stone, *Broken Lives*, 341.

92 Cited in Westmeath, *Reply*, 35 and 37.

93 *Ibid.*, 45 and 97.

94 Stone, *Broken Lives*, 333 and 338.

95 Biggs, *Concept of Matrimonial Cruelty*, 38.

96 Stone, *Broken Lives*, 344.

97 *Ibid.*, 297–8. Stone also suggests that she was more interested in 'parties, fashion, power, money and the rights of women than in sex', 302.

98 Cited in *ibid.*, 300. Lady Westmeath was also described by various witnesses in the 1827 case as able to express herself 'with warmth and even with bitterness and acrimony … but she had considerable self-command, and her natural temper and disposition are described as being good' (Westmeath, *Narrative*, 19).

99 Cited in Stone, *Broken Lives*, 306.

100 *Ibid.*, 300–2 and 308.

101 Westmeath, *Narrative*, 2.

7. A Terrible Beauty

1 Jan Cannavan, 'Revolution in Ireland, Evolution in Women's Rights: Irishwomen in 1798 and 1848' in Louise Ryan and Margaret Ward (eds), *Irish Women and Nationalism: Soldiers, New Women and Wicked Hags* (Dublin: Irish Academic Press, 2004), 35.

2 Nancy Curtin, 'Women and Eighteenth-Century Irish Republicanism', in M. MacCurtain and M. O'Dowd (eds), *Women in Early Modern Ireland* (Dublin: Wolfhound Press, 1991), 133–44.

3 Cannavan, 'Revolution in Ireland, Evolution in Women's Rights', 34.

4 Jan Cannavan, 'Romantic Revolutionary Irishwomen: Women, Young Ireland and 1848', in Margaret Kelleher and James H. Murphy (eds), *Gender Perspectives in 19th Century Ireland* (Dublin: Irish Academic Press, 1997), 214.

5 *Ibid.*, 216.

6 *Ibid.*, 218.

7 *Ibid.*, 219.

8 Cannavan, 'Revolution in Ireland, Evolution in Women's Rights', 43.

9 Mary Cullen and Maria Luddy (eds), *Women, Power and Consciousness in 19th Century Ireland* (Dublin: Attic Press, 1995).

10 Toby Joyce, '"Ireland's trained and marshalled manhood": the Fenians in the mid-1860s', in Kelleher and Murphy (eds), *Gender Perspectives in 19th Century Ireland*, 76.

11 Catherine Morris, *Alice Milligan and the Irish Cultural Revival* (Dublin: Four Courts Press, 2012), 126.

12 Joyce, '"Ireland's trained and marshalled manhood"', 76; Maria
    Luddy, 'Women and Politics in Nineteenth-Century Ireland',
    in Maryann Valiulis and Mary O'Dowd (eds), *Women and Irish
    History* (Dublin: Wolfhound Press, 1997), 92-3.
13 Joyce, '"Ireland's trained and marshalled manhood"', 76.
14 Anna Parnell, 'How They Do in the House of Commons: Notes
    From the Ladies' Cage', *Celtic Monthly*, May–July 1880.
15 *Ibid.*
16 Jane Côté, *Fanny and Anna Parnell: Ireland's Patriot Sisters* (Dublin:
    Gill and MacMillan, 1991), 95.
17 Roy Foster, *Charles Stewart Parnell: The Man and his Family* (Sussex:
    Harvester Press, 1976), 263.
18 Danae O'Regan, 'Anna and Fanny Parnell', *History Ireland* 1, Vol. 7
    (1999): 37-41; Margaret Ward, 'Anna Parnell: Challenges to Male
    Authority and the Telling of National Myth', in Pauric Travers and
    Donal McCartney (eds), *Parnell Reconsidered* (Dublin: University
    College Dublin Press, 2013), 47-60.
19 O'Regan, 'Anna and Fanny Parnell', 41.
20 C.L. Innes, *Woman and Nation in Irish Literature and Society*
    (Hertfordshire: Harvester Wheatsheaf, 1993), 112.
21 Roy Foster, *Charles Stewart Parnell*, 254.
22 'New Departure' refers to the policy of Glan na Gael leader John
    Devoy who urged support for nationalists in parliament who
    favoured land reform and Irish independence.
23 D.B. Cashman, *The Life of Michael Davitt and the Secret History of the
    Land League* (Glasgow: Washbourne, 1883 or 1884), 231.
24 *Ibid.*, 230.
25 Margaret Ward, *Unmanageable Revolutionaries: Women and Irish
    Nationalism* (London: Pluto Press, 1983): 4-39.
26 Côté, *Fanny and Anna Parnell*, 169.
27 *Irish World*, 25 February 1882.
28 Côté, *Fanny and Anna Parnell*, 207.
29 Beverly Schneller, *Anna Parnell's Political Journalism: Contexts and
    Texts* (Bethesda: Academica Press, 2005), 176.
30 Schneller, *Anna Parnell*, 176-7.
31 *Ibid.*, 179.
32 Ward, 'Anna Parnell', 49.
33 Côté, *Fanny and Anna Parnell*, 217.
34 Anna Parnell, *The Tale of a Great Sham*, ed. Dana Hearne (Dublin:
    Arlen House, 1986), 155.
35 Henry George to Helen Taylor, 1 October 1882, vol. xvii, item 81, Mill–
    Taylor Collection, London School of Economics and Political Science.

36 Helena Molony, Witness Statement 391, Bureau of Military History, Ireland, 14.

37 *United Ireland*, 5 August 1882.

38 Senia Paseta, *Irish Nationalist Women 1900–1918* (Cambridge: Cambridge University Press, 2013), 75.

39 Morris, *Alice Milligan*, 132.

40 *Ibid.*, 134.

41 *Ibid.*, 141.

42 *Ibid.*, 141-2.

43 *Ibid.*, 153.

44 *Ibid.*, 155.

45 *Ibid.*, 156.

46 *Ibid.*, 179.

47 Sheila Turner Johnston, *Alice: A Life of Alice Milligan* (Omagh: Colourpoiont Press, 1994), 96.

48 *Shan Van Vocht*, June 1897, reprinted in Ward (ed.), *In Their Own Voice*, 9.

49 Morris, *Alice Milligan*, 206.

50 Maud Gonne MacBride, *A Servant of the Queen* (London: Victor Gollancz, 1974) first published 1938, 96.

51 Karen Steele (ed.), *Maud Gonne: Irish Nationalist Writings 1895–1946* (Dublin: Irish Academic Press, 2004), 125.

52 Gonne MacBride, *A Servant of the Queen*, 176.

53 Karen Steele, 'Raising Her Voice for Justice: Maud Gonne and the *United Irishman*', *New Hibernia Review*, Summer 1999, 84-105.

54 *Ibid.*, 90.

55 *Ibid.*, 278.

56 Ann Matthews, *Renegades: Irish Republican Women 1900–1922* (Cork: Mercier Press, 2010), 34.

57 Margaret Quinn, Witness Statement 273, Bureau of Military History, Dublin, 1.

58 Steele, *Maud Gonne*, 140.

59 Morris, *Alice Milligan*, 273.

60 *Ibid.*, 269.

61 *Ibid.*, 267.

62 Molly Hyland, Witness Statement 295, Bureau of Military History, Dublin, 2.

63 Helena Molony, Witness Statement 391, Bureau of Military History, 4.

64 Ward, *Unmanageable Revolutionaries*, 79.

65 *Ibid.*, 67.

66 Helena Molony, Witness Statement, Bureau of Military History, 8-10.

67 Molly Hyland, Witness Statement, Bureau of Military History, 5.

68 *Bean na hÉireann*, 1, 3 January 1909.
69 Helena Molony, Witness Statement, Bureau of Military History, 64.
70 *Ibid*.
71 *Ibid*.
72 Carmel Quinlan, *Genteel Revolutionaries: Anna and Thomas Haslam and the Irish Women's Movement* (Cork: Cork University Press, 2002), 161.
73 Paseta, *Irish Nationalist Women*, 102.
74 Aine Ceannt, Witness Statement 264, Bureau of Military History, 9.
75 Ward, *Unmanageable Revolutionaries*, 91.
76 Mary Colum, *Irish Freedom*, September 1914, reprinted in Ward, *In Their Own Voice*, 44.
77 Aine O'Rahilly, Witness Statement 333, Bureau of Military History, 1.
78 Agnes O'Farrelly, *The Irish Volunteer*, 18 April 1914; reprinted in Ward, *In Their Own Voice,* 41.
79 Nancy Wyse Power, Witness Statement 541, Bureau of Military History, 9.
80 O'Farrelly, *The Irish Volunteer*, 18 April 1914.
81 Aine O'Rahilly, Witness Statement, Bureau of Military History, 1-2.
82 Louise Gavan Duffy, Witness Statement 216, Bureau of Military History, 2.
83 Aine Ceannt, Witness Statement 264, Bureau of Military History, 9.
84 Nancy Wyse Power, Witness Statement 541, Bureau of Military History, 10.
85 Aine O'Rahilly, Witness Statement 333, Bureau of Military History, 2.
86 Colum, *Irish Freedom*, September 1914.
87 *Ibid*.
88 *Irish Citizen*, 9 May 1914, reprinted in Ward, *In Their Own Voice*, 42. The name 'Irishwomen's Council' was used as well as Cumann na mBan in the early days of the organisation.
89 *Ibid*.
90 *The Irish Times*, 8 May 1914.
91 Francis Sheehy Skeffington, 'Open Letter to Thomas MacDonagh', *Irish Citizen*, 22 May 1915.
92 *Irish Citizen*, 23 October 1915, reprinted in Ward, *In Their Own Voice*, 46.
93 Eilis ni Riain, Witness Statement 568, Bureau of Military History, 3.
94 Nancy Wyse Power, Witness Statement 541, Bureau of Military History, 10.
95 Matthews, *Renegades*, 101.
96 Helena Molony, Witness Statement 391, Bureau of Military History, 20.
97 *Ibid*., 26.
98 *The Irish Times*, 'Stories of the Rising', 17 January 2014.
99 *Ibid*.

100 Matthews, *Renegades*, 112.
101 Hanna Sheehy Skeffington, *Bean na hÉireann*, November 1909;
     reprinted in Ward, *In Their Own Voice*, 32-4.
102 Mary Butler, 'Irish Women and the Home Language', in *The Field
     Day Anthology of Irish Writing*, vol 5: Irish Women's Writings and
     Traditions (Cork: Cork University Press, 2002), 85.
103 *Irish Citizen*, 23 October 1915, reprinted in Ward, *In Their Own Voice*.
104 Karen Steele, 'Constance Markievicz's Allegorical Garden:
     Femininity, Militancy, and the Irish Press, 1909–1915', *Women's
     Studies* 29, 2000, 427-51.
105 Maryann Valiulis, 'Free Women in a Free Nation', in Brian Farrell
     (ed.), *The Creation of the Dáil* (Dublin: Blackwater Press, 1994).
106 Ward, *Unmanageable Revolutionaries*, 126-7.
107 Margaret Ward, 'The League of Women Delegates and Sinn Féin
     1917', *History Ireland*, 4, 2 (1996), 37-41.

8. Knowing Their Place

1 The forms of schooling offered in nineteenth-century Ireland are
   often quite unlike those we are now accustomed to. William Carleton
   records in his *Traits and Stories of the Irish Peasantry* (1872) that
   'Nothing can more decidedly prove the singular and extraordinary
   thirst for education and general knowledge which characterises the
   Irish people than the shifts to which they have often gone in order
   to gain even a limited portion of instruction. Of this the Irish Night
   School is a complete illustration. The Night School was always
   opened either for those of early age, who from their poverty were
   forced to earn something for their own support during the day …
   or for grown young men who had never had an opportunity of
   acquiring education in their youth' (242). 'Secondary tops', national
   schools that offered the secondary school curriculum to senior pupils,
   operated throughout the 1940s and 1950s in Ireland.
2 See A.V. O'Connor, 'Influences Affecting Girls' Secondary Schooling
   in Ireland, 1860–1910', *Archivium Hibernicum*, Vol. 11, 1986, 86.
3 St Mary's College was initially intended as a novitiate for the
   Marist Fathers.
4 The European orders were: the Sacred Heart (1842); the Faithful
   Companions of Jesus (1844); St Louis (1859); St Joseph of Cluny
   (1860); La Sainte Union des Sacrés Coeurs (1862); Sacred Heart of
   Mary (1870); and the Marists (1873).
5 See, for example, A.V. O'Connor and S. Parkes, *Gladly Learn and
   Gladly Teach: Alexandra School, 1866–1966* (Dublin: Blackwater Press,

1984); A.V. O'Connor, 'The revolution in girls' secondary education in Ireland 1860–1910', in C. Clear (ed.), *Nuns in Nineteenth-Century Ireland* (Dublin: Gill and Macmillan, 1987); D. Raftery and S. Parkes, *Female Education in Ireland 1700–1900* (Dublin: Irish Academic Press, 2007); J. Harford, *The Opening of University Education to Women in Ireland* (Dublin, Irish Academic Press, 2008).

6   For example: curricular content, stereotyping in textbooks, equal pay etc.

7   The literature pertaining to this topic is extensive. See, for example, J. Kamm, *Hope Deferred: Girls' Education in English History* (London: Methuen & Co Ltd, 1965); M.C. Bradbrook, '*That infidel place': A Short History of Girton College, 1869–1969* (London: Chatto & Windus, 1969); R. McWilliams Tullberg, *Women at Cambridge* (Cambridge University Press, 1975); M. Bryant, *The Unexpected Revolution: A Study in the History of the Education of Women and Girls in the Nineteenth Century* (London: University of London Institute of Education, 1979); S. Fletcher, *Feminists and Bureaucrats: A Study in the Development of Girls' Education in the Nineteenth Century* (Cambridge: Cambridge University Press, 1980); J.N. Burstyn, *Victorian Education and the Ideal of Womanhood* (New Jersey: Rutgers University Press, 1984); J.S. Pedersen, *The Reform of Girls' Secondary and Higher Education in Victorian England: A Study of Elites and Educational Change* (New York, Garland, 1987); J. Purvis, *A History of Women's Education in England* (Milton Keynes: Open University Press, 1991); G. Avery, *The Best Type of Girl: A History of Girls' Independent Schools* (London: A. Deutsch, 1991); W. Geoffre, *The Private Schooling of Girls: Past and Present* (Oxford, RoutledgeFalmer, 1993); C. Dyhouse, *No Distinction of Sex? Women in British Universities, 1870–1939* (London: Routledge, 1995); D.M. Copeland, *London's Women Teachers: Gender, Class and Feminism 1870–1930* (London: Routledge, 1996); J. Martin, *Women and the Politics of Schooling in Victorian and Edwardian England* (London: Continuum, 1999); P. Hirsch, *Barbara Leigh Smith Bodichon: Feminist, Artist and Rebel* (London: Random House, 1999); M. Hilton and P. Hirsch, *Practical Visionaries: Women, Education, and Social Progress, 1790–1930* (London: Longman, 2000); A.B. Murphy and D. Raftery, *Emily Davies: Collected Letters, 1861–1875* (University of Virginia Press, 2004); J. Martin and J. Goodman, *Women and Education, 1800–1980* (Basingstoke: Palgrave Macmillan, 2004).

8   See J.N. Burstyn, *Victorian Education and the Ideal of Womanhood* (Croom Helm, 1980) for an insightful investigation of the expectations of gender in Victorian society.

9   R. Aldrich, 'The Three Duties of the Historian of Education', in *Lessons from History of Education: The Selected Works of Richard Aldrich* (London: Routledge, 2005), 18.

10 See *ibid.*, 4 and 18. P. Gardner, 'Reconstructing the Classroom
    Teacher, 1903–1945', in I. Grosvenor, M. Lawn and K. Rousmaniere
    (eds), *Silences and Images: The Social History of the Classroom* (Bern:
    Peter Lang, 1999), 125 and *The Lost Elementary Schools of Victorian
    England* (Croom Helm, 1984), 107.

11 D. Copelman, *London's Women Teachers: Gender, Class and Feminism,
    1870–1930* (Routledge, 1996), 152.

12 N. Hoffman, *Woman's 'True' Profession: Voices from the History of
    Teaching* (Harvard Education Press; 2nd edition, 2003), xv. See also
    R. Raughter (ed.), *Religious Women and their History: Breaking the
    Silence* (Dublin: Irish Academic Press, 2005), 50.

13 Ireland is not alone in overlooking the history of classrooms.
    Writing in 1992, Harold Silver wrote regarding the United
    Kingdom that 'it is difficult to believe that historians have made
    almost no attempt to reconstruct the classroom, the culture
    of the classroom, the social relations of the classroom'. See
    'Knowing and not knowing in the history of education', *History
    of Education*, 21, 1, 105.

14 Gardner, *The Lost Elementary Schools of Victorian England*, 1.

15 *Ibid.*

16 The dominance of social ties meant, according to Ó hÓgartaigh, that
    once educated middle-class women entered the 'professions and other
    leadership roles in Ireland, they did little to change the structure of
    society. Their inaction ensured that a professional career was possible
    only if one had the necessary contact for a professional apprenticeship,
    or the finances for advanced education.' M. Ó hÓgartaigh, 'A
    Quiet Revolution: Women and Second-Level Education in Ireland,
    1878–1930', *New Hibernia Review*, Vol. 12, No. 2, Summer 2009, 50-1.

17 M. Theobald, 'Teachers, memory and oral history' in K. Weiler and
    S. Middleton (eds), *Telling Women's Lives: Narrative Inquiries in the
    History of Women's Education* (Milton Keynes: Open University Press,
    1999), 18.

18 Cited in *ibid.*

19 *Ibid.*, 20-1.

20 *Ibid.*, 21.

21 Hoffman, *Woman's 'True' Profession*, xvii.

22 *Ibid.*, xviii.

23 See *ibid.*, 17.

24 Gardner, *The Lost Elementary Schools of Victorian England*, 121.

25 *Ibid.*, 125.

26 J.A. Preston, 'Reading teachers' mail: using women's correspondence
    to reconstruct the nineteenth-century classroom', in Grosvenor,

Lawn and Rousmaniere (eds), *Silences and Images*, 207. On female
teachers using corporal punishment see also Hoffman, *Woman's True
Profession*, 21.

27 See E. Watters (ed.), *Go Teach all Nations* (Paraclete Press, 2000), 51.

28 Burstyn, *Victorian Education and the Ideal of Womanhood*, 33.

29 It is difficult to assign a 'class' distinction at this distance. The majority
of parents who sent their daughters to secondary schools in the second
half of the nineteenth century were the professional, merchant or
'strong' farmer class, what today might be identified as middle- and
lower middle-class. Working-class children seldom attended school
beyond national level. See M.M. Kealy, *Dominican Education in Ireland
1820–1930* (Dublin: Irish Academic Press, 2007), 72-3, 76, 81.

30 The founding date of Siena is uncertain. For details of schools see
ibid., 85.

31 Sr M. Lillis, *Two Hundred Years A-Growing, 1787–1987: The Story of the
Ursulines in Thurles* (A Bicentenary Commemorative Publication
[n.p.] 1987), 29. The school finally accepted an offer to pay
£10 per year for three years and then £20 per year until the
account was cleared.

32 See O'Connor and Parkes, *Gladly Learn and Gladly Teach, passim*.
Alexandra College, founded by Anne Jellicoe in 1866, was
modelled on Queen's College, London (1848), the first college
established for the higher education of women in England.
As O'Connor notes, it 'began the movement to reform
girls' secondary education in Dublin', and indeed in Ireland.
A.V. O'Connor, 'The revolution in girls' secondary education in
Ireland, 1860–1910', in M. Cullen (ed.), *Girls Don't Do Honours:
Irish Women in Education in the 19th and 20th Centuries* (Women's
Education Bureau, 1987), 34.

33 In 1892 Katherine Murphy, educated by the Dominicans at Sion Hill
and Eccles Street, was awarded first place in the Royal University of
Ireland examination in modern literature. The response of the *Freeman's
Journal* was typical of the 'Catholic' press: 'We do not wish to make
any ungenerous comparisons but at a time when it is not unusual to
suggest that the convent schools are unequal to a programme of higher
education, it cannot be uncalled for to state the fact that on this first
occasion when the Alexandra College and a convent school came
into open competition for the great prize in connection with the
examination for the highest degree in Arts, the convent remains the
victor.' *Freeman's Journal*, 29 October 1892.

34 See J. Harford, *The Opening of University Education to Women in
Ireland*, 2.

35 See O'Connor, 'The revolution in girls' secondary education in Ireland, 1860–1910', in Cullen (ed.), *Girls Don't Do Honours*, 38.

36 *Catholic Directory*, 1848

37 Dominican Archives, Cabra, Dublin.

38 O'Connor and Parkes, *Gladly Learn and Gladly Teach*, 28.

39 Dominican Archives, Cabra, Dublin, *Cabra Annals*, 103.

40 *Ibid.*

41 *The Irish Times*, 4 May 1878.

42 Cited in Kealy, *Dominican Education in Ireland*, 80.

43 *The Irish Times*, 5 July 1879.

44 See Watters (ed.), *Go Teach all Nations*, 51.

45 Quoted in Raftery and Parkes, *Female Education in Ireland*, 77. Paul Cullen, Cardinal Archbishop of Dublin from 1852 to 1878.

46 Quoted in Kealy, *Dominican Education in Ireland*, 88. Edward McCabe, Cardinal Archbishop of Dublin from 1879 to 1885 and Cardinal from 1882.

47 *Ibid.*, 99.

48 *Ibid.*

49 Quoted in Raftery and Parkes, *Female Education in Ireland*, 82-3. The history of girls' schooling is replete with examples such as this. The system in the United Kingdom, which in terms of concerns regarding class and gender was very similar to that in Ireland. In 1910, for example, Sara Burstall, headmistress of Manchester High School for Girls, leading member of the Association of Headmistresses and 'prominent suffrage activist', told the National Union of Working Women that girls needed 'protection from the exhausting over-pressure of competitive examinations made by men for boys' schools. They needed time and leisure for the cultivation of literature and art and the deepening of the inner life of emotion and aspiration. In a word our girls' education must not be so closely modelled on that of boys.' Quoted in Copelman, *London's Women Teachers*, 223.

50 *Intermediate Education (Ireland) Commission. Appendix to the Final Report of the Commissioners. Part II. Miscellaneous Documents.* Stationery Office, Dublin, 1899. (C.-9513), Section E. – Digest of Minutes of Evidence, 246, Mrs. M. Byers, Principal, Victoria College, Belfast.

51 *Ibid.*

52 *Ibid.*

53 *Ibid.*, 270.

54 *Ibid.*, 274.

55 *Ibid.*, Section B. – Digest of Answers to Queries, 281.

56 *Intermediate Education (Ireland) Commission. Final Report of the Commissioners.* Stationery Office, Dublin, 1899 (C. – 9511) 21 X.-Over-pressure.

57 Loreto Archives, Dublin, *The Loreto Magazine*, Christmas 1896.

58 *Ibid.*

59 *Freeman's Journal*, 2 September 1886, quoted in Raftery and Parkes, *Female Education in Ireland*, 83.

60 *Ibid.* Girls attending Catholic schools at the period suffered a considerable disadvantage where Latin and mathematics were not taught, as these were awarded significantly higher 'points'.

61 Quoted in Kealy, *Dominican Education in Ireland*, 95-6.

62 D. Barry, 'Female Suffrage from a Catholic Standpoint', *Irish Ecclesiastical Record*, Vol. XXVI, July–December 1909, 300. Quoted in Harford, *The Opening of University Education to Women in Ireland*, 4.

63 See *ibid.*, 102.

64 Sacred Heart Archives, Mount Anville, Dublin, RSA/127: 'Roscrea 1861–1921: Memoirs written by Mrs. Moore', 9. On the importance of needlework in initial teacher education see the recollections of 'Dympna' in E. Kiely and M. Leane, *Irish Women at Work 1930–1960: An Oral History* (Dublin: Irish Academic Press, 2012), 71. However, there was much making and mending of garments for the poor and Our Lady's Needlework Guilds were not uncommon in girls' schools in the nineteenth and early twentieth centuries.

65 *Ibid.*, 65.

66 *Ibid.*, 24.

67 *Ibid.*, 34.

68 See B. Walsh, *Boy Republic: Patrick Pearse and Radical Education* (Dublin: History Press, 2013), Chapter Five.

69 *Ibid.*, 24.

70 *Ibid.*, 57.

71 *Ibid.*, 55.

72 *Ibid.*, 58.

73 *Ibid.*

74 D. Rudd, *Rochelle: The History of a School in Cork, 1829–1979* (Naas, 1979), 7.

75 *Ibid.*

76 *Ibid.*, 27.

77 See O'Connor and Parkes, *Gladly Learn and Gladly Teach*, 62.

78 Rudd, *Rochelle*, 39.

79 *Ibid.*

80 *Ibid.*, 83.

81 *Ibid.*, 52.

82 School Minute Book, 1897–98, September 13, cited in Rudd, *Rochelle*, 60.

83 *Ibid.*, 103 and 107. The authors of these recollections are not cited by Rudd.

84 *Ibid.*, 107.

85 *Ibid.*, 108.

86 *Ibid.*, 87.

87 *Ibid.*

88 *Ibid.*, 39. Again, Rudd does not cite the source of these quotes.

89 *Ibid.*

90 *Ibid.*, 41. Notes were sometimes passed between the young medical students and the girls from Rochelle at church; indeed, 'a highly respected and eminent Cork doctor' some time later 'carried on a violent flirtation with an extremely pretty girl, a great friend of mine' (Rudd, *Rochelle*, 41).

91 *Ibid.*

92 Quoted in *ibid.*, 70. Notably, pupils are now rising one hour earlier than in the previous decade.

93 *Ibid.*, 71.

94 *Ibid.*

95 Quoted in *ibid.*, 74.

96 Quoted in *ibid.*

97 *Ibid.*

98 *Ibid.*

99 'Capturing the Atmosphere and Rhythm of the Boarding School: Immaculata Rules 1914' in O. Burns and M. Wilson (eds), *Dominican Sisters Cabra 1819–1994* (n.p., 1994), 29-30.

100 *Ibid.*, 30.

101 *Ibid.* Lay brothers and sisters remain largely invisible to history, victims again of the grand narrative. A notable exception is C.T. Jack's 'The lay sister in educational history and memory', *History of Education*, 2000, Vol. 29, No. 3.

102 A.S. Neill (1883–1979), founder of Summerhill School, Suffolk. Patrick Pearse (1879–1916), founder of St Enda's School, Dublin.

103 Quoted in M. Lee, *Loreto Secondary School Bray: Commemorative Year Book, 1850–2000* (n.a., n.p., 2000), 10.

104 *Ibid.*, 8.

105 See Burns and Wilson, *Dominican Sisters Cabra, 1819–1994*, 24.

106 Sr D. Kelly, *The Sligo Ursulines: The First Fifty Years, 1826–1876* (Sligo: Ursuline Sisters, n.d.), 208.

107 Quoted in Kealy, *Dominican Education in Ireland*, 74.

108 K. Tynan, *Twenty-Five Years* (London: Smith, Elder & Co., 1913), 49.

109 *Ibid.*, 56.

110 F.H. O'Donnell, *The Ruin of Education in Ireland* (David Nutt, London, 1902), 154.

111 A reference to the Dogma of Papal Infallibility, defined by the First Vatican Council 1869–70.

112 'Papa and the Dogma', *Scribner's Magazine*, November 1870, 107.

113 'Sex and Wages', *ibid.*

114 *Ibid.*

115 Y.Y., 'The New Woman', *Loreto Magazine*, Midsummer 1895, 21-2. The spelling of 'Loretto' was changed to 'Loreto' in 1896. In 1883 the Catholic bishop of Meath, Revd Thomas McNulty, castigated 'the advent of the new woman who demanded equal rights with her brothers in admission to a study of the exact sciences and to the Pagan literature of Greece and Rome as well as to the realms of Law and Medicine and all the professions'. Quoted in M. Gibbons, *Loreto Navan: One Hundred Years of Catholic Progress, 1833–1933* (Navan: 1933), 111.

116 M.E., 'Another View of "Woman's Progress"', *ibid.*, 22-3.

117 M. Mulhall, 'Woman's Education', *Loreto Magazine*, Summer 1897, 14.

118 Final report of the Belmore Commission, 2.

119 Mulhall, 'Woman's Education', 14.

120 W.Z. Ella Hannon, 'Poetry – Its Effects on Education', *Loreto Magazine*, Midsummer 1898, 64.

121 *Ibid.*

122 B. Walsh, *Secondary Teaching in Ireland 1878–2010: An Oral History* (forthcoming).

123 *Loreto Magazine*, Summer 1900. The queen also visited Castleknock College, Dublin, where the ever-present religious/national tensions were well captured in *The College Chronicle* (1900), which recorded 'it was certainly a curious anomaly to see Her Majesty engaged in affable intercourse with a member of an order [the president, Fr Geoghegan] whose disabilities Her Government refuses to appeal … did it not seem strange to see her interested in a collegiate body to which, in defiance of reason and argument, Her Government resolutely denies university education' (J. Murphy, *Nos Autem*, 95). The queen also visited the Masonic Girls' Charity School in Dublin. See B. Bowden, *200 Years of a Future Through Education* (Dublin: Masonic Girls' Benefit Fund, 1992), 79.

124 School magazines of Clongowes Wood College and Belvedere College.

125 H. Kennedy, 'The Claims of the Irish Language', *Loreto Magazine*, Summer 1901.

126 C. O'Sullivan, 'A Summer School in Kerry', *Loreto Magazine*, Christmas 1902, 31-7.

127 O'Donnell, *The Ruin of Education in Ireland*, 24.

128 *Royal Commission of Inquiry into Irish Education*, 1870, part iii, 446.

129 *Ibid.*

130 W.Z. Ella Hannon, 'Poetry – Its Effects on Education', 64.

131 Muckross School archives, Dublin. *Persons, Places and Items of Interest, Muckross III* (scrapbook). Newspaper not identified, date 27 January 1965.

132 Walsh, *Secondary Teaching in Ireland 1878–2010: An Oral History*.

133 Sacred Heart archives, Mount Anville, Dublin. RSA/129 [1] Mistress of Studies: Copies of 'Board' documents, 24 January 1940.

134 Walsh, *Secondary Teaching in Ireland 1878–2010: An Oral History*.

135 *Dominican College Muckross Park: A Century of Memories 1900–2000* (Dublin: DBA Publications Limited, 2000); see 'Muckross Park, 1940s, memories of Alma McIntyre, Hilda Murphy, Bernadette Maire Packenham and Pat Warren', 21.

136 O'Sullivan, 'A Summer School in Kerry', 36.

137 Former Minister for Education Niamh Breathnach (interviewed 23 May 2011) recalled how a nun at the Dominican Sion Hill School encouraged her to enter public life. She and others were encouraged by 'the head nun to enter the USI' (Union of Students in Ireland) while studying at Sion Hill Froebel College in the 1960s. Sir Tony O'Reilly recounted in 1997 that 'all of the great influences in my life … have been … directly or indirectly related to the Jesuits'. See J. Quinn, *My Education* (Dublin: Town House, 1997), 304-5. Seamus Heaney cited the influence of his English teacher, Sean B. O'Kelly, and, in particular, that 'reading Chaucer, Wordsworth and Keats with him was … terrifically important' (*ibid.*, 172). The poet and former professor of modern literature at Trinity College Dublin Brendan Kennelly recalled that his secondary school was 'run by an amazing woman … Jane Agnes McKenna [who] handed us this ability to be haunted, to leave our hearts and minds open to Shakespeare, to Latin, to French' (*ibid.*, 222).

138 P. Parker, *The Old Lie: The Great War and the Public-School Ethos* (Hambledon: Continuum, 1987).

139 O'Connor, 'Influences Affecting Girls' Secondary Schooling in Ireland, 1860–1910', 96.

140 J. Martin, 'Interpreting biography in the history of education: past and present', *History of Education*, vol. 41, no. 1 (2012), 102.

Notes on Contributors

CLARA CULLEN

Clara Cullen is a former academic librarian whose present research centres on the history of cultural institutions in nineteenth- and twentieth-century Ireland, the history of Irish women in science in Ireland, the history of libraries and of education in nineteenth century Ireland, and the history of Dublin. As well as her recent publication, *The World Upturning: Elsie Henry's Irish Wartime Diaries, 1913–1919* (2012), she also co-edited *His Grace is Displeased: Selected Correspondence of John Charles McQuaid* (2012) with Margaret Ó hÓgartaigh, *The Building of the State: Science and Engineering with Government on Merrion Street* (2011) co-edited with Orla Feely, and contributions to *The Oxford History of the Irish*, Vol. 4 (2011), *Women and Science, 17th Century to the Present* (2011) and *Science and Technology in Nineteenth-Century Ireland* (2011). Among her forthcoming publications is '*A Veritable Genius': Sir Robert John Kane in Nineteenth-Century Ireland* (2015). Clara is an Associate of UCD Humanities Institute and this year's winner of the Royal College of Physicians of Ireland History of Medicine prize.

JENNIFER FITZGERALD

Jennifer Fitzgerald taught in the School of English, Queen's University Belfast from 1975 to 2002. She is currently an Adjunct at the Department of

Women's Studies, San Diego State University in California, USA. She has recently published an intellectual biography, *Helen Waddell and Maude Clarke: Irishwomen, Friends and Scholars* (2012) and edited *Helen Waddell Reassessed: New Readings* (2014).

KATHRYN LAING

Kathryn Laing is a lecturer in the Department of English Literature and Language, Mary Immaculate College, University of Limerick, Ireland. She is the editor of *The Sentinel: An Incomplete Early Novel by Rebecca West* (2002) and co-editor of *Edna O'Brien: New Critical Perspectives* (2006). She has published articles on Virginia Woolf, Angela Carter, Rebecca West and George Moore, and has co-published several articles with Faith Binckes on the late nineteenth-century Irish writer, Hannah Lynch. Currently she is co-writing a monograph on Hannah Lynch.

MARGARET Ó HÓGARTAIGH

Margaret Ó hÓgartaigh works in Harvard University and is the author or co-editor of six books including *Kathleen Lynn, Irishwoman, Patriot Doctor* (2006, 2011), *Quiet Revolutionaries: Irish Women in Education, Medicine and Sport, 1861–1964* (2011) and, with Clara Cullen as co-editor, *His Grace is Displeased: The Selected Correspondence of John Charles McQuaid* (2012) which has been reprinted several times. She is currently completing a biography of Nano Nagle, 1718–84, Progenitor of the Presentation Order of Nuns.

SUSAN M. PARKES

Susan M. Parkes is an Emeritus Fellow of Trinity College, Dublin. She is an authority on the history of Irish Education and was editor of *A Danger to the Men? A History of Women in Trinity College, Dublin, 1904–2004* (2004) and co-author with Dr Deirdre Raftery of *Female Education in Ireland, 1700–1900 – Minerva or Madonna* (2007).

DIANE URQUHART

Diane Urquhart is head of department and a reader in modern Irish history at the Institute of Irish Studies of the University of Liverpool. A graduate of Queen's University Belfast and a former postdoctoral fellow of the Institute of Irish Studies at Queen's, she has also worked as a researcher for the Women's History Project. Diane is the author of *Women in Ulster*

Politics, 1890–1940 (2000) and *The Ladies of Londonderry: Women and Political Patronage, 1800–1959* (2008). She has published numerous articles and edited and co-edited a number of collections relating to women in nineteenth- and twentieth-century Ireland, the most recent of which (with Gillian McIntosh) is *Irish Women at War: the Twentieth Century* (2010). She is currently writing a history of Irish divorce.

MARGARET WARD

Margaret Ward was the director of the Women's Resource and Development Agency, a regional organisation for women, based in Belfast, from 2005 until 2013. She has worked as an academic at Bath Spa University and the University of the West of England and was Research Fellow at the Institute of Irish Studies, Queen's University of Belfast. Her publications include *Unmanageable Revolutionaries: Women and Irish Nationalism*, biographies of Maud Gonne and Hanna Sheehy Skeffington and (with Louise Ryan) edited studies of *Irish Women and Nationalism and Irish Women and the Vote*. Dr Ward is a board member of Museums NI.

BRENDAN WALSH

Brendan Walsh lectures in the History of Education, Dublin City University. He is co-author of *Teaching Practice in Ireland*, editor of *Education Studies in Ireland: Key Disciplines and Degrees of Nonsense: the Demise of the University in Ireland*. His most recent book, *Boy Republic: Patrick Pearse and Radical Education*, was published in 2013.

Index

Abbot, Charlotte 186
Abelard, Peter 45
Agriculture and Technical Instruction,
    Department of (DATI) 34
Aimers, Annie Cecilia 123–4
Alexandra College, Dublin 14, 27, 30,
    33, 34, 35, 88, 97, 98, 106, 124,
    125, 177, 178, 181
Amnesty Association 158
Ancient Order of Hibernians 162
Andrews, Mary 19
Annal Rioghachta Éireann 61–2
Annals of fashionable gallantry 128
Annals of the Four Masters 61
Armstrong, Frances Elizabeth 25
As We Ride (Vernon and Cole)
    114–15
Association of Irish Schoolmistresses
    14, 99, 181–2, 187
Autobiography of a Child (Lynch) 72

Badham, Edith 117, 120, 121, 125
Baker, Lily 34
Balfour Education Act (1902) 101
Ball, Anne 19
Ball, Mary 19
Barlow, Jane 120
Barrington, Amy 102
Bartram, Helen 120
Bateson, Mary 54
Bean na hÉireann 161–2
Beasts and Saints (Waddell) 47
Belfast Academical Institution 21
Belfast Academy 21
Belfast Ladies' Institute 97
Belmore Commission 195–6
Bennet, Leota Kathleen 119, 120
Bentham, Dr Ethel 85–6, 87

Bermingham, Louise 35
Birmingham, George (James Hannay)
    39
Blackrock College, Dublin 171, 175,
    180
Bland, Lilian 19
Bone, Dr E. Honor 86
Boole, Lucy 19
Boyd, Dr Douglas 93
Brigidine Sisters 177
British Association for the
    Advancement of Science
    (BAAS) 20, 27
Brittain, Vera 39, 49
Brooke, William 131
Broomscod Collar, The (Olivier) 39
Brougham, Lord Chancellor 141, 146
Brown, Richard Beaver 90
Browning, Oscar 106
Bryant, Sophie 15, 120
Bullen, Denis 21
Bulley, Agnes Amy 120
Bureau of Military History 164
Burgon, John 12
Burnell, Jocelyn Bell 18
Butler, Mary 167
Byers, Margaret 14, 97, 118, 150, 181
Byrne, James 138

Cam, Helen 50, 51, 61, 64
Cambridge Association for Women's
    Suffrage 111
Cambridge Teachers' Syndicate 106
Cambridge Training College for
    Women 107
Campbell, Dr Emily 87
Campbell, John 87
Carlisle, Earl of, Lord Lieutenant 28

Catholic University School of
     Medicine 34
Ceannt, Aine 164
Cecil, Lady Emily (First Marchioness
     of Westmeath) 15, 131–47
Celtic Literary Society 158, 159
Century Magazine 192, 193
Charnock, R.S. 16
Chinese Classics, The She King, or Book
     of Odes (translated by James
     Legge) 40, 49
Chrimes, S.B. 50
Christian Observer 16
Clark, Dr Ann Elizabeth 87
Clarke, Brice 50, 57
Clarke, Harry 50
Clarke, Maude 15, 17, 37, 39, 48–56,
     61, 62–5
Clarke, Stewart/Chang 50
Clerke, Agnes Mary 19
Clough, Anna Jemima/Anne 96, 110
Coffey, George 34
Cole, Grenville A.J. 114
College of Science 29
Collingwood, R.G. 55, 56
Colum, Mary 163, 164, 165
Commission of Inquiry into Primary
     Education in Ireland 30
Commission on Manual and
     Practical Instruction (Belmore
     Commission) 195–6
Commission on the Department of
     Science and Art in Ireland 28
Coneys, Matilda 29, 30, 32
Coneys, Zoe Leigh 29, 32
Congregation of the Faithful
     Companions of Jesus 176
Connolly, James 91, 156, 167
Cook, Rachel 102
Cope, Eleanor 27
Corlett, Ada Barbara 97
Court of Arches 137, 142, 146
Court of Common Pleas 142
Cox, Bertie 187
Crommelin, Constance Maud de la
     Cherois 114
Crommelin, Nicholas de la Cherois 114
Cullen, Cardinal 180
Cumann na mBan 155, 164–7, 169
Cumann na nGaedheal 162
Cunningham, Elizabeth Margaret
     108–9, 125
Curtis, Edmund 60, 61
Cust, Aileen 19
Custody of Children Act 140

Dark Tide, The (Brittain) 39
Das Antitz der Erde (The Face of the
     Earth) (Suess) 115
Davies, Emily 96, 101, 104
Davies, Rees 62
Daviot, Gordon 39
Davitt, Michael 152
Dawson, Belinda 35
de Courcy, Revd Gerald 116
de la Mare, Walter 40
de Mailly, Heloise 115
de Meun, Jean 40
Deane, Margaret 118
Deed, Jessie Gertrude 109
Denys d'Auvrillac: A Story of French
     Life (Lynch) 81
Desert Fathers, The (Waddell) 47
Devlin, Anne 156
Dickson-Martin, Dr Emily Winifred
     34, 87–8
Discipline (Clarke and Waddell) 38–9
Divorce and Matrimonial Causes Act
     (1857) 130, 131, 144
Dodd, Edith Stuart 124
Dodd, Helen Letitia 124
Dodd, Isobel 124
Dodds, E.R. 57, 60
Dominican schools 178–9, 183,
     189–90, 191
Donoughmore, Lord 131
Dow, Gillian 68
Dowse, Judge Baron 130
Drapers' Company, London 99
Dublin High School 25
Dublin Mechanics' Institution 21
Dublin Workingman's Club 34
Dublin Zoological Society 20
Duffy, Gavan 75
Duffy, Louise Gavan 164

Earl, Lucie Anne 112
Ecclesiastical Court Powers Bill
     (1832) 146
Edgeworth, Maria 67, 82, 83
Edward II, King 52, 53
Edward III, King 52
Edwards, J.G. 50, 61
Egan, Katherine H. 25
Egerton, George 70, 72
Elgee, Jane Francesca ('Speranza') 149
Emily Lawless 1845–1913: Writing the
     Interspace (Hansson) 69
English, Dr Ada 34, 89–90
English Women of Letters: Biographical
     Sketches (Kavanagh) 82

Everett, Alice 19, 105, 126
Everett, John David 105

Farrell, Anne Frances 33
Fauset, Eileen 69, 80
ffrench-Mullen, Madeleine 90, 91
Fianna 156, 167
Field Day Anthology, The 69
Finlay, Elizabeth 112
Fisher, Dr Hugh 88
FitzGerald, Edward 63
Fitzgerald, Margaret 189
Fitzpatrick, Lily 188
Flower, Robin 59–60
Foley, Ruth 188
Fortune Grass (Lethbridge) 189
Fourteenth Century Studies (Clarke) 52, 54, 64
Frame, Robin 62
Francis, M.E. 67
Frazer, Aileen 33
Freeman's Journal 135, 183
French Life in Town and Country (Lynch) 81
French Women of Letters: Biographical Sketches (Kavanagh) 82

Gaelic League 155, 164, 167
Galbraith, Vivian 49–50, 51, 56
Gardner, Margaret Elizabeth 116
Gardner, Mary 122
Garrett, Elizabeth 89
George, Henry 153, 154
Gibson, Emily 102
Girls' Public Day School Trust (GPDST) 101
Girton College, Cambridge 96, 99, 100, 101–7, 123
Gladstone, William 154
Gonne, Maud 148, 157–8, 159, 160, 162, 168
Gore-Booth, Constance (Markiewicz) 11, 91, 156, 162, 166, 167
Gould-Bell, Dr Elizabeth 88–9
Government School of Science, Museum of Irish Industry 22–31, 35
Grace Lee (Kavanagh) 77
Gray, Betsy 149
Gray, Dr Sara 89
Gray, Frances Ralph 112, 113
Gray, James 112
Green, Alice Stopford 33

Greene, Robert 65
Greer, Germaine 8
Griffith, Arthur 158
Griffith, Margaret 49
Grimshaw, Beatrice 72
Grogan, Dr Amelia 89–90
Gwynn, Mary Louisa 11

Hall, Lady Margaret 42, 49
Hampton, Jill Brady 69
Hannon, Ella 196, 199, 200
Hansson, Heidi 69, 71
Hare, Frances Annie 25, 30
Hare, Halgena 25, 30
Hare, Mathias 25, 30
Hare, T.S.A. 25
Harman, Harriet 26
Harman, Henrietta 26
Harman, Hester 26
Harper, Isabella 92
Harrington, Tim 158
Haslam, Anna 150
Haslett, William Woods 109
Hayden, Mary 10, 11, 15, 118
Hayes, Gertrude 27
Hayes, Mary L. 27
Headlam-Morley, Agnes 49
Heavens and their Story, The (Maunder) 106
Hemphill, Anne 35
Henry Joy McCracken Literary Society 156
Higgins, William 20
Hobson, Bulmer 156
Hobson, Mary 156
Hoffman, Nancy 173
Hogben, Anna Grace 103, 121
Hore, Harriette 189
How Irish Scientists Changed the World 18
Huggins, Margaret Lindsay 19
Hughes, Elizabeth 106, 107
Hughes Hall, Cambridge 15
Humphreys, Sighle 166
Hurnard, Naomi 49
Hutchins, Ellen 19
Hutton, Mary 111
Hyde, Douglas 58, 160
Hyland, Molly 160, 161
Hymn Tune Mystery, The (Birmingham) 39

Inghinidhe na hÉireann (Daughers of Erin) 154, 155, 159, 160, 161, 162, 166

Intermediate Education (Ireland) Act (1878) 13, 20, 158, 175–6, 177, 180–4
Intermediate Education (Ireland) Commission (Palles Report) 181
Ireland under the Normans (Orpen) 60
Irish Association of Women Graduates 118
Irish Catholic Women's Suffrage Association 11
Irish Citizen 162
Irish Citizen Army (ICA) 91, 166, 168
Irish Ecclesiastical Record 184
Irish Freedom 162
Irish Innovators in Science and Technology 18
Irish Literary Society 58, 107
Irish Monthly 71, 74, 75, 76
Irish National League 154
Irish National Volunteers 163
Irish Parliamentary Party 151, 162
Irish Republican Brotherhood 150
Irish Scene in Somerville & Ross, The (Stevens) 69
Irish Society of London 99
Irish Times, The 13, 59, 94, 95, 179
Irish Universities Act (1908) 97, 118
Irish Volunteers 162
Irish Women's Association 155, 156
Irish Women's Centenary Union 157
Irish Women's Franchise League 162, 166, 167
Irish Women's Suffrage 162

Jane Eyre (Brontë) 80
Jellet, Lily 188–9
Jellett, Eva Josephine 34
Jellicoe, Anne 30, 97, 150
Jex-Blake, Sophia 85, 95
Jinny Blake: A Tale (Lynch) 66–7, 70–4, 79, 82
John XII, Pope 59
Johnston, Anna (Ethne Carbery) 155, 156, 158, 160
Johnston, Margaret 33
Joliffe, J.E.A. 50

Kane, Robert John 21, 23, 25, 26, 28–9, 30, 31–2
Kavanagh, Julia 67, 70–81, 83, 84
Kelly, Mary Ann ('Eva') 149
Kennedy, John Cochrane 103
Kennedy, Mary 103–4

Knowles, Matilda 19, 33
Knox, Betty 188
Kyllmann, Otto 43, 45

La Touche, Louisa Digges 33
Lab Coats and Lace 19
Ladies' Collegiate School (later Victoria College) Belfast 97, 177
Ladies' Land League 70, 151, 152, 154–5, 160, 168, 169
Lady Margaret Hall, Oxford 96
Laffan, May 69
Lancet, The 16, 89
Land League 90, 151–2
Lawless, Emily 67, 69, 71, 82
'League of Women Delegates' 169
Lee, Jane 111
Lee, William 111
Leeper, Alexander 27
Leeper, Jane Anne (Jeannie) 27–8, 35
Legge, Dominica 49, 64
Legge, James 40, 41, 49
L'Estrange, Camilla Alicia Vincentia 33, 34
L'Estrange, Jane Sophia Frances 33, 34
Lethbridge, Mabel 189
Letter to the Queen, A (Norton) 140
Lloyd, Alice Mary 112
Lloyd, Bartholomew 112
Local Government Association 162
Lock, Charles 59
London Anthropological Society 16
London Consistory Court 135
London School of Medicine 86
London University 98
Londonderry High School 106
Lonsdale, Kathleen 18
Loreto College, Dublin 33, 118, 124
Loreto Magazine 184, 192, 193, 197, 198
Loreto School, Bray 190
Lowndes, Kathleen M. 199
Lumsden, Louisa 102
Lydon, James 61, 62
Lynch, Hannah 66–7, 70–81
Lyndhurst, Lord Chancellor 141
Lynn, Dr Kathleen 34, 90–2, 95
Lyon, Mary 113
Lyon, Stanley 190
Lyrics from the Chinese (Waddell) 40, 49, 64
Lyster, Elizabeth 122

Macaulay, Mary (Lady Ogilvie) 48
McCabe, Archbishop 152, 180
McCallum, Elizabeth Archer 123
McCracken, Henry Joy 149
McCracken, Mary Ann 149, 156
McCutcheon, Katherine Sara
    Howard 109
McCutcheon, Revd Oliver 109
MacDonagh, Thomas 166
McGusty, Emily 32
McKenna-Lawlor, Susan 19
McKillip, Margaret 118
Mackintosh, Elizabeth 39
McKisack, May 48, 50, 54, 60, 62, 64
McLoughlin, Florence 60
MacNeill, Eoin 163, 164
Magee College, Londonderry 125
Maguire, Dr Katherine 34, 92–3, 94
Maitland, F.W. 50
Major, Edith Helen 104
Markiewicz, Constance (née
    Gore-Booth) 11, 91, 156, 162,
    166, 167
Marshall, Jane 187
Martin, Mary Jane 110–11
Martin, Revd J.D. 57
Masefield, John 114
Maunder, Annie S.D. (née Russell)
    18, 19, 105, 106, 126
Maunder, Walter 106
Maxwell, Anne 90
Maybury, Frances 189
Maynard, Constance 112, 113
Mayne, Rutherford 41
Meade, Maria Hamilton 116–17
Mechanics' Institutions 21
Mediaeval Latin Lyrics (Waddell) 38,
    44, 47, 64
Medical Act (1876) 85
Medieval City State (Clarke) 51
Medieval Group 49
Medieval Representation and Consent
    (Clarke) 53, 54, 56
Methodist College, Belfast 106
Milligan, Alice 155–6, 157, 158, 159,
    160
Mitchel, John 157
Modus Tenendi Parliamentum 52, 53, 54
Molony, Helena 160, 161, 162, 166
Molyneux, Frances 187
Moore, Margaret (née Nagle) 184–6,
    190
Moore, Sir John 94
Moran, Frances 188
More, Hannah 186

More Latin Lyrics: From Virgil to
    Milton (Waddell) 48
Morgan, Lady Sydney (Owenson)
    67, 70, 71, 82
Morris, William 102
Morrow, Genevieve Violet 33, 35
Mulhall, Marion 195, 196
Mulholland, Rosa 71
Mulvany, Isabella 33, 120, 181
Murphy, Josephine 190
Murray, Betty 49, 52, 63
Murray, Hannah 27
Murray, John F. 27
Murray, Mrs J.F. 27
Museum of Irish Industry (MII),
    Government School of Science
    22–31, 35
Mystery of the Modus, The 56

Narrative of the case of the Marchioness
    of Westmeath 131, 141–3
Natalie (Kavanagh) 79–80
Nation 149, 153
National League 158
National Teacher, The 174
National University of Ireland 97,
    118, 125
Nation, The (Duffy) 75
Neill, A.S. 190
New Woman project 69
Newnham College, Cambridge 96,
    100, 101, 110–17, 121
ni Riain, Eilis 166
Nicholls, Sophia 120
Northern Patriot 156
Norton, Caroline 15, 140, 141
Notes from the Ladies' Cage (Parnell)
    151
Nugent, George (Lord Devlin/
    Marquess of Westmeath)
    131–47
Nulty, Dr, Bishop of Meath 176

Ó Cleirigh, Tadgh 61
O'Donnell, P.H. 191
O'Donovan, John 62
O'Farrelly, Agnes 163, 164
Oldham, Alice 14, 33, 98, 118, 181–2
Olivier, Gillian 39
Oman, Charles 39
O'Meara, Kathleen (Grace Ramsey)
    67, 71, 74, 75, 77
O'Neill, Laurence 91
O'Rahilly, Aine 163, 164, 165
Orpen, Goddard 60

O'Sullivan, Clare 197–8
O'Toole, Jennie 155
Otway-Ruthven, Jocelyn 61, 62
Ovenden, Isabella 34
Overend, Letitia 95
Owenson, Sydney (Lady Morgan)
    67, 70, 71, 82

Pakenham-Walsh, Mary 115–16
Palles Commission/Report 14, 181
Parkes, Susan 15
Parnell, Anna 151, 152, 153, 155, 160,
    161, 163
Parnell, Charles Stewart 151, 154
Parnell, Fanny 151, 153
Parsons, Mary 19
Paterson, Rosa 121–2
Pearse, Patrick 190
PEN Club 107
Pepper, Henrietta 32
Perry, Alice 19
Peter Abelard: A Novel (Waddell) 38,
    45–7, 58
Phillips, Charles 128
Physicists of Ireland 18
Plowden, Francis 130
Political Prisoners' Aid Society 153
Politics of Writing: Julia Kavanagh
    1824–77, The (Fauset) 69
Pollock, Jane Rankin 107
Porter, J. Leslie 20
Power, Jennie Wyse 159, 162
Powicke, F.M. 37, 49, 50, 54, 61
Powis Commission 198
Praeger, Robert Lloyd 115
Presentation Sisters 177
Prosser, Dr Georgina 90
Pynchon, Thomas 63

Queen's Colleges
Belfast 20, 96, 119, 124
Cork 96, 118, 124, 125
Galway 96, 118, 124, 125
Queen's Institute, Dublin 30, 97
Queen's University, Belfast 37, 97–8
Quinn, Margaret 159

Raymond, Mary Sybil 103
RDS School of Design 25, 26
Reading the Irish Woman: Studies in
    Cultural Encounter and Exchange:
    1714–1960 68
Redesdale, Lord 144
Redmond, John 167
Reed, Adeline 175

Representation of the People Act
    (1918) 131
Reynolds, Hanna 152
Richard II, King 51
Richard of Bordeaux (Daviot) 39
Richardson, Anne Wakefield 112–13
Richardson, H.G. 50, 61
Robertson Commission 118, 126
Robertson, Mary 33
Robertson, Sir Benjamin 102
Rochelle School, Cork 186–9
Roman de la Rose (de Meun) 40
Rorke, Adelina 26
Rorke, John 26
Roseweyde, Herbert 47
Rosni Harvey (Lynch) 72
Rotunda Hospital Dublin 86
Royal Academy of Medicine 88
Royal College of Physicians and
    Surgeons, Edinburgh 86
Royal College of Physicians of
    Ireland 85
Royal College of Science for Ireland
    (RCScI) 22, 29, 31–5
Royal College of Science, London
    31
Royal College of Surgeons (RCSI)
    34
Royal Commission on University
    Education in Ireland 117
Royal Cork Institution 21
Royal Dublin Society (RDS) 20, 21
Royal University Act (1879) 158
Royal University of Ireland (RUI)
    20, 33, 35, 97, 107, 117–18, 126,
    187
degrees 98
university classes 124
Rudmose-Brown, T.B. 45
Ruin of Education in Ireland, The
    (O'Donnell) 191, 198
Russell, Annie Scott Dill (Maunder)
    18, 19, 105, 106, 126
Russell, George (Æ) 40, 58

Sacred Heart School, Armagh 178
St Angela's College, Cork 33, 118
St Kieran's College, Kilkenny 171,
    175
St Mary's College, Dundalk 171, 190
St Mary's Dominican College 33,
    118, 124
St Stephen's 94
Saintsbury, George 41
Salisbury, Lord 137

Salmon, Dr 186
Samuels, Arthur 131
Sand, Mary 33
Sayers, Dorothy 39
Sayles, G.O. 50
Scarlett, Mary 33
Science and Art (DSA), Department
    of 22, 24
Scribner's Monthly 192–3
Sex Disqualification Act (1919) 131
Shan Van Vocht 156, 158
Shannon, Agnes 34
Sheldon, William 134
Sidgwick, Eleanor 110
Sidgwick, Henry 96, 110
Siena School, Drogheda, County
    Louth 176
Sinn Féin 91, 155, 169
Sisters of Mercy 177
Sisters of St Joseph of Cluny 177
Sisters of St Louis 176, 191
Sisters of the Sacred Heart 176–7,
    191
Skeffington, Frank/Francis Sheehy
    154, 166
Skeffington, Hanna Sheehy 162,
    165–6, 167
Sketch of Lord Westmeath's Case, A 138
Skinnider, Margaret 167, 168
Smiley, Sara Robinson Beatty 122–3
Smith, Albert Dew 112
Smith-Bell, Dr Margaret 93
Smith, Gregory 37, 40, 42
Socialist Republican party 156
Society for Promoting the
    Employment of Women 97
Society of United Irishwomen 149
Sollas, Hertha Beatrice Coryn
    Johnson 115
Sollas, Igerna Brunhild Johnson 115,
    126
Sollas, William Johnson 115
Somerville College, Oxford 37, 48,
    96
Stars, Shells and Bluebells 19
Stone, Lawrence 131
Stoney, Dr Florence 121
Stoney, Edith Anne 120–1, 125
Stoney, George Johnstone 120–1
Stopford, Alice 33
Stopford-Price, Dr Dorothy 92–3, 95
Stott, Alicia Boole 19
Strand House School, Londonderry
    (Strand?) 177
Stritch, Clara A. 27

Stritch, Gretta D. 27
Stubbs, William 50
Suess, Eduard 115
Sullivan, W.K. 23
*Summer and Winter in the Two Sicilies,
    A* (Kavanagh) 75–6, 78
Susette Taylor Travelling Fellowship
    42
Sutherland, Lucy Stuart 49, 64
Swanwick, Anne 111
Swift, Jonathan 58

Talfourd, Thomas 140
Taylor, Helen 153, 154
Taylor, Revd George Pritchard 41
Teachers' Guild of Great Britain and
    Ireland 182
Tennant, Dr Elizabeth 94
Thompson, John 182
Thompson, Sydney Mary 19
Times, The 51, 54
To the Lighthouse (Woolf) 55
Tod, Isabella 97, 150
Tout, T.F. 50
Townsend, Alice Maud 111
Townsend, Chambrey Corker 102
Townsend, Isabella Frances Vere
    101–2
Townsend, Mary Hungerford 111
Trinity College, Cambridge 111
Trinity College Dublin 10, 15, 20, 27,
    35, 45, 61, 98, 101
    'ad eundem gradum' privilege 99,
        119–20, 121, 122
    admission of women 108, 119, 125,
        126
    commencements December 1904
        121–2
    'Examinations for Women' 97–8
Trinity Hall Dublin 108, 122
Twenty-Five Years (Tynan) 191
Tynan, Katherine 155, 191

Ulster Literary Theatre 41
Ulster Unionist Women's Council
    163
Ulster Volunteer Force 162, 163
Ulster Women's Council 163
United Ireland 152
United Irishman 158, 159
United Irishmen 149
Universities Act (1908) 35
University College Cork 97
University College Dublin 97, 118,
    125, 164

University College Galway 97
Ursuline Sisters 170–1, 177, 178, 191

Vernon, Blanche 114–15
Veterinary Medical Association of
    Ireland 199
Victoria College, Belfast 14, 33, 98,
    124, 181
Victoria High School, Derry 124
Victoria, Queen 129, 148, 159, 197
Vitae Patrum (Roseweyde) 47

Waddell, Billy 41
Waddell, George 41
Waddell, Helen 15, 17, 37–8, 40–8,
    49, 58, 62–5, 123
Wandering Scholars, The (Waddell) 38,
    43–4, 47, 58, 59, 60, 63
Ward, James 110
Ward, Mary 19
Warnock, Annie McClure 107
Webb, Dr Isabella (Ella) 94–5, 115
Webb, George 94
Welsh, Elizabeth 104
Wesley College, Dublin 177
Westfield College, University of
    London 43
Westmeath, Lord. see Nugent,
    George (Lord Devlin/Marquess
    of Westmeath)

Westtropp, Louisa 130
Wheeler, Henry Albert 123
White, Henrietta 14, 113–14, 118, 125
Wild Irish Girl (Owenson) 82
Wilkins, Eliza 33
Wilkins, Maurice 111
Wilkins, William 111
Wilkinson, B. 50
William of Windsor 52
Willis, Margaret 123
Willis, Robert 123
Wolfe Tone, Theobald 157
Wollstonecraft, Mary 15, 149
Woman in the Drama before
    Shakespeare (Waddell) 40, 41, 42
Wood, Henry 132, 134
Woodhead, Sarah 102
Woolf, Virginia 55, 56
Wynne, Catherine 90
Wynne, Owen 90
Wynne, Revd Richard 90
Wyse Power, Jennie 155, 162, 163,
    167
Wyse Power, Nancy 163, 165

Yeats, W.B. 58, 157
Young, Charlotte 102
Young, Georgina Tarleton 103
Young Ireland 149